PROBLEMS IN READING

PROBLEMS IN READING

BY

EDWARD WILLIAM DOLCH, PH. D.
College of Education, University of Illinois

AUTHOR OF
TEACHING PRIMARY READING
A MANUAL FOR REMEDIAL READING
THE PSYCHOLOGY AND TEACHING OF READING
BETTER SPELLING

THE GARRARD PRESS
CHAMPAIGN, ILLINOIS

1948

First Printing, 1948
Second Printing, 1949

MANUFACTURED IN THE UNITED STATES OF AMERICA

PREFACE

This book presents intensive discussions of a large number of important aspects of the teaching of reading. Some of these concern reading materials, some concern methods of teaching, still others deal with the whole reading program, as well as its relationships to education as a whole. In fact, the thirty-two chapters, each a distinct discussion, cover a wide range of interesting matters that deal more or less directly with reading.

The method of separate discussions has many advantages. Each topic is dealt with much more fully and intensively than would be possible in the usual systematic treatment of all phases of reading. In addition, all factors affecting a topic are brought to a focus, thus affording the reader a more well rounded understanding of the topic.

The various chapters of the book are often a re-presentation of material at one time published in an educational magazine. Such material has stood the test of time and criticism, and has been found of enduring value. Hence its presentation here. Other chapters have at one time been presented to an audience at an educational conference or other meeting. In each case, the audience received the material with interest, and expressed its sense of its value. Therefore, to reach a wider audience, the material is again published here.

Some of the chapters are discussions that the author worked upon in his intensive study of some topic but never published in any way. These are given as affording the reader an opportunity also to think upon the topic intensively and with profit.

An important and extensive study never before published is the one on Graded Reading Difficulty. Along with it is given the word list used in determining difficulty. The two together will afford teachers and others a yardstick to measure, on their own, graded difficulty of reading materials.

The author wishes especially to thank the many teachers and students and assistants who have helped in the studies here presented. Particular thanks are due to joint authors who consented to publication, H. A. Curtis (Chapter XXVII), Miss Maurine Bloomster (Chapter IV), and Mrs. Ida C. Dolch, (Chapter XII).

E. W. Dolch,
Urbana, Illinois.

CONTENTS

Part I

General Problems

CHAPTER I

HELPING THE GOOD READER IMPROVE

The term "good reader" in our title must be defined. We do not mean the good reader in the sense of the exceptional reader, the one who reads very well for his age or grade. He should be called the superior reader. Instead, we mean "good reader" as opposed to the "poor reader." So we are dealing perhaps with the "average good reader," meaning the one who reads well enough to do the work assigned and to get at least a passable minimum from our courses. In that sense he is a "good reader" but we feel that he is not good enough. At least he is not as good as he might be.

This average good reader is an important problem because there are so many of him. He makes up the bulk of the output of our schools. He is also important because if we could make him a better reader, our standards in nearly all subjects could be raised. And, as a result, the level of the mental life in our whole community might be raised. There-

---

From *Schoolmen's Week Proceedings*, University of Pennsylvania Philadelphia, Pa., 1946.

fore let us consider most seriously indeed how we can help this good reader to improve.

The first recommendation we should make for the average good reader is *greater facility.* Enable him to read more smoothly and easily. If we do not do a thing easily, we do not do it very often. So my first recommendation is that at every school level we so manage things that the average good reader actually does more reading, so that by much reading he becomes increasingly able to read with ease.

Three very definite outcomes are secured by greater facility in reading. First, reading will be more fun. Reading has always had to compete with other activities, but now it has to compete with the movies and the radio. Nowadays too many people "with nothing else to do" go to a movie rather than just sit at home. If they had more frequently experienced that reading is fun, they might stay at home with a book. Second, greater facility usually results in getting more out of reading. At any moment, the reader's attention is necessarily divided between the words and the thought. Greater facility means less and less attention to words and more and more attention to thought. Every average good reader could get more from his reading than he does. Greater facility will help him get more. The third result of the facility that comes from practice is that more is covered in any given time. An increase of twenty-five per cent in speed means reading more newspapers, more magazines, and more books in whatever time the individual does give to reading. So greater facility in reading usually means wider reading.

These results of greater facility will give year after year more of that vague but valuable thing called "background." Our average good reader is still woefully lacking in background. There is so much to be aware of in this world. The average citizen must be aware of so many things if he is to make good judgments. And the most direct road to the wide and varied background we all must have is wider reading. The good reader will not get this unless he is a still better reader than he is now.

We now come to the "how" of getting facility, and the first requirement is easier books in all subjects and at all levels. It is time the schools recognized that children learn more from an easy book than from a hard one. It is a queer mechanical idea that children get more from a book the more you put into it. They may get more from a grab bag the more you put into it, but the mind does not work that way. We are educated by our reactions, and difficulty of reading matter paralyzes reaction. The actual reading is not the activity we are after. We are after the associations in the child's mind which are stimulated by the reading. Of course, it is theoretically possible to get a book that is so easy that no activity will be stimulated, but we have not seen such books in the schools. Instead, we find the great majority of books so hard that much mental activity is blocked by too hard words and too strange ideas.

There is a test for a book suitable to children that we all can apply. Books suitable for children must seem very simple to an adult. To us, with our years of schooling and life experience, the child's book must seem very simple in ideas, very simple in words, and very simple in language construction. How many of the children's textbooks you have read seem so simple to you? Instead, teachers and others who select books for children usually select books suitable for themselves. This mistake is almost universal at all levels. College books are suitable for college professors. High school books are suitable for high school teachers, and most grade school books are suitable for the teachers rather than for the children. The great exception is in books for primary grades. Up through the third grade the text often fits the child as his coat fits him and his shoes fit him. But from that point on the likelihood is that the book is suitable to the superior student, who is quite close to the teacher in skills, and not to the average good reader of whom we are now thinking.

The other method for securing greater facility for the average reader is better salesmanship on our part. It is our job to sell the joys of reading to the world. Do we know our stock in trade? We want children to read the newspaper more. Do we know the good newspapers from the bad and how to show children the interesting parts of the newspaper? The publishers present a tremendous menu of magazines on every conceivable subject. Are we experts on the fascinating magazines in every field? The libraries are full of books new and old that will appeal to nearly every kind of child, but are we experts at finding the right book for the right child? I know that I am proposing what may seem a large order. But how can we avoid the necessity of knowing better the things we are trying to sell to children? Suppose we make such a proposal as this. Suppose every Monday we call to our class's attention some interesting thing we found in the Sunday paper. Suppose that every week we buy at the news-stand some magazine that looks interesting to children of the level we teach and tell the class what we find in it. Suppose we make it a rule every month to read at the library one book that we might want to recommend to the good average reader in our classes. Is this too much to expect for better salesmanship in increasing the facility in reading of our students?

Our second main suggestion for helping the good reader improve is to spend more time in all our classes on the word meanings met with in our daily work. One of the greatest stumbling blocks in the way of better reading is the readers' superficial and inadequate word meanings. The children read many, many words, but get only the shadow of what the authors tried to convey by them. We can work in at least three directions. One is for more concrete meaning behind the symbols in our books. The average good reader reads stories about people of many lands over the earth. But if the truth were known, these people look to the children very much like American citizens of the present year. The children simply have not seen these distant lands or adequate pictures of these lands, nor have they read telling descriptions. Instead, they know that a gaucho is an Argentine cowboy and to them he is very much like the American cowboy of the movies. They read of a French peasant and in their minds this French peasant is living in an American farmhouse of the kind common in their part of America. The same problem arises in history stories. To this average good reader, the London of Shakespeare is much like an American city, with sidewalks, and so on. If they think of George Washington's dentist, they will imagine him much like their own. Visual education has attacked this problem but it has not received nearly the support it should have. Every reading teacher should be a confirmed enthusiast for visual education so that her children may have more concrete meanings to their vocabulary.

Greater exactness of meaning could well be emphasized in all our work. Study of synonyms is considered old fashioned and it was undoubtedly made too formal. But teachers could well call attention in any reading lesson to an author's choice of words and why he used one word instead of another that he might have used. And the third direction for more study of word meanings is leading children to appreciate more of what lies behind the words they read. After all, a word is a symbol for a great collection of associations. The child may have some of those associations, but the man who wrote had many more. One clue to this wealth of association is the origin of the word and the family of words to which it belongs. This is not to mean that we will sidetrack meaningful and interesting reading by digression but only to suggest that as occasion offers we get the average reader to realize that there is often more in a statement he reads than he suspects.

A third major proposal for helping the good reader improve is to create a more thoughtful attitude toward the ideas over which he often skims so lightly. We often say that people do not read enough, though every year the quantity of reading increases. It is becoming more and more evident, however, that those who do read do not think enough about what they read. One way to secure such thinking is to build up a healthy skepticism. After all, whatever we read has been written by someone somewhere. One wonders what kind of a man he was. One wonders what he really knew about the subject. Do other people think the same? How much is fact, and how much is opinion? In the past we have devoted most of our time to making children feel that there is great authority in books. It is now time that we emphasize that not everything in a book can be accepted without criticism.

Another way to get the thinking that we so desire is to emphasize comparison of reading matter. Compare one newspaper with another, one magazine with others, one book with other books. There is such a flood of reading matter surrounding all of us that we must ask what part is more worthwhile. Nowadays schools are shifting from the limited required reading to optional reading over a great area. It is appropriate, therefore, that we ask about anything the child reads, "Was it worth reading or more worth reading than something else?" Teachers may be afraid to raise this matter of student judgment. But if the good reader is to become a better reader, one way is for him to develop some skill in selecting what to read.

A final suggestion for helping the good reader is to try to improve his taste in reading matter. Here we have the same problems as lie in the improvement of taste in any of the arts. First, we must accept the fact that the child's present standard will operate until he improves it. What he likes, he likes and he will be governed accordingly. Scolding a person for his present tastes does little good. Second, there must be exposure to something better but not too much better. In the field of reading we have tried to improve taste by exposure to something which the child simply could not like and which he therefore learned to dislike. In reading matter, as in music, we need a progression from the popular to the better popular, to the light classic, to the better classic, and then for some people sometimes, to the most difficult type of classic. The big problem in the field of reading, of course, is that what we usually call better reading is likely also to be harder reading. This is a handicap often overcome by having worthwhile literature read aloud, a method which takes time but may be worth the time it takes. The finest writing surely deserves oral presentation by a good reader.

In this progression from poor taste to better taste, the teacher has a modern aid of which she has not as yet made adequate use. In the past, she has had to get a class or an individual to read through the better book, perhaps four or five hundred pages of it, before she could get a reaction or make a comparison. She could often not make any comparison between the poor and the good just because she could not get the good books read. So she could not get the exposure that is demanded for improvement of taste. Now she can actually get this constant exposure and the resulting comparison by using the motion picture. A book is a story read and imagined; a movie is a story seen and heard. As stories, the two are practically the same thing. That is, the child will call each a good story or a poor story. But the big difference is that we can get our classes to see good movies and many of them, while in the past we could get very few students to read good books.

We suggest therefore that in the elevation of taste, we begin in the school by using movies, either shown at school or at the local theatre. The children see every week movies of their present level of taste.

Let us so manage that they also see movies of higher level. Then let us discuss and compare. Children quickly see the criterion of trueness to life when applied to movies. They may call a good movie slow or unexciting, but they will see that it is "good" in the sense of seeming true. They may prefer the wild excitement of the poor film, but they will readily admit that "it couldn't happen." With this intellectual evaluation made, the children will gradually see more good movies and gradually like them better. In time, their "literary taste" in movies will shift in the right direction. And we will then find that their "literary taste" in reading matter will also. If what they read "couldn't happen" they will care less for it. They will prefer that which might be "true." So the movie will have been a tool for cultivation of taste in reading that is a much more practicable one than the old required reading list.

To summarize, we have admitted that the present "good reader" is far from the good reader he might be. To help him, we have suggested first of all, greater facility through more practice at his level. Second, that he be encouraged to get more out of his reading through more attention to word meanings. Third, that we cultivate a more thoughtful attitude toward the ideas read, so that more is learned than now seems to be. And finally we have urged that we do more to elevate taste in reading so that the art of literature may have more impact on the general public that this good reader typifies. To do this, we suggest study of the art of the movie as a most handy and efficient means.

CHAPTER II

CONTROVERSIAL ISSUES IN THE TEACHING OF READING

One of the healthiest things a school can do is to face controversial issues in education. Facing such issues tends to dispel controversy over them because, first of all, we make a clear statement of just what the issue is. Then we begin to find truth on both sides. We begin to weigh evidence calmly. And we may soon agree to disagree in a friendly spirit, or we may effect a compromise which forms a basis of getting along together with as little friction as possible.

In seeking out these controversial issues in reading, we have taken the point of view of the teacher and the school administrator. The teacher and the administrator cannot postpone decisions until controversies are settled. They must do something about the teaching of reading "right now," even though they may not be very sure what is the right thing to do. The problem to be discussed here is, therefore: What are the questions about which the teacher and administrator feel uncertain, about which they feel there are two sides? These are the issues about which there invariably is controversy.

From *Supplementary Educational Monographs,* No. 56, 1942, Univ. of Chicago, Chicago, Ill.

READING VERSUS PUPIL DEVELOPMENT

The first controversial issue in the teaching of reading is one that is basic to a great deal of our school practice during the first three years. It is this: Is reading, or is child development, the chief concern of the primary grades?

For some decades it was freely said that the chief purpose of the primary grades was to develop skill in reading so that the child could, as promptly as possible, use reading skill in attacking many school subjects. For some years past, however, there has been rising a wave of disagreement with this view. Objectors to it have said that the happy, balanced development of the child is the one chief concern of the school, especially in the beginning years. They have boldly said that child life has been warped, hampered, and restricted by too much emphasis on reading. Students of children's mental health throughout the school system have pointed accusing fingers at the primary grades and have claimed that in those grades great personality maladjustments were started by teachers who were blind to child development while bending every effort to force children to learn to read. Believers in the paramount value of interest in all learning have said that the child comes to school with eager interests and that we at once start to kill them off or dry them up by our emphasis on reading, which, they say, is an activity foreign to real child interests at this stage. Parents have pathetically reported that children hate school and have pointed to failure in reading in the primary grades as a great cause for their dislike.

Most primary-grade teachers are aware of this issue, but they are bewildered because they feel themselves between two fires. They are, in most schools, actively urged to "push reading" as much as possible, and at the same time they feel the vital nature of child life and want to contribute as much as possible to its happy, wide development. How are they going to do both? Time given to one seems automatically to be taken from the other. They try to compromise but do not feel successful.

Here it must be said that activities and reading go together very well with children who are superior in vitality, in background, in quickness in learning, in maturity, and in other qualities. These children have no trouble in following a broad developmental program and in making fast progress in reading also. But we cannot let our eyes dwell on such fortunate children. We must think of the average and, above all, of the slow, the faltering, and the deprived. They are in our schools, in great number. We must plan for them and work with them. How can we secure for them both reading skills and a full-rounded child development that will lead to a satisfactory membership in adult society?

I do not know of any research that decides which of the two courses we should take. The issue is one of philosophy. What do we conceive the good life to be for children of primary grades? If the good life means quickly to become a reader, that is one thing. If the good life means to live widely and eagerly in a world that has only a minor place for books at this period, that is another thing. If a child can combine the two, very well. If a child can hardly do both, which shall we choose?

TIME WHEN READING INSTRUCTIONS SHOULD BEGIN

The second controversial issue is related to the first. It is this: When should we begin regular or systematic instruction in reading? This may not be an issue with the believers in the child-development emphasis, for they generally delay reading and begin it very gradually. But the time of starting is a pressing issue with those who believe in emphasizing reading because, if we want to get best results in reading, we need to know what effect time of starting has on our efforts to attain those results. Some persons may believe that this issue is not controversial; they may believe that the time of starting is clearly decided for the child by his reaching six and a half years in mental age or by his passing a reading-readiness test. But in this case a piece of research may have made an issue rather than have settled one. A study has been going on for some years which again raises the question: When should we begin systematic instruction in reading?

The research we refer to is being carried on in Winnetka, Illinois. Indications picked up here and there caused the Winnetka teachers to wonder whether a later beginning in reading might not give better final results. Consequently a group of children were allowed to continue their activity program without systematic instruction in reading until the middle of Grade II. As a check, each child in this group was paired, in the usual scientific manner, with one, two, or even three other children who began systematic instruction in Grade I. Careful records were then kept, year by year, of the experimental children and the control children. The seventh year of comparison has been made, and results have been published by Morphett and Washburne.[1] In brief, these results seem to say that the children who started systematic reading a year late caught up with the others in two years, then steadily passed them, and at the end of Grade VII were a year ahead of them in reading ability. With such acceleration in reading, how much greater success these children can be expected to have in junior and senior high school!

This delay of systematic reading until Grade II has been suggested by many persons on many different grounds. Here we have a careful study which seems to say that it is profitable to start later. Obviously, more research is needed. May we suggest

---

[1] Mabel Vogel Morphett and Carleton Washburne, "Postponing Formal Instruction: A Seven-Year Case Study," *Official Report of 1940 Meeting of the American Educational Research Association*, pp. 168-72. Washington: American Educational Research Association, 1940.

that it deal with the question of what we mean by "systematic" instruction in reading. Maybe our usual systematic type of instruction is really a second-grade type of instruction and therefore had better be given in Grade II. Is there not, then, a first-grade type of instruction which is still systematic and which will give even better results than delaying the usual instruction until Grade II? Here is a research situation that is delicate but that surely must be attacked if we are to settle this controversial issue.

BASIS OF PROMOTION IN THE PRIMARY GRADES

The third controversial issue is related to both of the preceding. It is this: Should we promote, especially in the primary grades, on the basis of reading achievement or on the basis of maturity, chiefly chronological age? This is a distinct issue because, whatever be your philosophy about the chief function of the primary grades and whatever be your practice about beginning reading, you come at the end of each year to the issue, "To promote or not to promote?" and must face the consequences of either decision. To promote all pupils, or almost all, on a maturity basis means that the spread of reading ability in Grade II runs from nonreaders to pupils reading at the third-grade level, in Grade III from almost nonreaders to fourth-grade readers, and so on. To retain in each grade the pupils who do not learn to read as well as they should means dissatisfaction of parents, if not of children, and the undesirable situation of having in a room older and bigger children who do not fit in.

Research, in the sense of careful observation and recording of experience, shows, first, that there are some teachers who can handle the wide range of ability accompanying promotion on the basis of maturity. Unfortunately, daily experience seems to show that there are many teachers who cannot handle that wide range and who, therefore, simply neglect the extremes. Research also seems to show that the method of organization called the "primary school" is a successful solution of promotion for the first three years. For three years the child moves from group to group but not from grade to grade. He progresses as fast as he can and is placed where he can progress best. When he succeeds in reading, he graduates from the primary school and goes on to Grade IV. We very much need full reports concerning the progress of individual children in these schools so that we may have a better knowledge of the inner workings of the plan.

THE TEACHING OF PHONICS

The fourth controversial issue concerns the teaching of phonics, but here the controversy is not the same as that of five or ten years ago. No thoughtful person now disputes that children must learn the sounds which letters represent. Instead, the dispute concerns the what, when, and how of sounding. These facts are well shown by a recent report published by Brownell.[2]

Research in the field of phonics has been held back, it appears, by the difficulty of measuring results. We want to determine the effect of teaching certain elements, in certain ways, at certain times, but to do so we must be able to decide whether the children learn to use those elements. Here is an opening for the ingenuity of any teacher or administrator. How well do your pupils use phonics? What phonic elements do they use? Devise satisfactory means for finding out, and you will have made a major contribution to the teaching of reading.

THE AMOUNT OF READING

The fifth controversial issue concerns amount of reading. Here is a question that needs research for its solution. True, we have plenty of studies showing that children who read a great deal improve in reading ability, but the skeptics will still point to children who have improved when abundant reading was not provided. The reason for their improvement is, of course, that those children went out and got their extensive reading for themselves, but we do not have clear statistical evidence of this fact. What we need is a study showing the total reading done by a great many children during a year and

[2] William A. Brownell, "Current Practices with Respect to Phonetic Analysis in the Primary Grades," *Elementary School Journal*, XLII (November, 1941), 195-206.

their improvement in reading. Each child would have to keep a diary of the reading that he did day by day in newspapers, magazines, and books, and this quantity of reading would have to be totaled up on some comparable basis. Then children would have to be paired on all factors except the one variable, quantity of reading. Such a study would probably show that children do *not* improve in reading without practice in reading. With this evidence we might have some method of convincing those who let the situation drift along as it has in the past, getting each child one book or two a year to make him a reader.

THE IMPROVEMENT OF EYE-MOVEMENTS

A sixth controversial issue is the rather old one of improving eye-movements. Much work has been done in the field of accelerating eye-movements, but we have "reports" rather than research. Research implies a careful control of the whole situation and not merely attention to one aspect of it. It is true that children have been pushed and that people have pushed themselves, and they have reported reading a larger number of words per minute. But reading implies much more than the number of words covered per minute. Reading is defined in many ways, but every way in which it is defined makes it essentially a thought-process, an operation of the mind. What happens to the thought-process when we push reading, either with a machine or with the reader's purpose? Here is the real controversial issue, and one on which we have no adequate research. It is true that some reports state that comprehension was kept constant as measured by a few new-type responses. Other reports say that the subjects think they comprehend as much or even more. These reports either give merely subjective evidence or small samplings of immediate recall. The evidence is pitifully inadequate.

In opposition to these scattered reports, we have the general principle that speed and comprehension are inversely related. All of us know that, when we want to comprehend more, we read more slowly and that, when we read fast, we expect to get less from the reading. Here by "comprehension" we do not mean immediate recall. We mean seeing thought relationships, drawing inferences, associating the new with the old. There are no data to tell what happens to this real reading when we push eye-movements by any means whatever. Of course special pushing methods may produce stronger attention and, to that extent, produce better results. But how long does this stronger attention last? Suppose the pushing device puts the reader "on his toes." Can he remain "on his toes" for an hour? These and other aspects of the issue of pushing eye-movements need careful study. Until we have better evidence, most of us will rely on much easy, interesting reading to speed up reading without hampering the various mental processes that true reading involves.

THE TEACHING OF STUDY SKILLS

The seventh and final controversial issue which we shall take up should perhaps be called a controversial *area.* It deals with the teaching of study skills. Here the high schools are particularly concerned, although the upper grades must also think of teaching how to study. At least three issues are involved: (1) When should we begin teaching study skills? (2) Which study skills should we teach? (3) Should we teach them in a reading period or in the content periods?

Research is plentiful on the general field of study, but it fails to answer these controversial issues. Concerning the first, the claim is made that we should not teach slow, careful reading until we have well established the rapid, smooth eye-movements of recreational reading. Behind this claim is the assumption that children must learn one habit of reading very well before we try to have them learn another very opposite habit of reading. But can we not teach the two habits in alternate periods? No one has the answer, and we really need the answer before we can intelligently plan when to begin teaching study skills.

Second, how many skills are there? What study skills do children actually use when they study their lessons? We simply do not know. Why not take the children into our confidence and try to have them find out and tell us how they study? At any rate, before we go to great lengths to teach study skills, there should be some evidence other than our own opinion as to what those study skills should be.

The third question of whether study should be taught in a reading or English class or in the subject-matter classes is now entirely in the realm of opinion and conjecture. The issue is being settled now in particular schools by a rule-of-thumb method which has much to commend it. Wherever a teacher is found who is enthusiastic about teaching study skills, in the reading class or in any class, there study skills are taught and no doubt are more or less learned. Wherever a teacher is found who is not enthusiastic, perhaps we had better not try to teach the skills anyway. This is just a recognition of the value of special knowledge and enthusiasm on the part of the teacher. But the teachers would have more knowledge about the problem and would be more enthusiastic about it if research could give us some facts in this controversial field.

CONCLUDING STATEMENT

Many other controversial issues exist in the field of reading. Many will immediately occur to you or will be recalled on a moment's thought. We are all deeply interested in the investigation of these issues because in the schools we must do something about them, and we want to do the right thing. Progress should be made, and progress will be made if we all try to contribute.

CHAPTER III

THE LANGUAGE COURSE

For a long time the school curriculum has contained five different subjects called reading, writing, spelling, language, and grammar. There have been books for each of these subjects, and for each there has been a period on the daily schedule, if not in all grades, at least at different points in the grade levels. Now there is a movement to combine the five subjects into one and call it simply Language. This movement has been gathering headway for some time. What is behind this change? Upon what grounds is it based? And how can this new plan be successfully carried out?

First of all, the new movement is a recognition of the simple fact that a child's language development is, next to his character development, the most important part of his school experience. Language is thinking, and most of our thinking is done in language. Of course it is possible for us to think in terms of things, and we often do so. We may think of "school" as a mental picture of the school in which we work. But most of the time, when we think of school we think the word *school* and the other words connected with that word. At this moment, for instance, you are thinking the thoughts which these words suggest. You are also thinking other thoughts —agreeing or disagreeing, making exceptions or additions. Your thinking is language, and your language is thinking.

We have long recognized in school work that language is thinking. Sometimes we say that a child is just reading words, and what we mean is that he is not thinking what he is reading. When we listen to children talk or ask them questions, we are not really listening to words. We are trying to follow the thinking that is going on in the child's head. We have long encouraged reading because it gives children ideas to think with. We have said that children do not really have ideas unless they can think with them. We have seen that intelligence implies skilful use of language because thinking and language are so closely related. In short, we have consciously or unconsciously been emphasizing language development as thinking development.

The new movement for a unified language course frankly places the thinking aspect of language ahead of all its other aspects. Of what use is it for a child to be able to read words if he cannot think the thoughts he reads? Of what use is it for him to spell words if he has no thoughts to express in writing? Of what use is correctness in language if there are no thoughts to express correctly? Too long have we been concerned about mere form. Too long have we dealt with the husks and not the kernel. We have taught the sounding of words, the spelling of words, the writing of words, the forms of words, the classification of words. But all of this is useless unless there is thinking. The modern movement deals with language as the development of thinking, first and foremost and all the time. This is a sound emphasis. It is an emphasis that has come to stay. There is nothing for us to do but to align our school practice with it. How can we do that?

How can the whole school language course, including the five subjects, reading, writing, spelling, usage and grammar, be built around the conception of *language as thinking?* The answer begins with reading readiness in grade one. The primer has simple sentences because most children of primer age think in simple sentences. But we have some beginners who do not seem to think in sentences at all. All you can get out of them is isolated words. Such children are not ready to read because reading means thinking the sentences and stories of the primer. Therefore developing reading readiness includes, among other things, telling of stories by the children, or talking together by the children, until we are sure they think clearly in simple sentences. Then, and then only, can we expect them to think freely the sentences in the reading book. *So language development begins in the reading readiness program.*

Then, the first reader has somewhat longer sentences than the primer, with phrases and perhaps some subordinate clauses. The second reader has slightly longer and more complex sentences. Year by year the thought units in reading books become gradually more and more complex. But is the language development of the children keeping pace with the increased demands of the readers? Are the children thinking in longer and more complex sentences? Very often they are not, and the teacher complains that some of the children are just reading words. But how can they do anything else when the reading is at one level and the thinking at another? Therefore the second requirement of a logical language course is the development of the children's thinking in every grade, from the first grade on. Good teachers have always conducted this training in thinking because they felt the great need for it, but there has been no real recognition of language development in the school curriculum. It is time that such recognition is given. We shall therefore point out three *definite ways in which a language development program may be set up in a school system.*

First, there should be in every grade a daily period for the telling and discussing of experience. The natural thing for children to think about is what has happened to them or what they have actually done. This will be in fact an experience period but may be called simply a conversation period. It may be called an Oral English period if a more formal title for it is desired. By whatever name, it is simply an opportunity every day for children to exchange thoughts or to stimulate each other to thinking about what is going on about them. If we are really interested in teaching language as the teaching of thinking our first solution is the daily experience period. Good teachers have always had such periods at convenient times or have taken time for real thinking together when the opportunity offered. Children in their classes have known that if anyone had any important thought or question, that all would be interested in, time would be found to discuss it. This has been splendid for language development, but it has been unofficial and even frowned upon at times. Instead, the school must now provide for such exchange of experience and thinking together. Every room and every grade needs a daily opportunity for thinking about the daily matters that are important to children and about which they wish and need to think. So the first step is provision for such a period, call it experience, conversation, or Oral English or what you will.

Second, the reading period can be specifically thought of as a language development period. If the content of the reading book is interesting, children will think about that content if given a chance to do so. We may have the children go over the words orally or silently but that is only a slight beginning. Then we must see that the children think the thoughts they have read or other thoughts suggested by what they have read.

Three kinds of questions can be asked in the reading period, each having its own value. There are *reproduction questions* which ask the child to tell what he has read, looking not at the book but at the class and teacher. Then there are *reaction questions* which ask him for ideas which are in addition to what is in the book. Best of all are the *child's own questions* which show if he has or has not had reactions or thoughts. To turn the reading period into a language period takes time but it is time well spent. It also takes tact to cause all the children to have some thoughts of their own and not to allow a few to do the thinking and the others merely to sit. But reading is language if the children think what they read and think about what they read. Here is the real reason for the reading text book throughout all the grades. The reader in the hands of all is really a thinking book rather than a reading book. Questions at the beginning or end of selections try to help thinking but the best help is the free discussion based on both teacher's questions and pupils questions. These make the reading period a real language development period.

Third, the period for every content subject may and should be a language period. Here we have much the same situation as in the case of reading. If there is a text book the children must think about the subject matter they read, and in this way the subject matter becomes language and helps language development. Then there are questions and comments and additional ideas; and thus there is more thinking and more language development. Incidentally, children's troubles with verbal problems in arithmetic come because the children do not or cannot *think* the problems. We help children to solve such problems by helping them *think* them. In junior high school especially it is important to consider content subjects as opportunities for teaching thinking. No one really has an idea if he can not use it in thinking. To make sure our pupils have the content ideas we must make sure they think with those ideas. Of course language development is not the whole of any content subject. The different sciences and arts deal with things that are new to children and that give them new ideas. But if the children think about these things as they should, they will be using language and improving their use of language. Thus, we have a threefold program for language development—*a daily experience period, language in the reading period,* and *language in all content periods.*

We all know exactly what most teachers will say in response to this plea that language as thinking be made the most important concern of their school. They will say that there is not time. The answer to that is very simple. How can there *not* be time to do the chief thing that the school is there to do? If the school as now planned does not have time for language development, the school will have to make time for it or cease to call itself a real school.

Another response which teachers may make is that they have too many children and that the children are too different in their rates of language development. This is a real difficulty. An experience period with 40 children requires management if it is not to be bedlam. Habits of courtesy and cooperation must be taught. Thinking and expression in a reading period is not so difficult if we divide the children into several reading groups, or if we use work books with readers, though poor readers often find them so hard that little interest or thinking is possible. Work books may also stimulate thinking in content subjects if such work books are thought provoking and do not have too hard reading matter. Too many work books are puzzle books in which whoever fills the blanks somehow wins. But the chief recourse of the able teacher in developing language thinking, even in a large class, is the leading of a class discussion which is so active and so interesting that each child is bursting with things to say even though only a few get a chance to say them out loud. The others are thinking their own comments, which means saying them to themselves.

If we grant that language development means thinking development and should be the chief concern of the school at all levels, excepting only character development, all the other "subjects" which we have taught so long as separate skills fall immediately into their proper place. First of all we recognize that the natural language for a child is primarily spoken language. The children talk before they come to school and they talk all during their school life. Immediately we realize that we want them to speak correctly, that is, to follow correct usage. Textbooks have been built by publishers for this purpose but they must be used with caution. A textbook may lead us to "teach the book" instead of teaching children. *If it is the children's language that we are thinking of, the children's language should be our starting point.*

Every school should have what is called a correction program. All the teachers study the children's actual expression and list the mistakes which are found. Conferring together, they arrange these mistakes in a list from the most serious to the least. Then they decide on a plan of attack, assigning certain mistakes to each grade for special attention. The children are told all about the correction program so that each one can see where he stands on this "ladder of correctness." The children may even participate in making the program. Then, all together, teachers and children unite to outlaw grade by grade the particular mistakes. Here is a genuine language situation. It is public sentiment that makes us speak correctly, and the children must provide the public sentiment in this case. If such a plan is followed, the teaching of correct usage is made an inseparable and natural part of the program of language development. In such a program a textbook can be used but not chapter by chapter and page by page. No textbook is ever made for your particular school but you can adapt the textbook to your school. Each class can refer to the part of the textbook which helps in attacking the special problem of usage they have on hand at the moment. This is a natural and logical plan for teaching usage.

The second most natural use of language for children is following or thinking what is heard or read. Thus *all reading will be adjusted to the child's language development.* We will stop giving fourth grade books to third grade thinkers. Instead we will give them third grade books until practice at thinking third grade will bring them up to thinking fourth grade. Language development or thinking development cannot be forced. It is a growth. You cannot make a child grow, you can only help him to grow, and books which are beyond his development do not help him much. This fact has been recognized in modern schools in two ways. In the class reading period, all children may have the same reader and think together. Some children may not know the words, but they see the pictures, hear the other children and can follow somewhat.

There is also a supplementary reading period in which each child reads at his own true level. Each has a book suited to his own interests and reading ability. Now he can think what he reads. He can follow the thoughts. He can think thoughts of his own. This is an invaluable part of every reading program that is part of a language development program. But the same system is also followed in content subjects. Whether in natural science or geography or history, the children may have a single text and think together about it. But they also use a room or school library. Thus if the colonies are to be studied, there will be found in the room library or school library books on the colonies at three or four different grade levels. Each child will read and think at his own suitable level and each child will tell the group about what he has read. Thus the second use of language as thinking is in reading in textbooks and in reading of other books that are at the child's real language level and therefore permit and encourage thinking.

If speaking is the first kind of language, and reading is the second kind, writing is the third. For children, writing practically means talking on paper. To get honest, accurate writing, we need the same occasions and methods we use with oral language.

If this is so, just how do penmanship and spelling come into the picture? Obviously these matters are only of use in helping children to express themselves on paper. How does that expression arise? The first need that children have for writing is the need for writing in school. Therefore let us go right ahead and plan penmanship and spelling for this school use. Here we have the reason for the introduction of manuscript writing, or printing as it should be called. In the first grade there is some school use for writing, and manuscript writing serves that school use easily and well. Children need early to put their names on pictures or to fill in work books or the like. The same school use continues in grade two and three. In fact, printing does very well for school use year after year.

Script will be needed for use outside of school but that use is a long time in coming. Children of grades one, two and three do not write letters outside of school, and seldom do those of grades four, five, and six. Parents who have struggled to get children to write letters know this all too well. Children as a group just do not write outside of school unless they are especially urged to do so. At some time the child will need to write script but in the past we have taught him that script years and years before he will need it. The teachers of any school should seriously study this situation and adjust the teaching of writing to the child's real need for this kind of language. Do not depend on textbook makers or "authorities." Find out the facts for yourself.

The same thing holds true for spelling. No one needs to spell until he needs to write. He needs to spell a word only when there is a considerable chance that he will write it. If one reads through a spelling list in most textbooks he will wonder how many years it will be before the children are going to need to write the words included. A good device would be simply to push all the spelling books up a year or two. But this doubt of its usefulness has caused many schools to abandon the usual list altogether. They say that the child needs to spell just what he writes and therefore when he needs to write a word is the time when he needs to learn how to spell it. Let him have a dictionary handy and as he writes let him look up the words he does not know. What these words will be no spelling text book can predict. This is a frank facing of the real language situation. But if a school does not want to take this view, it can use the usual spelling book but make an entirely different use of it. Suppose the speller contains 4,000 words. These words are valuable in reading and in thinking even if one never writes them at all. So the school may frankly use the speller for vocabulary building and word study, with the spelling an incidental matter only. This will make the spelling lesson contribute to language development. The children can use words in sentences or discuss them in such a way as to benefit a great deal from the time given.

We as teachers have a traditional interest in the drawing of lines that we call penmanship; we have a traditional interest in the putting together of letters that we call spelling; we are traditionally concerned with the putting together of words according to correct usage. But we must not let these traditional interests distract us from a main concern of the schools. In comparison with it, these matters are very minor and very unimportant. For what will it profit a pupil if he has beautiful penmanship, correct spelling, and accurate usage but has absolutely nothing to say. Speaking is thinking and reading is thinking and writing is thinking. Our main concern, after the teaching of character, must be teaching real language, which is thinking. We must start this in the first grade and continue it in every one. We can do it through the experience period, the reading period and in every other period as well. This is the real meaning of the new emphasis on language development or language as thinking.

Part II

Word Recognition and Phonics

CHAPTER IV

PHONIC READINESS

The idea has become commonly accepted that the child cannot begin to learn to read until he has reached a certain degree of mental maturity. That mental maturity has been called "reading readiness"; it is chiefly "school readiness" plus the ability to acquire a sight vocabulary, that is, to associate word sounds with word forms. When a child can make such associations under classroom conditions, he can begin learning to read. When he has accumulated a sight vocabulary of the most common words, he can actually read books if they are strictly limited to the simplest vocabulary. Thus, with sight learning of common words and with vocabulary control in reading materials, teachers can secure what is typically first-grade reading.

Schoolbooks do not, however, remain limited to the sight vocabulary of the first-grade pupil. New words must come in daily and at an ever-increasing rate. At the same time the amount of repetition of

---

From the *Elementary School Journal,* Vol. 38, No. 3. Miss Maurine Bloomster, joint author.

new words steadily decreases. As the number of words becomes greater, the appearance of the words becomes more and more similar. All these conditions—greater number, less repetition, and greater similarity of words—demand something more than the sight method of learning. They demand what is called "independence in word recognition," and that means some sort of phonic attack.

Phonic attack must come—but when? The general agreement is that it must follow some certain amount of sight recognition. Phonic attack means the use of generalizations about how letters are sounded. Inductive teaching has been found to be most effective; the teacher puts together words with similar letter sounds and leads the child to note the similarity. After the child has perceived that four or five words beginning with a certain sound begin with the same letter, he is supposed to have learned the generalization that all words beginning with that letter begin with the associated sound, and he is supposed to use this generalization in new word situations.

It is true that the use of phonics means the use of generalizations, that generalizations are best learned inductively, and that sight words are the basis of inductive reasoning. Do these facts mean that, as soon as the pupil has learned a few similar sight words, he can go right ahead with phonics? Actual classroom experience leads to the questioning of such a conclusion. Dozens of sight words of similar sound can be taught; the children can be led carefully through the process of inductive reasoning; and still many of the pupils simply cannot use phonics. The best teachers as well as average teachers have this experience. Some factor seems to have been neglected.

Studies have been made of the sight words needed and of the methods necessary for inductive teaching, but little attention has been paid to the mental abilities which the child himself uses in the process. To learn phonic analysis of words and to use the results of such analysis surely requires more mental ability than that used in sight recognition or, at least, a different type of mental ability. Experience in teaching indicates that this conclusion is correct. Learning of phonics comes later than the sight learning of words by a greater or a less interval. Some children use phonics to some extent in Grade I; other children learn to do so in Grade II; and still others do not seem to be able to use phonics until Grade III. These facts show that some factor is operating other than material or teaching method.

One hypothesis is that the ability to learn and to use principles of phonics is closely connected with the increase in mental age. General reading readiness, which is largely readiness for the sight learning of words, is generally supposed to be attained at the mental age of 6 or 6½ years. The school experience just cited suggests that phonic readiness comes at some time later than sight readiness. Then it may come at a later mental age. To try out this hypothesis, an experiment was conducted in the first two grades of a school in which the teaching of phonics had been uniform for at least two years and in which phonics had had some emphasis, though not an unusual amount. The plan was simply to measure, first, the children's mental development and, second, their phonic attainment, and to see whether one was in any way related to the other.

About May 1, a primary mental test was given to the children in each of the two grades. In the previous September the first-grade pupils had been given the Detroit First-Grade Intelligence Test, and the year before that the pupils now in Grade II had been given a primary mental test. Results from these previous tests were roughly brought up to date by the addition of the number of months from the time of giving the test to May 1. Thus mental ages for the pupils of both grades were secured from the average of two group tests. It must be understood that these results could not give anything like the accuracy which individual intelligence tests would make possible.

The phonic achievement in these two grades was determined by the use of experimental issues of Tests 1 and 2 of the Basic Reading Tests, Word-Attack Series.[1] Test 1 of this series consists of

[1] The Word-Attack Series of the Dolch-Gray Basic Reading Tests are published by Scott, Foresman and Company, Chicago, Illinois. They are group tests measuring three degrees of ability in sounding attack on new words.

words containing only the short vowels, preceded and followed by a single consonant. Each test word is in a line with three other words or word-like forms, each of which differs in only one letter from the test word. Hence the word wholes look so much alike that recognition by the method of pure sight is difficult for a beginner, and the child is usually compelled to sound out the forms in order to find the right form pronounced for him by the tester. Test 2 is of similar construction except that some of the test words contain short vowels and some long vowels with final *e* and that many words also contain consonant blends or consonant digraphs. In both tests sight knowledge is rendered largely useless by the great similarity of the word forms. In addition, the words in the test are familiar to children by meaning, but they do not appear on lists of words common to primary reading books. In Grade II the scores on the two phonic tests were averaged to give each child's phonic achievement. In Grade I only the easier test was used.

Because the second-grade group had had more teaching than Grade I, the groups could not be combined, but it may be assumed that the material and teaching factors for the members of any one group were practically constant. Therefore, for each group the mental age and the phonic achievement were correlated by the Pearson product-moment method. As a check on the results, the experiment was repeated in the following May. There was marked agreement between the results of the two experiments, as is shown in Table I.

TABLE 1

Correlation of Mental Age and Phonic Achievement of Pupils in Grades I and II in Two School Years

Grade	Number of Pupils	Correlation
I (first year)	30	.412±.102
I (second year)	24	.472±.106
II (first year)	28	.516±.096
II (second year)	33	.406±.098

When consideration is given to the difficulty of accurate measurement of young children in both the fields concerned, the relation between mental maturity and the use of phonics is reasonably high. The scattergrams made from the scores show a more significant fact: children of high mental age sometimes fail to acquire phonic ability but children of low mental age are certain to fail. The scattergrams seem to show the thing in which we are perhaps most interested, namely, the *minimum age for phonic readiness.* Children with mental ages below seven years made only chance scores; that is, as far as this experiment indicates, *a mental age of seven years seems to be the lowest at which a child can be expected to use phonics, even in the simple situations provided by these two tests.*

It has always been known that some first-grade pupils learned to use phonics, but it is also known that many children reach a mental age of seven years before the end of Grade I. Most of the others, though not all, reach the mental age of seven years in Grade II. Some do not reach the mental age of seven years until Grade III. Correspondingly, some children learn to use phonics in Grade I, most learn to use some phonics in Grade II, and a few do not learn to use phonics until Grade III.

These results seem therefore to check with school experience. They do not tell, however, exactly when the teaching of phonics should be *started.* Ear-training, which is the basis of phonics, may begin early. Children may be taught to notice the similarities between sounds some time before they are expected actually to use sounding generalizations. This study does suggest, however, that many schools are perhaps expecting results from phonic-teaching too soon.

CHAPTER V

WORD RECOGNITION AND PHONICS IN THE PRIMARY GRADES

To the child in the primary grades, reading means essentially "getting the story." Some primary-grade reading is nonfiction, but predominantly it is story-reading. The teacher prepares for a story by stirring the children's imaginations beforehand. The teacher asks about past experiences; she may show objects or pictures; she may tell of her own experiences; or she may tell a story of her own. If she is fortunate, she can take the children somewhere, to the fire house, for example, before reading a story about fire engines. The publisher of the reading book also prepares for the story, but he does it through the illustrations. He gets the most skilful and imaginative children's artist that he can, who makes the pictures as exciting as possible, and causes the children to imagine themselves in the story.

Sooner or later, however, the children must look at the words under the pictures. But many children do not see any need to look at those words. They know the story; they have imagined it; they are "in it" already; and they can look at the page and "read off" a story in a smooth, coherent, and convincing manner. Only it is not the story that the

---

From *Supplementary Educational Monographs*, No. 57, 1943, University of Chicago.

author put into the book. Some of these children can "read" the whole page after just a look at the picture. Others catch a word or two as they go along and make up what happens in between. Some read almost what the words say but add little changes or improvements of their own.

Sooner or later, such an imaginative child, who can make up the story as he goes, must come to realize that real reading is telling just exactly what is on the page and nothing else. The literal child, on the other hand, has been at this point all along. He has recognized the words that he knew and has stopped when he came to a word he did not know. The story did not carry him away; the words held him right to the line. Some teachers like this literal child because they feel that he has the right idea from the start. Other teachers like the imaginative child and feel that the literal child really does not have the right idea of reading. We can agree with both kinds of teachers; reading is in fact imagining things in our heads, but, on the other hand, imagination should follow the words that the author has put down for us. Reading is getting the right words and *then* getting the right meaning or story. Without the right words, the story will be wrong.

REPEATED ASSOCIATION

If reading, then, demands word recognition, how can we teach the child efficient habits of word recognition? In answering this question, we follow, in the primary grades, one basic principle: we teach word recognition by *repeated association.* As a child looks at a word form, the teacher or a pupil says the word sound. The form and the sound occur together; they are associated in the child's mind. This association occurs again and again, and presently, when the child looks at the word, the sound and, therefore the meaning, comes to his mind.

Here we can present the first important rule for efficient teaching of word recognition, namely, that *the principle of repeated association must be used skilfully.* One of the chief causes of poor reading is that teachers so often do not use this principle skilfully or efficiently. Strangely enough, many teachers do not even realize that they must provide this repeated association. Word form and word sound must be thought together.

The great secret of the ability of some teachers and the inability of others to develop a large sight vocabulary in their children is easily seen from a visit to their classes. The successful teachers get their children to look at all the words on the board or in the book as they are said. The children therefore get repeated association. The unsuccessful teachers may have just the same words on the board and the same words in the book, and just the same words may be read aloud, but the children are not looking at the right place at the right time.

When children come to Grade II or III without the sight vocabulary that they are supposed to have, the explanation in nearly every case is that they did not get repeated association of the words called for. They may have been sick and so missed the associations that the others had. They may have moved about and kept changing books and, therefore, kept meeting new vocabularies. Usually, however, they just sat in the room and looked around and hence did not learn. There is no substitute for repeated association of word form and word sound.

We may digress here to say that insisting on form-sound associations does not mean stripping the reading lesson of thought or of interest. Far from it! We must keep interest always present. We must keep thought-getting uppermost. The children must read for fun and experience, and they must *also* develop word recognition.

WORD COMPARISON

But some of us are not satisfied to rely upon repeated association alone. "Why cannot we hurry the process?" we say. "Why not point out similarities and differences?" Surely the method of repeated association means that the child subconsciously notices more and more about each word. Let us make the process conscious. Let us teach the characteristics of words directly.

So we come to our second principle for teaching word recognition, the principle of *word comparison.* Word comparison may be developed into a large and complicated science. Two avenues of study present themselves. First, we can ask children how they tell words apart and thus discover that they use this or that detail of the word appearance. Second, we can study the miscallings that children make in their reading and surmise what detail they failed to notice. As a result of these two kinds of study, the usual work of word comparison has been divided into a comparison of beginnings, endings, and middle letters. Teachers spend much class time in showing these word comparisons, encouraged usually by copious material in the manuals. Many pages of workbooks for the primary-grade years are filled with innumerable and ingenious exercises in word comparison.

We are not here discounting the value of word comparison but are seeking to present a saner viewpoint with regard to it than is sometimes seen in the class room. A great deal of time can be wasted in word-comparison exercises, since time spent on word comparison might also be spent in reading. Word comparison should be considered a necessary evil. We should not stop to compare words unless we need to do so. When we need to, let us do it. If we do not need to, let us read.

SOUNDS OR NAMES OF LETTERS

We now come to a disputed point in classroom practice. When we put the words "think" and "thank" on the board for word comparison, how shall we point out the difference? Shall we say that the first word has an *i* in it and that the second word has an *a*? In other words, shall we use the spelling to bring out our point?

Here is a situation in which we must do something. What should that something be? Now it is true that many children will come to school knowing the names of the letters. Their parents have taught them the letter names, and they will spell out the new words they see. Some teachers therefore accept the naming of letters, and in all their word comparison speak of the letter names. If the children know the letters anyway and are bound to think of them, and if mere visual comparison is what we want, such a practice will do. But is mere word recognition what we want?

Our real object is "recognizing words *independently*"; that is, coming to a word we do not know, with no one to tell us, and finding out by ourselves what that word says. In such a situation one can guess, of course, but that will not be finding out. If there is no one to tell us whether the guess is right, it is still a guess. Many children get the fixed habit of guessing and looking at the teacher's face. Her face will show instantly whether the guess is right or wrong, and, if it is right, the child feels that he has done the job well. He has found out by himself, he thinks, and the teacher might say the same. But reading the teacher's face is not reading a book. Finding out independently what a word is means finding out with no one to aid. Such finding out means only one thing: sounding out from the letters which make up the word.

In the sounding-out of words, the letter names will not help. It is strange that adults think that the letter names somehow correspond with the letter sounds. For instance, no reader realizes, probably, that the *name* for *h* does not have the *sound* of *h* in it at all. We would spell that sound "aitch" perhaps, but the letters of *tch* in this spelling do not contain the sound of *h*. Consider also the names of the five vowels. None of these five names contains the short sound—the usual sound—of the vowel.

Can a child use the letter names in sounding out a new word? Just try it. Say the letter names in any word, and try to get the sound of the word from them. For instance, try this word. We shall give the letter names. They are *see-you-bee-ee.* Now think of what you just did. First, you may have visualized the letters and then seen the word and read it off as a sight word. Or, you may have changed each letter name into a letter sound and thus made the word. But please note that in either case the letter names did not give you any *direct* help. You had to go through the letter names either to the word form or to the letter sounds. The old spelling method of learning reading gave the child the letter names, and it was found a very indirect and clumsy method. Why should we go back to letter names again when it is the letter sounds that we must use in attacking a new word?

PHONOGRAMS

We are aware that there is another school of thought on this question. Some of you may, in fact, be thinking, "Oh, no! The child must not use the letter sounds. He must use sounds of letter combinations." Yes, that is just what some teachers think concerning primary phonics. In so thinking, they are following teachers' manuals which are based upon certain researches made some years ago. But those researches have been very greatly misinterpreted. Any teacher can understand this by making a little research of her own. After all, our first problem is to teach children to recognize the words in their own reading books, is it not? So let us turn to the words in beginning readers. Let us see what those words tell us about phonograms. The way to make this test is actually to list the blends and the endings which appear in the books being used by the children.

We can tell you right now what your results will be. First, one-fourth of all your words will be polysyllables and hence too complicated for any system of phonogram endings to help. Another fourth of your words will be "individual" words, that is, words which are too unusual to fit any system of endings. So fully one-half of your words are outside any phonogram system. In the remaining half, practically all the twenty-one consonants will be used as initial letter sounds. Therefore these twenty-one letter sounds have to be taught as letter sounds no matter what phonograms you teach. You will nearly always find eighteen blends, most of which are used only once but a few of which may be used four or five times each. When you come to count the different endings, you will find anywhere from seventy to a hundred. More than half of these will appear only once during the whole year; five or six will appear as often as four or five times. Now suppose we add up all these different items. To use a phonogram system, we would have to teach 21 beginning consonants, 18 beginning blends, and perhaps 90 endings, or nearly 130 different items. But no one would teach an ending as an ending if it is used only once; so to attack these endings, we should have again to go to the single letter sounds. (See Chapter VIII for further figures on phonograms in primary books.)

The upshot of the facts just presented is that, if we want *independent* word recognition, the only way we can get it is to teach the child the sounds of the letters, with their common variations, about fifty in all. With the equipment of these simple sounds, he can attack any word, and, if that word is reasonably phonetic, he can figure it out.

NONPHONETIC WORDS

At this point we should emphasize another practical side of word recognition. It deals with the problem of nonphonetic words. Unfortunately many of the common words of the language are largely nonphonetic. In sounding by any system, we encounter trouble with these words. How, then, is the child to acquire independent word recognition in the face of this situation?

The solution of the conflict between sounding and nonphonetic words is, first, to defer sounding as long as possible. Let the children learn words by the sight method and keep on learning words by sight just as long as they can. This sight learning depends on the two principles that we have already discussed: repeated association and word comparison. If these two principles are skilfully used, it is astonishing how far children can go by sight alone.

The second practical solution is to use sounding, not so much for working out complete words, as for *checking guesses from context.* That is, do not tell a child to work out a new word from the letters. First, ask him what he thinks the word is, and then ask him to check with the letter sounds to see if it could be that word. This checking process need usually go only part way through the word. It works with nonphonetic words also because, except for a few words like "know" and "pneumonia," a word is phonetic in its beginning. Let us cultivate intelligent guessing and the use of sounding to catch mistakes. This method will aid in getting around the tremendous handicap of nonphonetic words.

Let us summarize briefly the discussion thus far on word recognition in the primary grades. First, it was pointed out that two principles show the way to efficient teaching of sight vocabulary: (1) repeated association of word form and word sound; (2) word comparison when needed, including comparison of the word part which causes difficulty. Then, when the child is reading alone and must work out words independently, we must teach a third principle: guessing from context and checking the guess by sounding out at least the beginning of the word. For this sounding-out of beginnings, the individual letter sounds are needed.

POLYSYLLABLES IN PRIMARY GRADES

Now we must consider one other problem with regard to independent word attack in the primary grades. It has been noted that one-fourth of the words in the first year are almost sure to be polysyllables. If we study the words during the second school year, we find that nearly one-third are polysyllables and in the third primary year, almost half of the new words are polysyllables. What shall we do with word recognition of the polysyllables which are met with in the primary grades?

First of all, we are bound to teach most of these polysyllables by sheer sight-word methods. This is the more possible because the long words do not resemble one another so closely as do the short words.

Second, many of the polysyllables in the primary grades will be compounds of monosyllables, such as "into," "without," "blackboard," and so on. A child needs only to be told to look for the parts of such a word, and he is likely to recognize one half instantly and can then concentrate on the other half.

Third, many of the polysyllables of the primary grades are what may be called "changed monosyllables." That is, any monosyllable that the children know may be changed by adding *s, ed, er, ing,* or some other inflectional ending. If we suggest to the child that the word is a familiar one that has been changed by adding something to the end, he will concentrate his eyes on the central part or on the beginning and will usually recognize the word.

Fourth, there is a great difference of opinion as to whether primary-grade children should be taught to attack true polysyllables, that is, polysyllables not made by compounding or by adding endings. A reasonable conclusion seems to be that, if the children in Grade III have already had a good grounding in the phonics of monosyllables and can attack the short words successfully, they should go on to the syllable division of long words. But if the third-graders have not successfully learned the attack on the short words, the division of the long words would only confuse them. In such a case the attention would have to be given to monosyllable phonics, and polysyllable phonics would have to be deferred until the next year.

See page 96 for description of materials for teaching sounding.

CHAPTER VI

PHONICS IN THE MIDDLE GRADES

It is doubtful whether any of us can appreciate the great change in reading books that the child finds between the primary and the middle grades. In the primary grades the books are chiefly storybooks. Subjects other than reading are introduced incidentally. There is much activity aside from reading, and books do not seems to play the major role during the five hours of school.

Beginning with Grade IV, however, this same child is presented with a real stack of books. Everything seems to be in a book. All day he seems to be putting away one book and taking out another. All at once, reading seems to be the chief thing that he is doing all day. And all at once, he finds that his reading ability, or lack of it, seems to be the immediate and all-important cause of success or failure in school.

Added to this sudden increase in the amount of reading, there is an equally astonishing increase in the difficulty of the reading matter. There is the famous "fourth-grade hump," the sudden difficulty of reading matter that strikes the children without warning. The difficulty keeps on climbing fast through Grades V and VI.

From *Supplementary Educational Monographs,* No. 57, 1943, University of Chicago.

When to the word burden of the regular readers we add the word burden of the subject-matter books —geographies, histories, arithmetics, health books, and so on—we see that the task of word recognition in the middle grades is far beyond that in the primary grades. What, then, can the middle-grade teacher do about the word-recognition problem? As the children meet new words, line by line, paragraph by paragraph, page by page, what should be her system, her method of attack?

UNKNOWN MEANINGS

First of all, many new words will be of unknown meaning. These words are not recognition problems but teaching problems. The child cannot *recognize* a word of which he does not already know the sound and the meaning.

Usually the teacher will know from experience which these teaching words are, and she will first tell the pupils the correct pronunciation and then will explain the meaning, or she will have some of the more advanced pupils do this. Letting the children do it has advantages, but this should not be an exhibition of superiority on their part. Sometimes the teacher will not be sure which words present meaning problems, and she will have to find out when the class comes to the word. In any event, a word of unknown meaning is not a word to be "recognized," since we can recognize only what we already know.

Second, the remaining words are "recognition words." They are known to the children by sound but not by sight. The usual method of dealing with these recognition words is simply "telling." Either the teacher tells or some bright pupil says the word out loud, or the teacher asks who can tell.

This common habit of "telling" all new words is the cause of the equally common habit of "skipping" in silent reading. Some teachers naïvely say, "Jimmy can read so well silently but cannot read orally at all." That is a queer statement. Anyone who can read one way, can read the other. What that teacher should say is, "Jimmy skips so successfully when reading silently, but of course we don't let him skip when he reads orally." Our present system of appraising reading by silent-reading tests perpetuates and even encourages this habit of skipping. The usual silent-reading test gives a paragraph and a few questions, and many children can answer most of the questions even if they can read only half the paragraph.

What shall we do, then, if we are determined that the children shall do their own recognizing—that we are not going to cripple them by doing it for them?

MONOSYLLABLES

First, we must note that some of the words to be recognized will be monosyllables and some will be polysyllables. These two kinds of words should be considered separately because they have to be dealt with differently. The monosyllables will be few. They form a very minor part of the new words during later grades. Many of these unusual monosyllables are also *teaching words,* as mentioned above, because the children do not know their meaning, as in the case of such words as "monk," "flare," "gloat," and the like.

If the children have had a good course in monosyllable phonics in their primary-grade years, it will be well to have these monosyllables attacked in the usual way. If, however, the children have not had successful monosyllable phonics, it is useless to try to go back and teach it to them. In fact, a practical rule may be to teach all monosyllables as sight words. This is a small job and is easily done.

Second, our chief concern in helping the children with the words which they must recognize themselves is teaching them how to attack the polysyllables, of which there are an immense and never-ending number. Every year and in every subject there will be new words which are polysyllables. Throughout life there will be more and more polysyllables. The children must learn how to attack these words if they are ever to be successful independent readers. Here our teaching divides itself into three distinct parts.

a) We find that some of the polysyllables are simply two monosyllables put together, that is, compound words. If the teacher just suggests that there are two parts, as in "schoolhouse" or "sometime" or the like, the child will look for the two parts, recognize the monosyllables, and so be able to read the word.

b) We find that many long words are merely "changed monosyllables"; that is, they are monosyllables with a prefix or a suffix. Recognition of this group can be taught either by exercises or by attack during reading. There are, in fact, a rather limited number of suffixes that can be taught, such as the inflectional endings, *-ed, -ing, -er, -est, -es;* the "change-of-part-of-speech endings," such as *-ly* in "sharply," *-ness* in "goodness"; and so on. The point is that the teacher will be on the lookout for familiar monosyllables in some changed form, and, when she sees one, she will call attention to the change, if the pupil does not recognize the situation himself.

TRUE POLYSYLLABLES

Third, we come now to the true polysyllables, and these form the chief problem of word recognition in the middle grades. They form the main problem because they usually do not have familiar parts. They are long strings of letters in which the average child finds no help or comfort. They appear as a confusing configuration. To the child they seem actually a jumble of letters, without rhyme or reason.

How can we help children to attack the long string of letters that is a new word and to recognize that it is really a word which they have heard and perhaps used themselves? The first thing is to break the word up into parts. Ear training is usually needed to teach children that long words are made up of parts. Make a game of telling how many parts a long word contains when you say it rapidly. Say, for instance, "manufacture," "elementary," "signature," "mortification," and the like.

In sounding out a new word, for the beginner there are four steps. First: How many parts? The answer is: As many as there are vowels. We should give the answer in this simple way, though there are the complications of the silent final *e*, double vowels, diphthongs, and the like. Working with a class, the best way at first is to write the word on the board and to put a check over each sounded vowel. That will show graphically how many parts.

The second question is: Are there prefixes or suffixes? The reason for taking this step is that prefixes and suffixes are cut off as units and take with them the consonants that belong to them. For instance, the prefix *com-* takes the *m*, the prefix *un-* takes the *n*. In this way certain consonants are taken care of. Thus, if there are prefixes or suffixes, they should be cut off by vertical lines as the second step.

The third question is: What to do with the remaining consonants? The general answer is that all consonants go with the next vowel if they can be pronounced with it. Usually, however, if there is one consonant, it goes with the next vowel; but, if there are two consonants, they are divided. This does not deny the rule that all consonants go with the next vowel if they can be pronounced with it, for usually the two or more consonants coming together cannot be pronounced together. Some persons teach the general rule, and others teach the division of two or more consonants, both arriving at about the same result. So with the word on the board, let vertical lines be drawn to divide the syllables or parts.

After the word is divided, the small parts can easily be sounded by the sounds of the letters. Most of the syllables will be but two or three letters long. They are, in fact, much simpler than monosyllables. The fourth step deals with the sound of the vowel, following the rule that open syllables are long if accented, while closed syllables are short. This is most natural since an open syllable—one ending in a vowel—means that the speaker keeps his mouth open and thus tends to prolong the sound. A closed syllable, one ending in a consonant, means that the speaker closes his mouth in saying the consonant and thus tends to shut off the vowel and make it short. But, the objector says, how can the pupil tell whether the open syllable is accented or not? We cannot teach him rules for this, and so he may come to a wrong conclusion. You all know the story of the foreigner who always put the "emphásis on the wrong syl-láb-le." But there is an answer.

THE PROBLEM OF ACCENT

What to do with emphasis in sounding out a long word is well explained by Thorndike, who says:

> A pupil who is slowly pronouncing a word syllable by syllable with accents on each syllable in order to learn its constituent parts or its spelling may properly replace the sound of *e* by the more specific sound which the *a* or *e* or *i* or *u* would have if accented, and may replace the sound of *i* by that of *ē* in words like "detain," "presume," and "receive."[a]

This fact of formal, accented pronunciation was recognized as far back as Dr. Johnson. What the pupil actually does is to accent each syllable as he works out the word. He makes every open syllable long. As a result, he does not try to get the exact sound of the word. We must remember we are talking about word recognition—the recognizing of words already known by ear. We are not talking about entirely new words. As said earlier, such words are teaching words, and the teacher will give the correct sounding. This sounding-out by syllables is merely to recognize. Therefore the child may get the sound "in-de-pen-dent" and at once say "independent." He may get "ir-ri-ga-tion" and say at once, "Oh, irrigation." He sounds out each syllable, says the syllables together, and recognizes the word. That is, he will recognize it if he knows it by ear. If he does not know the word by ear, he must go to the dictionary. No one can trust himself to sound

---

[a] E. L. Thorndike, *Thorndike Century Junior Dictionary*, p. ix. Chicago: Scott, Foresman & Co., 1942 (revised).

out a strange English word and get the exactly correct sounding, both because of not knowing where to accent and because of irregular parts.

The attack on new words in the middle grades may, therefore, be summarized as follows:

I. If the words are new meanings, teach sound and meaning at once.
II. If the meanings are known and the sound is familiar—
  A. Tell them if monosyllables.
  B. If polysyllables—
    1. And if compounds, point out familiar parts.
    2. If changed monosyllables, point out prefixes and suffixes.
    3. If true polysyllables—
      a) Mark number of vowels,
      b) Separate prefixes and suffixes,
      c) Divide remaining consonants,
      d) Work out by letter sounds.

Here a word of practical caution must be given. The sounding-out of long words should be a game, a sort of cross-word puzzle. There should be a little every day, but not a boring quantity. The teacher may still tell most of the new words or have a pupil tell them, because there are so very many in any reading lesson. But from time to time, as often as seems advisable, she should challenge the pupils to work out a word by themselves.

SOUNDING IS A SKILL

The teaching of word attack on long words, as we have outlined it, would be easy except for a little-understood fact. Word attack is a skill, not a mere branch of knowledge, and learning any skill is a matter of taking time. One learns a little, and then a little more, and keeps on improving. The child will thus learn a little of word attack each year, and keep on learning. We may tell the whole story in Grade IV, but we shall have to tell the story again in Grade V and in Grade VI, and perhaps in Grades VII and VIII. We also tell the child over and over again how to use his saw, and each time he uses it a little better. So word attack is taught and retaught, and what counts is not how often we teach it but how the child learns to use it. Facts may be learned in a few days or weeks. Skill is learned in years of practice.

Is this skill in word recognition worth the trouble? Let us envisage the years ahead of the child in the classroom. He will go on through years and years of school. He will then go on for years and more years of life. All this time he will be presented with books, magazines, newspapers, and all these will be full of new long words. Remember that the dictionary contains six hundred thousand words. No one will ever get over meeting new words. When he meets those new words, he must do one of three things. He may skip, he may guess, or he may sound out for himself. Which do we want him to do? That is why it is worth the trouble to teach and reteach word attack on long words until the skill is learned by all.

See page 96 for description of materials for teaching sounding.

CHAPTER VII

PHONOGRAMS OR LETTER PHONICS

Phonics are customarily taught in the three primary grades. In those grades the children are learning to read the more commonly used words of our language. Phonics are taught, therefore, in direct relation to these commonly used words. There have been statistical studies to determine what phonics should be taught. These studies deal with the most commonly used words. The well known study of Vogel and Washburne [1] analysed the vocabularies of twenty primers and first readers. The extensive study by Gates and others was based upon "A list of words that occur with highest frequency in the reading material likely to be encountered in the primary grades."[2] Many present systems for teaching phonics are based upon these studies. Other systems are based upon exactly similar material because they use the words in some individual set of primary readers and follow the methods of study set forth by Vogel, Washburne and Gates.

From this situation a very pertinent question arises. We find the schools teaching phonics which

---

From the *Elementary English Review*, Vol. 15, No. 4.

[1] *Elementary School Journal*, February 1923. Vogel, M., Jaycox, E., and Washburne, C. W. "A Basic List of Phonetics for Grades I and II."

[2] *New Methods in Primary Reading*. Arthur I. Gates. Bureau of Publications, Teachers College, Columbia University, 1928.

are based upon an analysis of the common words, which are predominantly *monosyllables,* or monosyllables with inflectional endings such as *-ed,* or *-ing.* But we must remember that it is during the nine years which *follow* the primary grades that phonics is going to be needed both for extensive reading and for study of content text books. Therefore, *a phonic system which is built upon monosyllables is to be used upon new words which are predominantly polysyllables.* How far this is true can be seen by a study of the Combined Word List.[3] This list combines eleven of the best known vocabulary studies and gives in one alphabet more than 19,000 words (dictionary basis). Of that number, more than 16,000, or about 81 per cent are polysyllables. These 16,000 are predominantly the words which the child will meet in his reading from the fourth grade on. They are the words which he is going to have to sound out. Our question is therefore, "Are the phonics which are now taught the kind best suited to help in the attack on these polysyllables which will present an unavoidable problem in all reading after the primary grades?" (See Chapter VIII for further figures on per cent of polysyllables.)

To answer this question a study has been made of recent textbooks. From a newly published six-volume series of arithmetics, a sampling of 6,000 running words was taken, a thousand words from

[3] *A Combined Word List.* B. R. Buckingham and E. W. Dolch. Ginn and Company, Boston, 1936.

each book composed of ten sections of 100 words, these sections scattered throughout the book. Four volumes of a new set of geographies were sampled in the same way, giving 4,000 running words. Four volumes of a new history series likewise gave 4,000 running words. The total was therefore 14,000 running words. Of this number 3,931, or 28 per cent were polysyllables. These polysyllables were listed and separated into syllables according to the practice of a standard dictionary. This resulted in a total of 8,509 syllables or 1,255 different syllables. Now it is understood that many polysyllables are sight words by grade four or later. Therefore the actual polysyllables among 14,000 words to be sounded out by pupils is not as large as the group we are discussing. Yet it may fairly be said that the syllables which we thus secured are in very large measure ones which children using these text books will have to sound out if they are going to read these books independently. Our question then becomes, "To what extent can phonics as now taught aid a child in sounding out these syllables found in a sampling of the text books he will be called upon to use?"

It is reasonable to say that two kinds of phonics are now taught in the primary grades. One kind may be called letter phonics. This includes the sounds of single letters and the sounds of consonant and vowel digraphs, which, though combinations of letters, have a single sound. The second kind may be called the teaching of phonograms, meaning combinations of vowel and consonants. This meaning of phonogram is the one we shall use here since it is a common usage, despite the technical definition of phonogram as any symbol which represents a sound. Teaching of letter phonics is characteristic of all systems. Practically all systems then go on to teach phonograms by assembling sight words into what are called phonetic families. The *-at* family for instance, may include *cat, hat, sat,* and so on. The *-ight* family might include *sight, right, fight,* etc. Some few persons have insisted that these families should be based upon word beginnings, as in the *ca-* family which include *cat, can, cap,* etc. This belief has had little acceptance in practice and the use of the "ending families" is practically universal.

Our question then resolves itself into this. "Since primary phonics mean letter phonics or phonogram phonics, can these types of phonic teaching help in the sounding out of polysyllables which children must do in the nine years of school after the primary grades?" Since all words are made up of letters, it is obvious that letter phonics will help to some extent in the sounding out of any words, short or long. We are all familiar with children's attempts to sound out big words letter by letter and know the difficulties involved. It is a practicable method, though a clumsy one.

But how about phonogram phonics? Can that type of phonics help with polysyllables? To answer this question we first had to secure a list of accepted and widely taught phonograms. The studies before mentioned of Vogel and Washburne, and Gates furnished us with a list of "important" phonograms. As a further check we compiled a list of all the phonograms assigned to the first two years by the teacher's manuals of seven important sets of readers. From these three sources the following list of twenty-four most "important" phonograms was compiled.

"IMPORTANT" PHONOGRAMS

Including all, except letters, digraphs, and blends, which appear on the Vogel and Washburne list, the Gates list, and in at least one of seven manuals for grades one and two.

-ing	-or	-at	-en	-old	-it
-er	-ir	-ay	-in	-ake	-ill (il)
-ed	-ar	-ight	-un	-and	-op
-all (al)	-ell (el)	-an	-on	-et	-ow

There might be some disagreement as to the inclusion or the exclusion of a few of these phonograms, but this list is representative. It includes every phonogram which was both on the Vogel and Washburne list and on the Gates list and which was mentioned in even one of the seven manuals.

We must here emphasize that all of these phonograms begin with a vowel. This is because they are all endings of monosyllables. By putting consonants before these phonograms many common monosyllables can be formed. By comparing monosyllables with different initials but the same ending, these phonograms may be derived. It is therefore not too much to say that the phonics of phonograms as taught at great length in the primary grades teach the children to recognize the endings of common monosyllables. The first three on the list are the only exceptions to this statement. They are *-ing*, *-er*, *-ed*, which are inflectional endings.

We may now ask, "Will this list of important phonograms, taught in the primary grades, help in the sounding of polysyllables?" We have just told how, by sampling arithmetics, geographies and histories, we found a total of 8,509 syllables in the polysyllables represented in only 14,000 running words. We have only to check our twenty-four "important" phonograms against this list of syllables to get something of the answer. We shall use the total number of syllables instead of the number of different syllables because the total better represents the situation that confronts the child.

In the teaching of phonograms there is a very common belief that we are teaching syllables which will be met with later on. Therefore, we must ask *"Are the 'important' phonograms the same as syllables in longer words?"* Table I which follows conclusively shows that they are not. In fact, in only 11.6 per cent of the cases do syllables and phonograms correspond, and more than half of this correspondence can be credited to the first four phonograms, which are signs of inflection and are therefore added at the end of words of all lengths. Of the other twenty phonograms only one, *-in*, reaches even one per cent of the total cases. Six of the phonograms never appeared at all as a syllable.

Clearly, if we exclude the inflectional endings, we may say point blank that the "important" phonograms are not syllables in polysyllabic words.

TABLE I

How Far the 24 "Important" Phonograms Help in Pronouncing the 8,509 Syllables

Phonogram	Times found as a syllable	Per cent	Times as a part of a syllable	Total per cent
-ing	240	2.8	17	3.0
-er	223	2.6	467	8.0
-ed	125	1.4	204	3.8
-or	16	.2	164	2.1
-ir	2		15	.2
-ar	21	.2	177	2.0
-at	14	.2	68	.5
-et			60	.6
-it	15	.2	77	.8
-an	71	.8	283	3.9
-en	50	.6	273	3.5
-in	93	1.1	160	1.8
(not counted in -ing)				
-un	21	.2	102	.5
-on	3		320	1.9
-all (al)	74	.9	143	2.5
-ell (-el)	23	.3	40	.7
-ill (-il)	4		86	.9
-op	5	.1	17	.3
-ow			95	1.1
-ay			20	.2
-ight			7	.1
-old	1		8	.1
-ake			1	
-and			20	.2
	1001	11.6	2826	38.7

Teachers who believe that in teaching phonograms they are teaching syllables are very much mistaken. The reason for this result is easily seen. The rule for syllable division is that consonants between vowels go with the vowel that follows if they can be pronounced that way. This means that in most cases syllables *begin with consonants.* But our list of "important phonograms," the ones so widely taught, all *begin with vowels.* Therefore we might well expect that these phonograms could not be the same as syllables. This is what the statistical study found.

There is, however, a most unorthodox way in which these phonograms might be helpful. These phonograms do appear in polysyllables, but not as syllables. In fact, in the 8,509 syllables these phonograms appear 2,826 times. For instance, two phonograms appear in the word "important" and a child might sound out the word in this way "im-p-or-t-an-t" although the word should be divided "im-por-tant." A child might find three phonograms in the word "permanent" and sound it "p-er-m-an-en-t" though the dictionary divides it "per-ma-nent." A child might find three phonograms in "material" and divide it "m-at-er-i-al" instead of "ma-te-ri-al." These examples show that though phonograms are seldom syllables, they may help in pronouncing syllables. We here find *-or* as part of *-por* and *-er* as part of *-per.* The phonogram *-an* is in *-tant* and *-en* is in *-tent.* At the same time we find that these phonograms at times combine part of one syllable with part of another, as the *-an* in "permanent" and the *-at* and *-er* in the word "material." This is very likely to happen because all these phonograms begin with a vowel and end with a consonant. True syllables, as we have said, generally begin with a consonant and often end with a vowel. Therefore the phonograms, which begin with a vowel, are quite likely to cut across syllable lines.

If children have been taught to see these monosyllable endings during the primary years, we must expect them to see the same letter combinations in the long words that they meet. This study suggests that these twenty-four phonograms might be of help in this kind of pronouncing in perhaps *one-third* of the syllables in content text books. But do we want children to use letter combinations that at times cut across syllable divisions? Are these phonograms, vowel-consonant combinations derived from the endings of monosyllables, of sufficient use to justify any reliance upon them in an attack on polysyllables?

SIGHT SYLLABLES VERSUS LETTER PHONICS[4]

A previous section discussed the question whether the "important" phonograms, which have been identified by research and which are commonly taught in the primary grades, can be of much help in sounding out polysyllables. That study showed that these twenty-four "important" phonograms

[4] From the *Elementary School Journal*, Vol. 41, No. 1.

corresponded to only 11.6 per cent of the 8,509 syllables in a sampling of 14,000 running words in elementary-school textbooks in arithmetic, history, and geography; that 6.8 per cent of these were accounted for by the three endings *-ing, -er,* and *-ed;* and that, therefore, only 4.8 per cent corresponded to the other twenty-one. This unexpected situation was easily explained by the fact that all these phonograms begin with vowels, whereas most syllables in the English language begin with consonants. This research showed that, even if these phonograms might stand for parts of syllables or even parts of two different syllables, they still accounted for only 38.7 per cent of the cases, 61.3 per cent being unaccounted for.

If phonograms are not going to "unlock" polysyllables, it might be thought advisable to learn what the common syllables really are so that the schools may teach them. We are all sure that we know many common syllables so well that we recognize them by sight in any strange word. A second study was therefore made of the 8,509 syllables previously discussed. Among these were found 1,255 different syllables. Were there not among this number certain common syllables which might be taught to children in order to help them with the new long words in their reading?

The first step was to select the one hundred most common of the syllables and to see just how common they are. The result was Table 2, which shows that,

TABLE 2

One Hundred Most Common Syllables and Total Frequency of Occurrence of Each in a 14,000-Word Sampling of Textbooks in Arithmetic, Geography, and History

Syllable	Frequency of Occurrence	Syllable	Frequency of Occurrence	Syllable	Frequency of Occurrence	Syllable	Frequency of Occurrence
a	186	dif	23	ing	240	riv	26
ā	31	dis	21	lar	23	ry	46
af	25	dren	35	lem	21	sion	19
age	38	e	24	long	23	son	24
al	74	ē	23	lōw	47	sup	21
am	33	ed	165	ly	105	ta	21
an	71	el	23	ma	20	ter	100
ar	21	en	50	man	125	ther	20
be	45	er	223	ment	39	ti	31
ber	39	ern	27	mer	29	tion	87
ble	27	ers	20	min	18	tle	31
bout	31	es	48	mon	20	to	18
ca	25	est	53	mount	18	ton	20
can	22	ex	73	o	23	try	20
chil	36	fa	21	ō	40	ture	42
cit	19	fer	19	on	18	tween	20
co	18	fig	47	oth	32	ty	28
col	21	fol	37	pēo	22	u	39
com	33	for	18	per	36	un	21
con	47	franc	19	pic	27	ure	63
coun	27	gle	20	ple	61	us	21
de	42	go	18	prob	27	val	25
dec	26	i	144	re	76	ver	34
der	44	im	22	ri	22	vid	20
di	75	in	93	ries	21	y	174

when the 100 most common (of the total of 1,255 different syllables) were listed, the syllable *-ing* occurred most frequently (240 times) and that the last place was shared by a group used 18 times each: *co, for, go, min, mount, on,* and *to.* Examination showed this list to be unsatisfactory because frequent appearance of a single word in the sampling would give high frequency to the syllables in that word. For instance, *prob-* and *-lem* are on the list solely because of the word "problem," and *-tween* is on the list solely because of repetition of the word "between." Yet the sounding-out of a word is a difficulty only the first few times it is met. From that point on, the word may not need to be sounded but may have become a sight word.

It seemed that a better list of the 100 commonest syllables could be obtained if each word were counted only once; at least such a list would be better than that given in Table 2. The tabulation on this basis is given in Table 3. In this case the most common syllable was again *-ing,* used in 135 different words, and the least common of the 100 was a large group of syllables each of which appears in only six different words.

Aside from the single letter *a,* the most common syllables on this list are, as might be expected, the inflectional endings *-ing* (135), *-ed* (90), and *-er* (72). Other prefixes and suffixes which are often emphasized as of much importance in sounding polysyllables do not appear with notable frequency; for instance, the prefixes: *in-* (38), *re-* (30), *de-* (29), *con-* (29), *ex-* (26), *com-* (20), *pro-* (13), *un-* (8), and *dis-* (7); and the suffixes: *-ly* (59), *-tion* (38), *-ment* (17), and *-ful* (8).

TABLE 3

The 101 Most Common Syllables and Number of Different Words in Which Each Appears in a 14,000-Word Sampling of Textbooks in Arithmetic, Geography, and History

Syllable	Number of Different Words	Syllable	Number of Different Words	Syllable	Number of Different Words	Syllable	Number of Different Words
a	74	den	6	li	9	sion	7
ac	8	der	15	low	8	son	7
ad	6	di	20	ly	59	sup	7
af	6	dif	6	ma	15	sur	9
age	8	dis	7	ment	17	ta	14
al	31	e	25	mer	9	tain	7
an	20	ed	90	na	10	tem	7
ap	7	el	10	ni	6	ter	24
ar	9	en	25	no	6	ters	6
at	7	er	72	ny	7	ti	16
be	10	ers	16	o	27	tion	38
ber	12	es	26	or	12	tle	7
ble	12	est	17	pa	7	to	14
ca	10	ex	26	pe	10	ton	8
cal	8	fer	6	pen	11	tov	8
can	6	for	13	per	13	ture	8
cap	6	ful	8	ple	10	ty	21
car	8	ger	7	po	7	u	19
cer	6	i	58	port	6	un	8
col	13	ies	6	pro	13	va	7
com	20	im	10	ra	11	ver	11
con	29	in	38	re	30	vi	6
cor	6	ing	135	ri	16	y	25
coun	6	is	9	ries	9		
cu	6	it	11	ry	21		
de	29	la	9	se	6		

A study of this list led inevitably to the question whether there really are a great number of syllables which are common enough to be taught for their value in sounding out polysyllables. At first glance it would seem that any syllable which appears in only six different words in a total of fourteen thousand running words, as do the least frequent on this list, would not be of sufficient importance to be learned as a syllable. However, fourteen thousand running words make up only about fifty pages of an ordinary textbook, and to be able to use the sound of a syllable in six different words within fifty pages would certainly be of help in pronouncing. If one examines even the less frequent syllables on the list, it is found that practically all of them are syllables which are instantly recognized as being in rather common use. One reads down the list without hesitation, evidently recognizing these letter combinations by sight without having to work them out. These considerations would lead to the conclusion that this list does give 101 common sight syllables which experienced readers at once recognize.

The fact that this list of 101 Commonest Syllables as found by this study are really sight syllables to an experienced reader emphasizes the well-known fact that the experienced reader does recognize instantly many syllables in the long words he meets. That is, there are sight syllables just as there are sight words. But does that mean that we should teach these syllables by the same methods we begin teaching sight words. With words, we found there were a few hundred common ones that every one should know instantly by sight. Are there similar sight syllables?

If we multiply each syllable on this list by the number of words in which it appeared and then added up the result, we find that these 101 common syllables appeared in 1664 words, (provided that no two of them appeared in the same word). What proportion of the 14,000 word sample do these 1664 words represent? We cannot be sure because we do not know the amount of repetition of each word in the 14,000 word sample. But these are all polysyllables, and the chances of much repetition of the words is not great. Some would be frequently used, but others would appear but once. Even if the average frequency were three times, the percentage would still be only 35 per cent.

We must conclude that if this "most common" list is not more common, they are in no way comparable to the most common sight words. But we found 12,550 different syllables in the 14,000 word sampling. That leaves 12,450 other syllables. And this was but a small sampling of a small group of books. If it were larger, there would undoubtedly be thousands more syllables. Can these be taught by means of lists? Obviously not.

LETTER PHONICS AND SYLLABICATION

The other type of primary phonics, letter phonics, is and always will be of constant usefulness in reading. Every adult will find himself using letter phonics when he meets strange words. Even if most of the word is familiar, he will use letter phonics on the unfamiliar part. In primary teaching, letter phonics have been at times discredited because of the difficulty children have in blending. But with the yearly increase in mental age, difficulty in blending becomes less and less. This continued usefulness of letter phonics should be frankly recognized at all levels of school work.

But letter phonics are not our only possibility for attack on polysyllables. There remains an attack on the sounding of polysyllables which has been much neglected. It is the thorough teaching of syllabication. The need for breaking up long words into parts is with the child constantly in every book subject from the fourth grade on through high school, through college, and through later life. Yet if you will ask teachers, you will find very few at any level who have any clear conception of how to divide a word into syllables. They know the sounds of the long words they meet and when a child asks how to say a certain word they tell him. They do not realize that in reading by himself the child must either skip the unknown word and go on or must give some sort of incorrect sounding to it. The teacher's chief advice is "in case of doubt, go to the dictionary."

What the schools definitely need is a teaching of the phonics of polysyllables. The work can be begun as soon as the children are mature enough to concentrate on division of words into parts. It needs to be continued year after year until there is real facility in this attack on long words. Rules may be taught, but much practice is necessary to develop skill. Facility in attacking polysyllables will go far in eliminating much of the remedial work in reading in the upper grades and in high school. Here is a neglected field of instruction. We have neglected it because we have assumed that the job had been done in the primary grades. Experience shows that the job has not been done. The figures which we have presented show that the job can hardly be done by the methods now universally employed. Children need to sound out polysyllables during all their years of reading. We must definitely plan to train them to do so.

Having urged the teaching of syllabication as the true attack on the sounding of polysyllables, we must emphasize that it is a means to an end. After we break words into syllables for a long enough time, we begin to find many syllables familiar. They become at last *sight syllables.* We see them quickly in new words and know at once how they sound. One of the sight syllables that we recognize instantly when we see it at the beginning of a long word is *pro.* Another that we see so often on the end of long words, is *-tion.* When we see a new long word, therefore, we are likely to recognize some of the syllables instantly and have to sound out only one or two others. Syllabication leads to the learning of sight syllables. Letter phonics serve as an expedient when all else fails. But phonograms are of doubtful help in the attack on polysyllables that is essential for independent reading at all levels.

CHAPTER VIII

PHONICS AND SPELLING

Many teachers have noticed that when they begin to pay special attention to the teaching of phonics in reading, the spelling of their classes improves. Teachers of remedial reading almost uniformly find that the children who are poor in reading are poor in spelling, and these teachers find that teaching phonics benefits both reading and spelling. What can be the connection between these two abilities that are considered so important in the school? And if there is a connection between phonics in reading and the improvement of spelling, what kind of phonics brings about the most helpful connection?

One possible relation between phonics and spelling is very apparent. In the beginning grades, phonics deals with the sounding of monosyllables. In the first years of spelling, it is the common monosyllables that have to be spelled. Then, as reading goes on into the middle grades, it is the polysyllables that have to be sounded out, since the children know the common short words as sight words. And as spelling continues into the middle and upper grades, it is the polysyllables that have to be spelled, since the short words have already been learned. So when phonics deals with short words, so does spelling. And when phonics must deal with long words, so must spelling also. This is an important fact, and it will be the basis for our discussion of the connection between phonics in reading and ability in spelling.

Let us now consider the characteristics of phonics in the primary grades, and see how they may be related to ability to spell. Beginning phonics, of whatever kind, consists essentially of word comparison. Words of similar beginnings, middles, or endings are written one above the other, and the child is asked to note carefully the like parts and the unlike parts. This work is simply constant training in careful perception, that is, in careful looking at words and at the parts of words. All phonics gives this training, and the more careful and systematic the phonics, the more of this training is given.

Without phonics, the children tend to look very vaguely at words. In fact, the word to them is a general shape. This general shape may be longer or shorter than others, it may have parts sticking up or down, or it may have other things that catch the child's eye. But it is very definitely not a collection of clear-cut letters, as it may be to the adult reader. Reading systems which do not use phonics may teach sight words, and the children may learn to tell one of these general shapes from another. But there is little likelihood that many of the children will feel the need for a careful scrutiny of the words they read. It is this careful looking that the word comparison of primary phonics makes absolutely necessary.

What, then, is the nature of beginning spelling? As already suggested, the first words that are spelled are the common words of the language. These are the short words which are used a great deal in anything we write. Naturally, these same short words are used in anything we read. The spelling words are the reading words. There is a little delay, in that the reading words of one year do not become spelling words until the next year, but these early reading words are so common that they are still being constantly met with in the reading at the same time that they appear in the spelling lessons. So the first words learned in reading are the first words learned in spelling.

How are these first words in spelling learned by the children? If the children learn them incorrectly, they read off the letters, one after the other, and over and over again. This is lip-spelling and is very common just because it is so easy to do. The child can "study" his spelling this way with little attention and with no thought. He just reads letters over and over. If, however, the children learn their spelling correctly at this stage, they will look hard at the words and get a mental picture of each word which includes all the letters. They can then use this clear mental picture when they want to write the word, or if they write a word incorrectly, this clear mental picture will tell them at once that they have made a mistake. This method is called sight-spelling.

At once it is evident why primary phonics helps primary spelling. The careful looking that phonics requires gives the children the clear mental pictures that spelling requires. Without phonics, the mental pictures are vague and general, and a vague mental picture is of no use in spelling. With phonics, the mental pictures are just what is needed for good spelling. Thus, as we have seen, the words of primary reading are the words of beginning spelling; and the method of learning words through the aid of phonics is the method which teaches the right way to spell these same common words.

At this point, we must ask our second question: what kind of monosyllable phonics brings about the most helpful connection between reading phonics and improvement in spelling? The facts we have just pointed out show that any kind of phonics helps by causing careful looking at words, but there are two rather definite kinds of primary phonics which may have somewhat different effects. One kind, which is usually called phonogram phonics, emphasizes combinations of sounds rather than simple sounds. For instance, it teaches the combination "bl" rather than the simple sounds "b" and "l." It teaches the combination "ot" rather than the simple sounds "o" and "t." In point of fact, it teaches these combinations *in addition to* the simple sounds. Study of the words in any set of readers will show that no set of sound combinations can take care of all the words. For instance, the seven first books of one new series, all of them intended for the first year of reading, contain 241 monosyllables. Of these, 81 are "individual" words, in the sense that they are not like any reasonable number of other common words. For example, "there" and "where" have similar endings, but no other common words have this ending, and so it would not be reasonable to teach the ending "ere" as a combination. Of the remaining 167 monosyllables, the endings might be found in other common words. We emphasize *might be* because in fact they are not found very often in others within these seven books. Their actual appearances are as follows:

Endings appearing	
5 times	3
4 times	6
3 times	10
2 times	24
Once	50
	93 different endings.

This system of using combinations of sounds also teaches the blends of consonants before the endings. In these same words, we found 18 different blends used. Adding this number of blends and the number of different endings, we would get 111 combinations of sounds. But 134 of these words did not begin with blends. They began with simple consonant sounds. So these 20 simple consonant sounds have to be added to the 111, to give us 131 items to teach. We do not, however, believe that any phonogram system would teach all of these combinations. Such systems claim to teach only the more common. Therefore the other words with less common endings would have to be sounded by use of the simple sounds, and so these simple sounds would have to be taught after all.

There used to be a belief that if the common endings of monosyllables were taught, these would help later as syllables of polysyllables.[1] Research has shown, however, that this is not the case. The only common endings that appear again are "-ing" and "-ed," and these only because they are inflectional endings. The other endings of monosyllables cannot appear as syllables in long words for the very simple reason that the endings of short words *begin with vowels* (they are made by cutting off the beginning consonants). But when we divide long words into syllables, we join the consonants to the following vowel, and hence the syllables in long words *begin with consonants,* not with vowels. So the endings of short words are of no longer use after the short words have been taught.

The other system of sounding used in primary work teaches the simple sounds and works out all the phonetic words from these sounds. This system gives only about 50 items to teach, the sounds indicated by the 26 letters and a few common variations, and these are usable at any and at all times for sounding. This system points to the obvious fact, presented above, that no set of complex sound units,

---

[1] See Chapter VII.

or phonograms, can possibly take care of even the majority of phonetic words in the primary years. For most of these phonetic words, the simple sounds have to be taught and used anyway. So why bother with complex sound units of doubtful usefulness? Why not put the time and effort on the simple sounds that must be taught anyway?

Now which system, the phonogram system or the simple-sound system, aids most in spelling of the beginning spelling words? It would seem obvious that the method which emphasizes the simple sounds would help spelling most, since this method causes the child to look most closely at each word. The method of using combinations might also have them look at simple elements part of the time, but part of the time it would be asking them to look at the more complicated units. Either method helps, but the simple-sound method would seem to help the most.

An added fact to be remembered about beginning phonics is that it always involves ear training. In any phonics lesson, the words are pronounced carefully and clearly. The total word-sound is carefully listened to so that the hearer may distinguish long vowel sounds from short vowel sounds, how the word starts and how it ends, and so on. This ear training is absolutely necessary if the child is to use his phonics in building new word sounds out of simpler sound elements. Neglect of ear training explains why some children seem to "learn" phonics but never seem to be able to *use* phonics. The need of ear training for phonics in reading is thus apparent, but does it have any relation to spelling? As we have seen, beginning spelling is built upon the visual image of the words. In spelling long words, however, the sound images of words are used and must be used. Through developing attention to correct sound images, this early ear training in phonics is of great value to spelling later on.

We have found it relatively easy to trace the reason that phonics in primary reading helps in the first years of spelling. The case is far less simple when we consider *the phonics of long words,* and the spelling of long words such as becomes necessary later on. For after the primary grades, both reading and spelling difficulties concern long words. This fact is shown by figures from a very simple investigation. Several reading series were studied for percentage of monosyllables and polysyllables. The figures for the different series were so much the same that they can well be averaged as follows:

	In Readers for Grade					
	I	II	III	IV	V	VI
	%	%	%	%	%	%
Per cent of Polysyllables	34	38	49	64	76	83
Per cent of Monosyllables	66	62	51	36	24	17

These are figures counting each word only once, since naturally at all levels the short words are repeated more frequently than the long ones. And these figures should be compared with a similar study of several series of spellers. These averaged as follows:

	In lists in Spellers			
	1st 1,000	2nd 1,000	3rd 1,000	4th 1,000
	%	%	%	%
Per cent of Polysyllables	28	74	87	96
Per cent of Monosyllables	72	26	13	4

These figures show clearly that only in the primary grades do monosyllables figure prominently. After that, the problem in reading is to sound out polysyllables, and the problem in spelling is how to spell out polysyllables.

The first great difference between the polysyllable spelling problem and the monosyllable spelling problem is that the polysyllables to be spelled do not correspond very closely with the polysyllables in the reading lessons. We have pointed out that the first words of reading were the first words in spelling, so that reading these words taught us how to spell the words. But after the first few years, the situation changes. The spelling book keeps down its number of words, of necessity, to 3500 to 4000, and these words are the ones most used in writing. But the vocabulary of the reading books does not keep down to this small number. The reading vocabulary may exceed the spelling vocabulary several times over. By the end of Grade IV, the children will have met over 4,000 different words. By the end of Grade VI, this number may be 6,000. By the end of Grade

VIII, it may be 10,000. It is true that the 4,000 words of the spelling list are somewhere in this large reading vocabulary, but there is not the same rather perfect correspondence and the same great repetition of a few words as was found with the first 1,000 reading and spelling words. There is hence much less likelihood that the child will have carefully studied in the reading lesson just the words he will write in the spelling lesson.

This lack of correspondence of reading vocabulary and spelling vocabulary increases in another direction. Much of a child's spelling during this later period is in his writing of stories, reports, examinations, and the like. He uses what may be called his "active spelling vocabulary," and this may range far beyond the limits of the 4,000 spelling list. It will cover all of his interests and hobbies. It will cover his out-of-school experiences, his travels, and his family affairs. It will also cover all of his school subjects. Again, many of the words of the child's active spelling vocabulary which are not on the spelling list may still be in the reading vocabulary of his reading books, but there will be still little close correspondence.

In addition to lack of word-list correspondence between reading and spelling, there is not, with polysyllables, the close "time correspondence" between reading words and writing those words that there is with the common words of the language. With the common words, a word read this week or month will also be spelled this month or year. With the less common words, a word read this month may be spelled year after next, or it may have been spelled last year. When the reading vocabulary ranges over ten thousand words, and the active school spelling vocabularies range over six or eight thousand words, the "time correspondence" is likely to be very poor, and thus meeting the word in reading will be far away from meeting the word in spelling. In short, seeing the word at one time will not help much in spelling the word when it is needed at another time. (See Chapter XXVII on the time when spelling words are learned.)

How, then, can phonics help spelling when we are concerned with the polysyllables of the language? The help comes, very simply and directly, through use of the same method of attack in both cases.

First, phonics of polysyllables requires that the child look very carefully at the word and divide it into syllables. It required that the child then attack each syllable and work it out from the letters which indicate the simple sounds that make it up. Most syllables in long words are simple and are made up of simple sounds. This is not true of special endings like "tion," which we teach as units, and which we do not ask the child to work out. But it is true of practically all other syllables. The great bulk of syllables are actually phonetic, and can be worked out. In this respect, polysyllables are in great contrast to monosyllables, of which a large proportion can never be worked out and have to be learned as wholes.

The phonic method of attack on long words thus (1) gives training in working out syllable sound units from the simple sound units indicated by the letters, (2) gives training in holding these syllables sound units in mind while they are blended into a word, and (3) this blended word sound leads the child to recognize some known word as the word intended. Note that the purpose is recognizing some known word. If some known word is not suggested, the pupil must consult the dictionary. No one should ever depend on his sounding to tell him a new word-sound, as he may make some errors or some part of the word may be irregular.

The interesting thing here is that phonetic analysis of a polysyllable in reading is almost certain to lead first to the formal pronunciation of a word. This is the pronunciation recognized as far back as Dr. Johnson as being "regular and solemn," suited to the pulpit or to oratory. This formal pronunciation sounds each syllable distinctly, and tends to stress each syllable. It is an "exaggerated" pronunciation, if you will, but not a "wrong" pronunciation. After the reader sounds out this formal pronunciation, such as "con-sti-tu-tion-al," for instance, he recognizes the word and drops at once into the colloquial or cursory pronunciation.

Now the spelling of polysyllables, as it happens, follows these same steps in almost exactly the reverse order. What do we do when we wish to spell an unusual word, one that we cannot "see" clearly in our mind's eye? First, we say the word, syllable by syllable, that is, we say the word with its formal pronunciation, accenting one syllable at a time. We even say each syllable in a sort of exaggerated form in order to find out more clearly how it is spelled. Then, we try to write each clearly sounded, emphasized syllable by "phonetic translation," that is, we change sound into letters representing sound. Here we find at once that it is the simple sounds we use. Few open syllables (ending in a vowel) have more than one consonant and one vowel; few closed syllables (ending in a consonant) have more than a beginning consonant, a vowel, and an ending consonant. The simple elements are used and serve in the vast bulk of cases.

From this explanation, it is clear that the phonetic method of attack on long words in reading is the reverse of the sounding method of attack in spelling. Training in one gives training in the other. This is not strange, since, in language, sounds must be spelled and spellings must be sounded.

This discussion of reading and spelling of polysyllables has a further implication concerning the kind of phonics which helps best in this relation between phonics in reading and the spelling of words. We have shown how both in sounding out syllables for reading, and in spelling out syllables in spelling, the simple elements represented by letters are used. We can therefore point out that this skill with simple sound elements is best acquired through work with a kind of primary phonics that teaches use of the simple elements represented by letters. After all, monosyllable phonics, as such, disappears after the few short words have been learned and have become sight words. But polysyllable phonics is used by us all of our lives, both in reading and in spelling, and since simple elements are thus used for all our later reading and spelling, why not learn them from the very beginning?

Two games for the teaching of phonics are published by the Garrard Press, Champaign, Ill.: Phonic Lotto, played like any lotto game, teaches all the sounds of the vowels and word combinations; the Group Sounding game, played like bingo, teaches the thirteen steps in sounding, from initial consonants to division of three-syllable words. This game gives the teacher a complete plan for teaching phonics. Either game is useful in a wide range of grades. The game method motivates learning.

Part III

Vocabulary

CHAPTER IX

A BASIC SIGHT VOCABULARY

NEED FOR A BASIC SIGHT VOCABULARY

Teachers of all grades, from Grade II on, find pupils who have very small or no sight vocabularies. The teachers wish to remedy this condition by drilling on the sight words that will be of most value to these children in their reading. But which are those sight words? The vocabulary of a particular primer will not do because the child's reading is now chiefly in books other than the basal series with which he started and also because the vocabularies of most primers contain many words that, though needed at the primer stage, are later not of general usefulness. No standard word list will do because all such lists contain five hundred words or more, too many to be given drill as a sight vocabulary.

SOURCES OF THE LIST

As a point of departure, it may well be assumed that the most essential of the words that are basic

---

From the *Elementary School Journal*, Vol. 36, No. 6, University of Chicago.

to children's reading, and therefore needed as a sight vocabulary, will surely be included in *all* the best lists of words used by children. A comparison of those lists was therefore the logical means of securing a basic sight vocabulary. The first list considered was naturally the vocabulary published by the Child Study Committee of the International Kindergarten Union,[1] which is a summary of many studies in this field. This list contains 2,596 words, which are the most frequent of 7,000 different words found to be known to children before entering Grade I. It was found that, if the words of a frequency of 100 or more (inflected forms being combined) were chosen from this list, a total of 510 words was secured, which is about the number of words on the other two lists which were used. The second list was the first five hundred of the Gates list,[2] which is too well known to need description and which has been used as a basis for many studies in reading vocabulary. The third list was that compiled by Wheeler and Howell,[3] consisting of the 453 words most frequently found in ten primers and ten first

[1] Child Study Committee of the International Kindergarten Union, *A Study of the Vocabulary of Children before Entering the First Grade.* Washington: International Kindergarten Union (1201 Sixteenth Street, N.W.), 1928.

[2] Arthur I. Gates, *A Reading Vocubulary for the Primary Grades.* New York: Teachers College, Columbia University, 1926.

[3] H. E. Wheeler and Emma A. Howell, "A First-Grade Vocabulary Study," *Elementary School Journal,* XXXI (September, 1930), 52-60.

readers. This list probably represents as well as does anything later made available to us the actual reading materials common in Grade I and therefore the vocabulary upon which, presumably, all later grade reading is built. Each of these three lists is compiled on a dictionary basis (that is, regularly inflected forms of a single root are combined), and a comparison of the three lists could easily be made. From this comparison the following list was secured and arranged according to parts of speech included.

A Basic Sight Vocabulary of 220 Words, Comprising Words, Except Nouns, Common to the Word List of the International Kindergarten Union, the Gates List, and the Wheeler-Howell List

CONJUNCTIONS

and
as
because
but
if
or

PREPOSITIONS

about
after
at
by
down
for
from
in
into
of
on
over
to
under
*upon
with

PRONOUNS

he
her
him
his
I
it
*its
me
my
*myself
our
she
that
their
them
these
they
this
*those
us
we
what
*which
who
you
your

ADVERBS

again
*always
around
away
*before
far
fast
first
here
how
just
much
never
no
not
now
off
once
only
out

so
soon
then
there
today
*together
too
up
very
*well
when
where
why
yes

ADJECTIVES

a
all
an
any
*best
*better
big
black
blue
both
brown
*clean
cold
*eight
every
*five
four
full
funny
good
green
hot
kind
*light
little
long
many
new
old
one
*own
pretty
red
right
round
*seven
*six
small
some
ten
the
three
two
warm
white
yellow

VERBS

am
are
ask
ate
be
been
bring
buy
call
came
can
carry
come
could
cut
did
do
does
*done
don't
draw
drink
eat
fall
find
fly
found
gave
get
give
go
*goes
going
got
grow
had
has
have
help
hold
*hurt
is
jump
keep
know
laugh
let
like
live
look
made
make
may
must
open
*pick
play
please
pull
put
ran
read
ride
run
said
saw
say
see
shall
show
sing
sit
sleep
*start
stop
take
tell
thank
think
*try
*use
walk
want
was
*wash
went
were
will
wish
work
would
*write

* The twenty-seven words marked with asterisks were included in only two of the lists.

This list may well be called "basic" because it includes the "tool" words or "service" words that are used in all writing, no matter what the subject. Conjunctions join clauses regardless of what the clauses are about; prepositions introduce phrases of every kind; pronouns stand for any and all persons and things; adverbs modify every kind of verb; and adjectives modify every kind of noun. Verbs denote action or being of every sort of subject, and the auxiliaries, practically all of which are included in this list, are used with all the verbs of the language.

This list is not perfect, since no list secured from frequency counts can be flawless. The chances of use that enter into frequency counts cause some unimportant words to secure higher frequencies than some more important words. For instance, "jump" cannot be considered a word of wide usefulness, yet on these vocabulary lists it ranked with words like "do" or "make." Word-counting will always give some such cases. Word-counting is also certain to leave out of a list some words of importance which should be included but which did not happen to be used often enough in the sample of material counted.

If the criterion of appearance on all three lists had been rigidly adhered to, the twenty-seven words marked with asterisks would have been cut from the list. This elimination would have been unfortunate, since these words appear in the first 510 of the International Kindergarten Union list and in the first 500 of the Gates list. Many of these words obviously belong with others on the basic list. "Which" belongs with "who" and "that," "done" and "goes" belong with "did" and "go," "start" belongs with "stop," and "write" with "read." The numbers under ten belong with the other numbers listed. For this reason these twenty-seven words are included in the basic list; they add a few that seem as important as others on the list.

It is to be especially noted that this basic sight vocabulary includes *no nouns.* Nouns cannot be of universal use because each noun is tied to special subject matter. If new subject matter is used, new nouns must be used. Unfortunately, teachers have spent a great deal of energy in teaching the nouns in primers as sight words, and then, as the later books take up new materials, new nouns must be used and not those that have been learned. Perhaps one reason that many children in the intermediate grades do not know by sight the words on this basic list is that the emphasis on sight teaching has been on nouns instead of on these "tool" words. Some few nouns, such as "thing" or "man," do recur a great deal, but in the case of most nouns the rule applies that they are "local" to a particular activity

95 Nouns Common to the Three Word Lists but not Recommended for a Basic Sight Vocabulary

apple	day	home	school
baby	dog	horse	seed
back	doll	house	sheep
ball	door	kitty	shoe
bear	duck	leg	sister
bed	egg	letter	snow
bell	eye	man	song
bird	farm	men	squirrel
birthday	farmer	milk	stock
boat	father	money	street
box	feet	morning	sun
boy	fire	mother	table
bread	fish	name	thing
brother	floor	nest	time
cake	flower	night	top
car	game	paper	toy
cat	garden	party	tree
chair	girl	picture	watch
chicken	goodbye	pig	water
children	grass	rabbit	way
Christmas	ground	rain	wind
coat	hand	ring	window
corn	head	robin	wood
cow	hill	Santa Claus	

These widely used nouns may be taught with the Picture Word Cards, Garrard Press, Champaign, Ill. 50 cents.

or interest. The nouns common to the three lists are mainly local to young children's interests and to first-grade activities. They are in no sense basic to all elementary-school reading. That the reader may see this fact for himself, the list of nouns is given below. However, children who have failed to get a good start in reading can well be taught these words because they do occur frequently in reading books.

It is not claimed that the basic list of 220 words includes *all* the words that the elementary-school pupil should know by sight; the claim is only that he should at least know these. Consequently, when a child in any grade is found lacking in sight vocabulary, he should be tested to see which of these words he does know and should then be trained to recognize instantly by sight the words that he does not know. Methods for doing this are explained in Chapter XIV, the First Step in Remedial Reading.

For greater usefulness in checking words in reading books, we present below this same list in two other arrangements. The first is in a single alphabet. The second is in two groups of easier and harder words according to a Wisconsin study that tested over 3,000 children in Grade I and over 3,000 children in Grade II. The teacher may use this divided list to tell which words to emphasize or which ones to expect children to learn first.

The Basic Sight Vocabulary of 220 Words in a Single Alphabet

a
about
after
again
all
always
am
an
and
any
are
around
as
ask
at
ate
away

be
because
been
before
best
better
big
black
blue
both
bring
brown
but
buy
by

call
came
can
carry
clean
cold
come
could
cut

did
do
does
done
don't

down
draw
drink

eat
eight
every

fall
far
fast
find
first
five
fly
for
found
four
from
full
funny

gave
get
give
go
goes
going
good
got
green
grow

had
has
have
he
help
her
here
him
his
hold
hot
how
hurt

I
if

in
into
is
it
its

jump
just

keep
kind
know

laugh
let
light
like
little
live
long
look

made
make
many
may
me
much
must
my
myself

never
new
no
not
now
of
off
old
on
once
one
only
open
or
our
out

over
own

pick
play
please
pretty
pull
put

ran
read
red
ride
right
round
run

said
saw
say
see
seven
shall
she
show
sing
sit
six
sleep
small
so
some
soon
start
stop
take
tell
ten
thank
that
the
their
them
then
there
these
they
think

this	upon	we	will
those	us	well	wish
three	use	went	with
to		were	work
today	very	what	would
together		when	write
too	walk	where	
try	want	which	yellow
two	warm	white	yes
under	was	who	you
up	wash	why	your

These basic service words may be taught with the Basic Sight Vocabulary Cards or with the Group Word Teaching Game (both published by the Garrard Press, Champaign, Ill.; the cards for 50c and the game for 75c).

The great importance of these 220 basic service words is shown by the table below which gives the percentages that the 220 are of the total number of running words in school text books in four subjects.

*Percentage That the Basic Sight Vocabulary Is of Running Words in School Textbooks in Four Subjects**

Subject of Textbooks	Number of Books	Grade I	Grade II	Grade III	Grade IV	Grade V	Grade VI
Reading	4	70	66	65	61	59	59
Arithmetic	2	......	......	62	63	57	57
Geography	2	......	......	......	60	59	54
History	2	......	......	......	57	53	52

* Based on a thousand-word sampling of each book, including inflected forms of the basic sight words in which the sight word appears unchanged.

It is indeed surprising that such a small group of words play such a large part in reading. In fact, almost half of any book, magazine or newspaper is made up of these words. Hence every child should learn to recognize them instantly by sight.

A Basic Sight Vocabulary of 220 Words in Two Groups. According to a Study by Mrs. Lois G. Nemec, State Supervisor of Schools, and Thirty-four Supervising Teachers in Twenty-two Wisconsin Counties.

Easier 110			Harder 110		
a	had	said	about	has	say
after	he	saw	again	have	seven
all	help	see	always	hold	shall
an	her	she	am	hot	show
and	here	six	any	how	sing
are	him	sleep	ate	hurt	sit
around	his	so	because	keep	small
as	I	some	been	kind	start
ask	if	soon	best	know	take
at	in	stop	better	laugh	tell
away	into	ten	both	let	thank
be	is	that	bring	light	their
before	it	the	buy	live	there
big	its	them	came	made	these
black	jump	then	carry	many	think
blue	just	they	clean	may	those
brown	like	this	could	much	together
but	little	three	cut	must	try
by	long	to	does	new	upon
call	look	today	done	never	us
can	make	too	don't	now	use
cold	me	two	draw	off	very
come	my	under	drink	once	want
did	myself	up	eight	only	warm
do	no	walk	every	open	wash
down	not	was	fall	our	well
eat	of	we	far	over	went
fly	old	when	fast	own	were
for	on	white	find	pick	what
four	one	who	first	please	where
from	or	will	five	pull	which
funny	out	yellow	found	put	why
get	play	yes	full	ran	wish
go	pretty	you	gave	read	with
going	red	your	give	right	would
good	round		goes		write
green	run		got		work
			grow		

CHAPTER X

THE FIRST THOUSAND WORDS FOR CHILDREN'S READING

Control of vocabulary in children's textbooks is for the purpose of making sure there are not too many unknown words. Such vocabulary control therefore requires that we have some list of words that are known to children. For many years no such list existed and publishers used instead the first thousand of the famous Thorndike list. These words were the commonest in reading matter, according to the types of reading matter studied by Thorndike, but were not necessarily the most common words for children's reading matter. Most of Thorndike's material was adult reading matter, and to a considerable extent reading matter for quite educated persons.

It was soon noted by users of Thorndike's first thousand that the list contained many words not familiar to children. To correct the list in this respect, a list of words used by children themselves was used, that famous list of the International Kindergarten Union, containing 1759 words (on dictionary basis, without proper names, contractions, and slang). These words had actually been found to be used by children either in kindergarten or the home before the age of six. Edgar Dale checked Thorndike's first thousand against the Kindergarten

Union list and found on both a total of only 755 words.

An experiment was made in using the Dale list of 755 words in checking the vocabulary of children's readers. It was found that because of the small size of the list, not enough difference was shown between books of various grades. It was accordingly decided to increase the size of the list to 1,000, to make it comparable to the vocabulary checks formerly made with the Thorndike first thousand.

To increase the Dale list to 1,000 required the addition of 245 words known to children. Fortunately there was another study from which these words could be drawn. This was called the Interview Vocabulary List because the words were secured through interviews with children during the first few months of the first grade. The purpose of this study was to find out which words children *knew*, as opposed to the ones they might happen to use.

In the Interview Vocabulary Study, the first step was to secure a "testing list" which would contain all the words which beginning first graders might conceivably know. From these words which they might know, we could discover by testing which ones they actually did know. This testing list was secured from the Combined Word Study List (Ginn & Co., Boston, Mass.) which contains 19,000 words, resulting from the combination of the Thorndike list, the Horn list, and nine other well-known vocabulary studies. The words of the Combined Word Study List were first classified into 305 topical groups, such as food, government, transportation, and the like. From these 305, the ones that were touched upon by child life were selected. Then from each of these groups, all words were selected that beginning first graders might possibly know. The result was our "testing list" for the Interview Vocabulary study.

An experienced tester then presented the words of the testing list to children during the first half of the first grade. She used trays of objects, sheets of pictures, lists of standard questions, and the like to determine if the children knew the *meaning* of the words. Each child was tested individually to get most accurate results. One child after another was tested until the chances were 42 to one that 75 children out of 100 knew the word. After two years work (that is the first semester of two different beginning groups), the Interview Vocabulary list was secured, of words *known in meaning to beginning first graders.*

Having the words to add to the Dale list to secure our list of 1,000, the next problem was, which words to add? The method was again topical analysis. The Dale list was separated into topics of child life and interest. Then the words on each topic were studied and "holes" or omissions were discovered. These omissions were corrected by adding the appropriate words from the Interview Vocabulary List.

The following pages show on the left side of the page the topically arranged words of the Dale List. Opposite each topical group, on the right side of the page, are the words that were added from the Interview Vocabulary List.

The resulting "First Thousand Words for Children's Reading" have been used very satisfactorily in the Graded Vocabulary study reported in Chapter XXI. It is the most carefully prepared and tested vocabulary of words covering children's life and interests that is now available.

TOPICAL ANALYSIS SHOWING DERIVATION OF THE

FIRST THOUSAND WORDS FOR CHILDREN'S READING

THE CHILD'S PERSON

Dale List Words on Left	Interview Words on Right
Body	
head, neck, face	chin, cheek
mouth, lip, tongue	tooth, teeth, throat
arm, hand, finger	thumb
leg, knee, foot, feet	toe, lap
shoulder, body, bone	
skin, hair	
heart	stomach
tall, fat	
Senses	
eye, see, saw, seen	
look, blind, watch	
ear, hear, heard, listen	
sound, loud, quiet	noise

The total list in one alphabet will be found in Appendix A.

Dale List Words on Left	Interview Words on Right
nose	smell
touch	
Body Actions	
stand, stood, sit, sat	jump, kick, climb
walk, step, run, ran	
hold, point, reach, pull	
start, stop, turn	
move, still	
hurry, fast, slow, quick	
Clothes	
clothes, fit, tear, wear	wore, mend
cloth, silk	
coat, suit	shirt, overalls, pants
dress	skirt, sweater
shoe	stockings, socks
bow, tie	ribbon
hat, cap	umbrella, handkerchief
	button, zipper, pocket

HOME ENVIRONMENT

House and Home	
house, home, roof	address, garage
building, build, built	porch, chimney
gate, yard	fence, outdoors, indoors
room, hall	stairs, kitchen, dining
floor, wall, door, window	
	cupboard, broom, sweep
Furniture	
bed	pillow
chair, table	furniture, stove, rug
bell, ring, clock	lamp
	drawer, curtain, mirror
People and Family	
family, name, people	
man, men, woman	women

Dale List Words on Left	Interview Words on Right
child, children	
boy, girl, baby, born	birthday
father, mother	grandfather, grandmother
sister, brother, uncle	aunt, cousin
old, young, mind	
fellow, self, neighbor	

FOOD AND EATING

Meals and Eating

breakfast, dinner	lunch, supper
eat, food, feed, taste	hungry, ate
drink, water	thirsty

Cooking and Services

cook	bake, pot, pan
cup	plate, dish, bowl, napkin
cut, serve	knife, fork, spoon

Foods

bread, butter	sandwich, cracker
milk, fresh	cream, cocoa
fruit	juice, lemonade
apple	banana, peach, orange
sugar, sweet	candy, chocolate
cake	cooky, pie
meat	
salt	soup
	potatoes, tomatoes
	lettuce, peas, beans

HEALTH AND CLEANLINESS

clean, wash	dirty, soap, towel
	tub, bath, bathe
sleep, dream	nap, wake, awake, tired
hurt, blood	accident, bandage, bleed
	bump, slip, sore
sick, strong, well	pain, ache, cough
doctor	nurse, dentist, medicine

Dale List Words on Left **Interview Words on Right**

RECREATION AND SOCIAL LIFE

Recreation

play, game	toys, doll, balloon
ball, catch, throw	
	bicycle, skates, scooter
sing, song, music	radio
band, dance	
race, win	
	circus, clown, parade
	picnic, tent, camp
	ticket
	puzzle
	funny

Speech

ask, answer, reason	question
speak, talk, tell, told	spoke, whisper
say, said	
laugh, cry, smile	
call	

Social Life

party, company, crowd	
visit, friend	
present, gift, surprise	
please, thank	
note, letter	
dear, kiss, love	
sir, lady	Miss, Mr., Mrs.

COMMUNITY ENVIRONMENT

City Environment

town, city, sign	
street, corner, cross	
church, bless	
	policeman, mailman

Dale List Words on Left	**Interview Words on Right**
Non-City Environment	
country, land, world	
farm, farmer, field	barn
garden, ground, dust	dirt, dig
road, path, bridge	
hill, mountain, valley	
ocean, sea, wave	
river, lake	pond, creek
Business Affairs	
bank, office, mill	
store, shop, market	grocery, drug, butcher
trade, buy, sell, sold	
pay, cost	
cent, quarter, money	nickel, dime, dollar, penny
rich, poor	
Trains and Transportation	
captain, ship, boat, sail	
drive, car, ride	automobile, engine, truck
tire, wheel	
station, train	trip, bus
	airplane
	wagon

SCHOOL

School, general	
school, class, seat	grade, flag, desk
teach, teacher	
	blackboard, chalk
	paste, scissors, ruler
lesson, learn	
book, story, page, word	
read, count, write	copy, pencil
	rub, rubber, eraser

Dale List Words on Left	Interview Words on Right
Pictures and Drawing	
picture, draw, paint, color	crayon, rag
bright, dark, light	
black, white, gray	
blue, red, yellow	
brown, green	

NATURE

Dale List Words on Left	Interview Words on Right
Animals	
animal, cow, horse, pen	pig, pony, calf
sheep	lamb, wool
dog	bark, pet, puppy
	cat, kitten, rabbit
bear, lion, wild	elephant, monkey, fur
fish, tail	frog, turtle
	mouse, deer, squirrel
Birds and Insects	
nest, egg	feather, robin
bird, fly, wing, bill	hen, chicken, rooster
	duck
	bug, ant, butterfly
bee	sting
Plants	
plant, seed, grow, grew	leaf, leaves, root
tree, oak, branch	nut
flower, rose	
grass, grain, corn, wheat	
Weather and Sky	
north, south, east, west	
earth, sky	
sun, moon, star, shine	shadow
cloud, wind, blow, clear	
air, weather	
hot, warm, cold, cool	
storm, rain, ice, snow	

Dale List Words on Left	Interview Words on Right
Time	
morning, noon, afternoon	
evening, night	
day, week, month, year	
minute	hour
today, tomorrow, yesterday	
season	Christmas, Thanksgiving
spring, summer, winter	Easter
date, time, sometime, ago	
now, then, soon	
never, always, early, late	

WAR AND FIGHTING

war, march, soldier	
fight, kill, die, dead	
brave, afraid, fair	
king, crown, queen, chief	

GENERAL THINGS, QUALITIES, AND RELATIONSHIPS

Containers and Parts	
box, bag, basket, case	bottle, pail
part, top, bottom	
back, front, side, edge	
cover, open, close, shut	wrap
fill, full	empty
outside	inside
Materials and Qualities	
paper	card, string
sand, stone, rock	brick
iron, chain	
gold, golden, silver	
wood, board, stick, post	hammer, nails
thick, thin, soft, hard	
dry, heavy	wet

Dale List Words on Left	Interview Words on Right
coal, fire, burn, smoke	burnt
glass	leather
Numbers	
one, two, three, four, five	
six, seven, eight, nine	
ten, twelve	eleven
twenty, hundred, thousand	
first, second, last	third
Number and Amount	
thing, some, something	
nothing, none	
any, anything	
every, everything	
number, half, whole	
double, pair, both	
all, several, few, lot	
enough, each	
much, many, more, most	
once, only, often	
piece, pound	
Size, Shape, and Space	
big, large, little	
great, small	
size, shape, space	
square, circle, round	
center, middle	
end, line, straight	
measure, mile	
place, row	
up, down, low, high	
near, far	
left, right	
here, there	
alone, together, next	
wide, deep, long, short	

MISCELLANEOUS PARTS OF SPEECH

Dale List Words on Left	Interview Words on Right
Miscellaneous Nouns	
spot, mark, hole, load	danger
chance, matter, kind	
way, course	
Miscellaneous Adjectives	
bad, good, better, best	
happy, glad	sorry, angry
nice, fine	
beautiful, pretty, plain	ugly
same, different, yes, no	
a, an, the	
true, wrong	
ready, sure, careful	careless
easy, new, busy, lost	
Pronouns	
he, him, his	
she, her	
it, its	
I, me, my, mine	
we, us, our	
you, your	
they, their, them	
myself, herself, himself	
this, these, those	
who, whom, whose	
which, what, that, where	
neither, either	
other, else	
Conjunctions	
and, but, yet, for, or, nor,	
when, because, while, if	
than, though, whether	

Dale List Words on Left	Interview Words on Right
Prepositions	
above, against, behind	
beside, between, over, under	
by, on, upon, in, into	
after, before, along, past	
through, with, without	
across, around, at, to, from, of	
till, until, like, except	
Interjections	
oh	hello, goodbye
Adverbs	
as, away, also, another	
again, almost, already	
about, ever, even	
instead, just, not, off	
out, quite, rather, real	
so, such, too, very, why	

VERBS

Auxiliaries	
am, are, is, was, were	
be, been	
will, would, shall, should	
can, could, may, might	
have, has, had	
do, does, did, done	don't
seem	
must, ought	
Mental Operations	
believe	
care	
choose	
expect	

Dale List Words on Left	Interview Words on Right
feel, felt	
forget	forgot
guess	
hope	
know, knew	
mean	
remember	
suppose	
think, thought	
want	
wish	
wonder	

Miscellaneous Verbs

act	
beat	
begin, began	begun
belong	bend
bit	bite
break, broken	broke
bring, brought	
cause	
change	
come, came	
carry	
drop	
fall, fell	
finish	
find, found	
fix	
follow	
give, gave	
get, got	
go, went, gone	goes, going
hang	hung
help	
hide	hid

Dale List Words on Left	Interview Words on Right
	hit
hunt	
keep, kept	
	knock
lie, lay, laid	
lead	led
leave	
let	
lift	
live	
make, made	
meet, met	
miss	
need	
own	
pass	
press	
pick	
put	
rest	
roll	
save	
send, sent	
set	
shake	shook
show	
spread	
stay	
strike	
take, took	
try	tried
use	
wait	
waste	
work	

The total list, in a single alphabet, will be found on the following pages.

ALPHABETICAL LIST OF THE FIRST THOUSAND WORDS FOR CHILDREN'S READING

a
about
above
across
accident
ache
act
address
afraid
after
afternoon
again
against
ago
air
airplane
all
almost
alone
along
already
also
always
am
an
and
angry
animal
another
answer
ant
any
anything
apple
are
arm
around
as
ask
at
ate
aunt
automobile
awake
away
baby
back
bad
bag
bake
ball
balloon
banana
band
bandage
bank
bark
barn
basket
bath
bathe
be
beans
bear
beat
beautiful
because
bed
bee
been
before
began
begin
begun
behind
believe
bell
belong
bend
beside
best
better
between
bicycle
big
bill
bird
birthday
bit
bite
black
blackboard
bleed
bless
blind
blood
blow
blue
board
boat
body
bone
book
born
both
bottom
bottle
bow
bowl
box
boy
branch
brave
bread
break
breakfast
brick
bridge
bright
bring
broke
broken
broom

brother
brought
building
built
bump
brown
bug
build
burn
burnt
bus
busy
but
butcher
butterfly
butter
button
buy
by

cake
calf
call
came
camp
can
candy
cap
captain
car
card
care
careful
careless
carry
case
cat
catch
cause
cent
center
chain
chair
chalk
chance
change
cheek
chief
chicken
child
children
chimney
chin
choose
chocolate
Christmas
church
circle
circus
city
class
clean
clear
climb
clock
close
cloth
clothes
cloud
clown
coal
coat
cocoa
cold
color
come
company
cook
cooky
cool
copy
corn
corner
cost
cough
could
count
course
country
cousin
cover
cow
crackers
cross
crayons
cream
creek
crowd
crown
cry
cup
cupboard
curtain
cut

dance
danger
dark
date
day
dead
dear
deep
deer
dentist
desk
did
die
different
dinner
dig
dime
dining
dirt
dirty
dish
do
doctor
does
dog
doll
dollar
done
don't
door
double
down
draw
drawer
dream
dress
drink
drive
drop
drug
dry
duck
dust

each
ear
early

earth
Easter
east
easy
eat
edge
egg
eight
either
elephant
eleven
else
empty
engine
end
enough
eraser
even
evening
ever
every
everything
except
expect
eye

face
fair
fall
family
far
farm
farmer
fast
fat
father
feather
feed
feel
feet
fell
fellow
felt
fence
few
field
fight
fill
find
fine
finger
finish
fire
first
fish
fit
five
fix
flag
floor
flower
fly
follow
food
foot
for
forget
forgot
fork
forth
found
four
fresh
friend
frog
from
front
fruit
full
funny
fur
furniture

game
garage
garden
gate
gave
get
gift
girl
give
glad
glass
go
goes
going
gold
golden
gone
good
goodbye
got
grade
grain
grandfather
grandmother
grass
gray
great
green
grew
grocery
ground
grow
guess

had
hair
half
hall
hammer
hand
handkerchief
hang
happy
hard
has
hat
have
he
head
hear
heard
heart
heavy
hello
help
hen
her
here
herself
hid
hide
high
hill
him
himself
his
hit
hold
hole

home
hope
horse
hot
hour
house
how
hundred
hung
hungry
hunt
hurry
hurt

I
ice
if
in
indoors
inside
instead
into
iron
is
it
its

juice
jump
just

keep
kept
kick
kill
kind
king
kiss
kitchen
kitten
knee
knew
knife
knock
know

lady
laid
lake
lamb
lamp
land
lap
large
last
late
laugh
lay
lead
leaf
learn
leather
leaves
leave
led
left
leg
lemonade
lesson
let
letter
lettuce
lie
lift
light
like
line
lion
lip
listen
little
live
load
long
look
lost
lot
loud
love
low
lunch

made
mailman
make
man
many
march
mark
market
matter
may
me
mean
measure
meat
medicine
meet
men
mend
met
middle
might
mile
milk
mill
mind
mine
minute
mirror
miss
Miss
money
monkey
month
moon
more
morning
most
mother
mountain
mouse
mouth
move
much
Mr.
Mrs.
music
must
my
myself

nails
name
nap
napkin
near
neck
need
neighbor
neither
nest

never
new
next
nice
nickel
night
nine
no
noise
none
noon
nor
north
nose
not
note
nothing
now
number
nurse
nut

oak
ocean
of
off
office
often
oh
old
on
once
one
only
open
or
orange
other

ought
our
out
outdoors
outside
over
overalls
own

page
pail
pain
paint
pair
pan
pants
paper
parade
part
party
pass
past
paste
path
pay
peach
peas
pen
people
pencil
penny
pet
pick
picnic
picture
pie
piece
pig

pillow
place
plain
plant
plate
play
please
pocket
point
pond
pony
policeman
poor
porch
post
pot
potatoes
pound
present
press
pretty
pull
put
puppy
puzzle

quarter
queen
question
quick
quiet
quite

rabbit
race
radio
rag
rain

ran
rather
reach
read
ready
real
reason
red
remember
rest
ribbon
rich
ride
right
ring
river
road
robin
rock
roll
roof
room
rooster
root
rose
round
row
rub
rubber
rug
ruler
run

sandwich
said
sail
salt
same

sand
sat
save
saw
say
school
scissors
scooter
sea
season
seat
second
see
seed
seem
seen
self
sell
send
sent
serve
set
seven
several
shadow
shake
shall
shape
she
sheep
shine
ship
shirt
shoe
shook
shop
short
should
shoulder
show
shut
sick
side
sign
silk
silver
sing
sir
sister
sit
six
size
skates
skin
skirt
sky
sleep
slip
slow
small
smell
smile
smoke
snow
so
soap
socks
soft
sold
soldier
some
something
sometime
song
soon
sore
sorry
sound
soup
south
space
speak
spoke
spoon
spot
spread
spring
square
squirrel
stairs
stand
star
start
station
stay
step
stick
still
sting
stocking
stomach
stone
stood
stop
store
storm
story
stove
straight
street
string
strike
strong
such
sugar
suit
summer
sun
supper
suppose
sure
surprise
sweater
sweep
sweet

table
tail
take
talk
tall
taste
teach
teacher
tear
teeth
tell
ten
tent
than
thank
Thanksgiving
that
the
their
them
then
there
these
they
thick
thin

thing
think
third
thirsty
this
those
though
thought
thousand
three
throat
through
throw
thumb
ticket
tie
till
time
tire
tired
to
toe
today
together
told
tomatoes
tomorrow
tongue
too
took
tooth
top
touch
towel
town

toys
trade
train
tree
tried
trip
truck
true
try
tub
turn
turtle
twelve
twenty
two

uncle
under
ugly
umbrella
until
up
upon
us
use

valley
very
visit

wagon
wait
walk
wake
wall

want
war
warm
was
wash
waste
watch
water
wave
way
we
wet
wear
weather
week
well
went
were
west
what
wheat
wheel
when
where
whether
which
while
whisper
white
who
whole
whom
whose
why
wide

wild
will
win
wind
window
wing
winter
wish
with
without
woman
women
wonder
wood
wool
word
wore
work
world
would
wrap
write
wrong

yard
year
yellow
yes
yesterday
yet
you
young
your

zipper

CHAPTER XI

THE VOCABULARIES OF TEACHING UNITS

A very definite suggestion to students of vocabulary arises from the present movement toward the organization of elementary school work about what are usually called units. We all know the enormous mass of literature which has developed about the unit idea. Every educational magazine carries in every issue, it seems, descriptions of the way teachers somewhere have organized their teaching by units. New text books in almost all fields are divided into units, and professional books concerning unit teaching appear continually.

We shall not attempt to explain exactly what a unit is since this is a matter of much controversy. But unit teaching seems to be, in essence, the organization of learning around more or less clearly defined topics. The purpose is to give the learning more meaning in the life of the child. This greater meaning arises partly from the growing tendency to have children get more concrete experiences — sensory, manual, social, and otherwise — along with unit study. It also seems to arise from the greater organization of experience that topical study seems to bring about. These tendencies toward more experience and more organized experiences are with us and will undoubtedly remain with us. Therefore

---

From the *Elementary English Review*, Vol. 16, No. 2.

units of some kind are probably here to stay. The great discussion now is as to what units should be used, how they should be related, how they should be conducted, and so on. We do not wish to discuss those questions here. We simply wish to point out the significance of units for vocabulary study.

Vocabulary study is the study of concepts. It has mistakenly been called the study of words, with the notion that words are merely groups of letters that happen to be found on printed pages. From a typesetter's point of view, words are groups of letters, but no one who ever used a word thought of it as a mere group of letters. In use, a word is a concept or idea. It represents a mental reality to the user and should represent a mental reality to the reader. To the user, it is a symbol for something in his past experience. Its importance is the past experience it represents. To the reader it is also important as a representation of experience. To the student of vocabulary it is of interest in the same way. Therefore study of vocabulary means study of concepts or experiences.

These units which are now so popular in the school are centers of child experience. Each unit serves as a gathering point for experiences which are related, which the child can have together and think of together. Each unit is therefore a center of thought. It forms a rallying point for related concepts. Therefore it becomes a kind of vocabulary center as well.

It was with this point of view that we made a study of the vocabulary of some of the more commonly used school units. We started with the basic assumption that the characteristic subject matter of each unit would show itself in a characteristic group of concepts which might be called the vocabulary of the unit. Of course if a concept used in the unit were no different from one that the children were already familiar with, such a concept would not be characteristic of the unit and would not form a part of its vocabulary. But if new concepts or new subject matter are met with, two different situations appear. One is that the new concepts will be represented by new words. This is the situation that most persons think of when they hear the phrase, vocabulary of a unit. For instance, they think of *obi* as part of a Japanese unit. But the second situation is also very common and very important. It is the case in which new material or new concepts are represented by a familiar word with a new meaning. For instance, we might find no new word for an Indian hoe. The unit must therefore use the word *hoe.* We can use simply the word *hoe* with the understanding that a special meaning is intended, or we can use the phrase *Indian hoe.* In our own tabulation it seemed unnecessary continually to qualify words with the adjective signifying the unit. We therefore listed the familiar words with the understanding that the special meanings of the words for the particular unit were implied. Thus a unit vocabulary would contain these two kinds of words, the words that were new altogether and the old words with new meanings.

The first unit with which we experimented was the Indian unit. This is perhaps the unit most widely used in all schools, doubtless because of its appeal to children. We set out to discover just what was taught in the Indian unit and to find the vocabulary that would indicate the concepts involved. Please note that we did not seek to say what *should* be taught in the Indian unit, but only what *is* taught under present conditions. No merely encyclopaedic or reference material was used. Eighteen books were used, all directly concerning Indian units in school. Four of these described studies of the Indian unit. Four of these were readers made up of Indian stories and ten of these were books about Indians prepared especially to be read by grade children. There is much more material than this on the Indian unit in school, but it was felt that this sampling was large enough for experimental purposes. It contained material on woods Indians, plains Indians, and pueblo Indians. Further study should be made to differentiate types, but this tabulation did not try to make such a distinction. Anyone using the resulting list should bear this fact in mind.

Each of these books was gone through carefully and all the words listed which conveyed some idea about Indian life, that is, some idea about the way in which Indian life was different or is different from our own life. These words were of the two kinds discussed above, entirely new words and old words with new meanings. Here we encountered a definite problem in any unit study. Practically all treatment of life different from our own deals with the differences. Few books, if any, devote time to pointing out the many ways in which the life of other people is just like our own. All races, for instance, love their children, but this fact is seldom mentioned. If the children get their clothes wet, the parents doubtless make them change to dry clothes. All races have indigestion if they eat the wrong things. Thus in countless ways lives of all groups of men are quite like the lives of other groups. This similarity is often commented on by travelers among strange peoples but it is seldom if ever mentioned in the books about them. Thus all study of other peoples tends to emphasize differences. This study also emphasizes those differences. This is not a defense for doing so; we merely point out a fact that should be recognized. This defect is inherent in unit teaching if not in all teaching in the schools.

After each individual book had been thus studied and a list derived from it, these lists were put together into a single unit vocabulary of 225 words. Immediately one strange fact appeared. There was surprising lack of agreement between the various books. No single word on the list appeared in all eighteen of the books about Indians. Two words appeared in ten of the books but not in the other eight. These were *moccasin* and *blanket.* The next in frequency were the words used in eight books: *tepee, tribe,* and *weaving.* But we must note that eight is a minority of the eighteen books. Then there was little logic in the appearance of other words. *Bow* appeared in six of the books and *arrow* in seven but *arrow-head* only in two. Some of the discrepancy is due to the fact that some units dealt with forest Indians, some with plains Indians, and some with pueblo Indians. But this fact nowhere accounts for the great inconsistencies. We must conclude that chance of mention was the largest element. One teacher or one author telling about Indians happened to mention some items while other teachers and authors mentioned other items. They used the material that opportunity offered. The results were necessarily incomplete.

If one wishes to consider frequency of appearance as a measure of importance, he would have to consider that some facts of Indian life have more than one common name. For instance, *brave* and *warrior* are used by different books to mean the same thing. *Tepee* and *wigwam* are used interchangeably even though not correctly so. Therefore, if frequency of use is to be considered, some words should be counted together. However, we have come to the conclusion that frequency on this list is a very poor measure of importance. The various treatments of the unit were so incomplete that frequency seems entirely too much a matter of mere chance.

Our second unit was chosen as a type of a great group of common units and is one quite different from the first. It is the unit on wheat. For this unit on wheat nineteen books were studied. Of these, six are separate booklets on wheat, intended for use in grade school, three are descriptions of wheat units as carried out in schools, six are wheat units in books on the social studies, and four are definite sections on wheat in geographies of America. As with the Indian unit, there are many more discussions of the wheat unit than those we used, but these nineteen represented a fairly good sampling for experimental purposes.

In this second tabulation, as in the case of the Indian unit, two types of words were found. Some new materials or concepts were represented by new words, whereas others were represented by familiar words with new meanings. For instance, *threshing* and *bolting* are new ideas which come from the unit, but *seed* and *flour* are old words which have a new meaning that is a part of the wheat unit. The criterion in selection of words was always whether the concept involved was an integral part of study of the unit subject. Each book was studied with these ideas in mind and a vocabulary list made from it. Then from all the books a composite unit vocabulary of 151 words was made.

As might be expected there was more agreement than in the case of the unit on Indians, but no single unit word appeared in all nineteen of the books. The most frequent word was *seed,* which appeared in fifteen books. The next most frequent was *grain* which appeared in thirteen books. *Bread* and *straw* appeared in eleven books. *Threshing machine* appeared in ten. *Flour* and *bundles* appeared in only nine books. When we consider that all nineteen of the books were presumed to describe the whole story of wheat from planting to final use by human beings, this lack of a common unit vocabulary is very surprising. As in the case of the Indian unit, we must presume that separate authors emphasized different things and that they simply forgot to mention many fundamental aspects of the subject. Here also we have the listing of the same concept under various words that may or may not be identical. *Bolting* and *sifting,* for instance, may be the same thing, but *seeder* and *drill* may at times be used interchangeably and at other times may mean quite different machines. Thus, all things considered, frequency of use, as shown by our list, must not be taken as an entirely satisfactory measure of importance.

The third unit that we studied was the Dutch or Holland unit. Here twenty-one books were studied. Of these, six were descriptions of the unit as taught in certain schools; five were geography reading books for grade children; nine were descriptions of Holland in geographies; and one was a teacher's manual on Holland. In tabulation the same methods were followed: selection of words essential to the teaching of the unit, whether entirely new words or old words with new meanings. The result was a list of 120 words. Here again we found no unit words in all the books. The nearest was the word *canal* which appeared in eighteen out of the twenty-one. Next came *dike* in fifteen books, *windmills* in fourteen, and *wooden shoes* in thirteen. *Fishing* and *tulips* appeared in eleven books, and all the rest of the 120 words in still fewer, which means in less than half of the possible number. This was indeed surprising. One would expect *cheese* to be mentioned in any treatment of Holland but only eight out of twenty-one books used the word. Even *tulips* was used more often, in eleven books. So the results from the third unit studied agreed with those from the Indian and wheat units, that there was no agreement as to what special words were needed in teaching the unit. One treatment mentioned some concepts, another treatment mentioned others. Again there was repetition of concepts under different words, sometimes with identical meanings and sometimes not. *Harbors* and *havens* are doubtless the same. *Boats* and *barges* are not always identical. This factor must be remembered in considering frequencies.

For what purposes are these unit lists useful? First, they should be an aid to the teacher in checking upon her own knowledge of the unit. Any teacher who wishes to teach a unit should read over the unit vocabulary list and make sure that she knows what all of the words mean, that is, that she knows all the concepts represented by them. If she does not, she can use reference books and make her technical knowledge concerning the unit more complete. Second, these lists may serve to prevent the very inadequate treatment of units which we have mentioned above. The low frequency of important words which one would think would certainly have been in nearly all of the books suggests much oversight on the part of the persons planning or writing up these units. It is not that we wish to crowd material into units for every grade, but that we should have the most important facts of each unit represented. Third, we should like these lists to be the basis of an inquiry by those interested as to how adequately we are now treating the subject matter of these units. Are we really taking up only the more picturesque or peculiar phases of Indian life or Dutch life or of wheat production? This list of concepts was made up from existing treatments of these topics for grade children. Do we not need better treatments than this, which could be represented by much better word lists? These lists are therefore suggestive as the beginning of study rather than the conclusion of it.

Possible Vocabulary of the Indian Unit

Gathered from 18 books and descriptions of Indian units

(The number of books or units containing the word is shown after each word.)

(In noting frequency of mention, the appearance of the same object under different names must be considered and the frequencies sometimes combined.)

adobe 5
arrow 7
arrowheads 2
arrow shaft 1
ax 2

baby board 3
baskets 5
beads 4
beadwork 2
birchbark buckets 2
Black Cloud People 1
blanket 10
Blue Man 1
bone awls 1
bone needle 1
bone fishhooks 1
bonnet 1
boomerangs 1
bow 6
bow drill 1
bowls 4
bowstring 2
brave 3
bracelets 3
brooches 1
broom 1
buckskin 3
bull boats 2

cache 1
cacique 1
calendar 1
calumet 1
canoe 6
celts 1
cement 1
ceremonies 1
chanters 1
chants 1
chief 4
chisels 1
clowns 1
cold moons 1
coracle 1
corncakes 2
council 2
coup sticks 2
cradle 2

dances 6
darts 1
deermeat 2
dibble 1
dice 1
digging stick 2
dishes 1
drawings 1
dressing skins 1
drums 5
dyes 5

Evil Spirts 1

Father Sun 1
feast 6
flint 2
flute 2
fringe 2
fur rug 1

gardens 1
ghosts 1
girdling 1
Good Spirits 2
gorgets 1
gourd rattle 1
granaries 1
Great Spirit 3

hammock 1
handicraft 1
handstone 1
Happy Hunting Ground 2
harpoons 1
harvest 1
Harvest Moon 1
hatchet 3
headdress 4
hoddle (weaving stick) 1
hoes 1
hogan 3
hooks 1
horn spoons 1
hunt 4
hunter 4

images 1

jars 1
juggling 1

kettles 1
kiva 2
knives 2

lacrosse sticks 1
ladders 1
language 1
leggings 5
lodge 4
Long Ago People 1

Long House 1
looms 3

maize 1
many snows 1
mats 3
medicine 1
medicine bag 2
medicine man 4
metate 1
moccasin 10
moon of cracking trees 1
moon of flowers 1
moon of snowblindness 1
mortar 1

necklace 4
nets 1

ollas 1
ornaments 2
ovens 2

paintings 2
papoose 3
papoose case 1
parfleche 2
peace pipe 2
pemmican 5
pestle 1
picture writing 1
pinchers 1
pinon nuts 2
porcupine quills 2
pottery 5
pouches 1
pow-wow 1
prairie potato 1
pueblo 2

quills 1
quill stitch 1
quiver 3

rabbit stick 1
racquet ball 1
rain makers 1
rattles 3
Red People 1
religion 1
robes 1
rugs 1

sacred tobacco 1
scalp lock 1
scouts 3
sewing awls 1
sewing bag 1
Shaman 1
shell spoons 1
shields 1
shirt 2
signals 1
signs 1
silversmith 1
skillet 1
skin bucket 2
skin dressing 1
skin ropes 1
skipping bone 1
skirts 1
sled 1
sleeps 2
smoke signals 2
snowshoes 1
spade 1
spear 2
spearheads 1
Spirit Land 1
spoons 1
squaw 1
string 1
Storm People 1
symbols 1

tabu 1
tanning 2
tepee 8
thong 1
Thunder Bird 2
tinder 1
tobacco pouch 1
toboggan 1
tomahawks
tom-tom 4
torches 1
totem 1
trading 1
trail 3
traps 1
travois 4
treaties 1
tribe 8
tumpline 1
turtle shell cup 1

village 5

wampum 2
war bonnet 1
war gods 1
war paint 1
war party 1
war path 2
war whoops
warm moons 1
warrior 7
water jars 1
Water Spirits 2
wattle traps 1
weapons 1
weaving 8
White Spirit 2
wigwams 5
Wilderness People 1
winter camps 2
winter count 1
wooden dishes 1
wooden yokes 1

Possible Vocabulary of the Wheat Unit

Gathered from 19 books and descriptions of Wheat units

(The number of books or units containing the word is shown after each word.)

(In noting frequency of mention, the appearance of the same object under different names must be considered and the frequencies sometimes combined.)

baker 1
bakery 2
bran 5
bins 5
binder 6
binding 2
biscuits 3
Black Stem Rust 1
bleaching 1
blight 1
bolter 1
bolting 2
bolting machine 2
bread 11
Bread Basket of America 1
breadstuff 1
bundles 9
bushel 2

cake 3
carbohydrates 1
cereals 8
Ceres 2
chaff 5
chinch bug 1
cleaning 4
coarse flour 1
coffee cakes 1
combine 6
cracked wheat 1
crackers 2
cradles 3
cream of wheat 1
crushing 4
cutting 6

divider 2
dough 2
drill 4
drying 1
duram wheat 2
dust storms 1
Dutch oven 1

elevator 6
endosperm 1

farina 1
fertilization 1
flails 5
flour 9
flour mill 4
foodstuff 1

gluten 2
gluten test 1
graham flour 2
grain 13
granary 2
grasshoppers 1
grinding 8
growing season 2

hand mill 1
hand stone 1
harvest 5
harvesting 7
heads 7
heading machine 1
Hessian Fly 1

kernel 4

laboratories 2
loaf 5

macaroni 3
middlings 2
middlings purifier 2
mill 5
miller 1
milling 6
millstones 2
mixing machine 1
molding machine 1
mortar 5
mowing knives 1
muffins 3

noodles 2

ovens 1

pastry 1
peels 1
pestle 5
pies 1
planting 1
protein 2
purifiers 1

quern 2

reaper 7
reaping 3
reaping, primitive 1
reel 2
ripening 2
rolled wheat 1
roller mill 1
rolls 1
rotation of crops 1
rounding machine 1

saddle stone 1
scab 1
scouring 2
scythe 3
seed 15
seeder 2
separator 2
sheaves 4
shock 8
shocking 3
sickle 4
sifting 4
slicing machine 1
smut 1
sowing 7
sowing, primitive 1
spaghetti 2
spring wheat 6
spring wheat section 2
stacks 1
stalk 6
starch 1
starch test 1
storing 3
straw 11
strawstack 4
stubble 1
swath 1

thresher 2
threshing 5
threshing floor 1
threshing machine 10
twine 1

waffles 1
washing 2
weighing 1
wheat belt 3
wheat berry 3
wheat gum 1
wheat plant 2
white flour 1
whole wheat 1
whole wheat flour 3
winnowers 2
winnowing 1
winter wheat 7
winter wheat section 2

yeast 1

Possible Vocabulary of the Holland Unit

Gathered from 21 books and descriptions of Holland units

(The number of books or units containing the word is shown after each word.)

(In noting frequency of mention, the appearance of the same object under different names must be considered and the frequencies sometimes combined.)

barge 8
beds 2
bicycles 1
boats 3
bridge 4

canal boats 2
canal path 2
canals 18
cheese 8
cheese press 1
churn 3
cod fish 1

dairying 7
dams 2
delta 5
diamond cutting 8
dikes 15
dishes 1
ditches 7
docks 2
dog carts 4
dredgings 1
Dutch painters 2

Edam cheeses 5

fields 1
fiords 1
fishermen 1
fishing 11
fishing boats 1
fishing ports 1
fishing villages 1

games 2
gardens 1
grinding grain 2

harbors 1
havens 1
herring fish 1
houseboats 1
houses 1
hyacinth bulbs 3

iceboats 2
ice-chair 1
irrigation 3

kermis 1
klompen 1

lakes 1
land of windmills 1
larder of Europe 1
locks 4
lowlanders 1
lowlands 5

market gardening 2
markets 4
marsh lands 3
meadows 1
milk cans 3
milk sleds 1
milk carts 2
moorland 1

one-way sidewalks

pasture land 2
peasant farmers 2
peasants 1
peat 5
peat polder 1
piles 3
polder farmers 1
polder lands 2
polder pastures 1
polders 9
polls 1
pumps 1
puppet shows 1

quays 1
Queen of Holland 2

rivers 3

sand dunes 8
sea dikes 1
shelf beds 1
skating 6
skating races 1
stilts 2
St. Nicholas 1
stork 7
swamps 2

towlines 1
tram chugs 1
tulips 11

village 4

water gates 1
weddings 1
windmills 14
wooden shoes 13
wooden stockings 1
wooden yoke 1

Zuider Zee 10

CHAPTER XII

THE BIBLE IS EASY READING

For centuries the Bible was practically all the reading matter that the common man had. We can be sure that most men in those times, with the very slight schooling available, were not very good readers. But they read the Bible with satisfaction and enjoyment. For a long period the Bible was the chief text in the schools. Methods of teaching were primitive, but the children learned to read with this text book. Our own present experience with reading the Bible is that somehow it appears simple reading and easy to understand. In fact many things point to the conclusion that the Bible is easy reading matter.

Interest in easy reading matter has led to study of what makes material easy to read. Naturally the first suggestion was vocabulary. Other things being equal, the easier the words, the easier the reading matter. Numerous studies have been made in this field. The widespread belief expressed above, that the Bible is easy to read, suggests at once that we apply these vocabulary studies to the Bible and see if the belief will be upheld. Will our feeling about the Bible be verified from a study of its vocabulary?

As an approach to the study of the Bible as easy reading matter, it was felt that the best known part

---

From the *Elementary English Review*, Vol. 15, No. 8. Ida C. Dolch, joint author.

should be studied first. People have always read the New Testament much more than the Old Testament because after all it is the New Testament upon which the Christian faith is based. In the New Testament, the Gospels have been the favorite reading matter because they present the life of the Master and contain His words. We therefore chose one of the Gospels for study, the Gospel of St. Mark.

Our first task was to tabulate the vocabulary of the Gospel of St. Mark on what may be called the dictionary basis; that is, inflected forms were combined as is done in the dictionary. Immediately we had our first verification of the belief that this Gospel is easy reading matter. The total number of different words found was 1237. In this day of complex civilization the child first coming to school knows twice that number when he hears them. A single third grade reading book will often have more than twelve hundred different words. And yet in the relatively limited vocabulary of 1237 words the Gospel of St. Mark presents the whole story of the life of Christ and gives in His words His plan for human salvation.

One might say that though the vocabulary of this Gospel is limited, the words are difficult ones and not those which a child would know. Here we have some most interesting checks. A committee of the International Kindergarten Union gathered into one list the results of many studies as to what words children understand before they come to school at six years of age. Their list contains 1785 words (on dictionary basis), and obviously does not include all the words these pre-school children really know, since other studies have found pre-school children knowing an average of more like twenty-five hundred. Yet these pre-school words of the Kindergarten Union List comprise 46 per cent of all the different words in the Gospel of St. Mark. That is, almost half of all the different words in this Gospel are those well known to small children before they enter the first grade.

A second interesting check is possible. We have a study of words written by school children, through eight grades, called the Free Association Study. It provides a list of 9,520 different words. Here again we know that there must be additional words which children failed to think of when they wrote their lists. Yet these school children's words make up 86 per cent of the different words in the Gospel of St. Mark. That is, almost nine out of every ten words in the Gospel are known to children before they leave the grades.

One last query might occur to the reader. "Even though most of the words in the Gospel are everyday, easy words, may it not be that there is also a group of strange archaic words which would make the reading difficult?" On this point, too, we have a check. There is a book called *The Teacher's Word Book of 20,000 Words.* This list gives the most frequent words used in a study of an enormous amount of reading matter of all kinds. Twenty thousand words is a very small number indeed. A man who studied a sample of pages from the Encyclopedia found over 50,000 different words. A desk dictionary may contain 100,000 different words, while the complete dictionary contains 450,000 different words. It will be seen, therefore, that the 20,000 commonest words must be very common indeed.

Let us check the vocabulary of the Gospel of St. Mark against the list of 20,000 commonest words. Doing this we find that almost 99 per cent of the vocabulary of the Gospel is included in the list. In fact, only 13 words are *not* in the list. And yet nearly all of these thirteen are variations and combinations of list words. One group may be represented by *deceitfulness* which is in fact an easily understood derivative of the word *deceitful*, which is on the list. Others of the thirteen are like *whensoever*, which is really a combination of several list words. Only two words are distinctly outside of the list of 20,000 words. They are *shew bread* and *wine vat*. And the parts of these compounds are on the list.

We are therefore not mistaken in thinking that the Bible is easy reading, at least so far as this familiar Gospel is concerned. Almost half the words are known to pre-school children, nine out of ten are known to grade school children, and all but thirteen appear on a list of the 20,000 commonest words of the language. This is a convincing verification. We can be sure that all *can* read the Bible—if they will.

Part IV

Remedial Reading

CHAPTER XIII

POOR READERS ARE "MADE"

That there are poor readers in the upper grades and in high school is a fact that we must accept but also a fact that we should understand. The explanation is not as simple as many people suppose. First of all, we cannot blame the whole situation on children's mental dullness. Many of the poor readers are of average ability or better, as we can find out if we test them carefully. Others of the poor readers are of less mental ability but they are not reading nearly up to the level that their actual ability would permit. The school has simply not made use of the learning capacity which we can show they possess.

In the second place, we cannot blame the children for lack of interest and application. Children who are poor readers show interest and application toward many things, but not toward reading. Obviously, the school years have failed in making reading something that appeals to interest and application. The school has not been able to use the child's potential mental ability nor his potential interest. In short, poor reading cannot fairly be blamed on the child who is the poor reader. Instead, poor readers chiefly have been "made" by the environment that has surrounded them in past years, both at home and at school.

It will help in understanding "how the poor reader got that way" if we briefly trace the various causes that brought him to this situation in which he now is. We will not find every one of these causes in every case of poor reading but a surprising number will be found in the past history of almost any poor reader.

1. A TOO EARLY START

It is common knowledge among parents that when they wish a child to begin any kind of activity, they must be careful not to start it too early. If they do, the child is "set against" the activity, and then, progress is likely to be very slow indeed. We find this in getting a child to do things for himself, in getting him to play with other children, in getting him to play musical instruments, etc. A too early start results in dislike and in slow progress instead of rapid progress.

In the case of many children, a too early start is made in the teaching of reading. The child will like the pictures in a book. He will like to read the story in the pictures or listen to the story read to him. Then with little training or preparation, he is asked to look at the marks under the pictures and tell what each set of marks says. He may even succeed in this when there are only four or six words under the picture. But very quickly, in a few weeks time, there are four or six lines under the picture, with twenty-five different words or more. The process goes too fast for him. One word looks very much like another. He fails to remember what has been read the way other children do. He is confused and repelled by the job. If you visited his reading lesson, you would see him looking around the room or inattentive in some way, anxious to get away from the thing he cannot do. He is, in fact, set against reading. Soon he is the "one child out of four or five" in grade one who is classed as a failure. He may repeat first grade or he may be pushed on to grade two because every seat in the first grade room is required for another child who has reached school age and must be put somewhere.

If the teacher of advanced reading will investigate the school record of the poor readers, especially asking their former first grade teachers about them, she will usually find a story such as we have given. Of course, the first grade teacher may say the child did not have the ability or did not apply himself. It is true, he may not have had the ability to learn to read as fast as the other children read, but he could have learned to read at a slower rate. He did not apply himself, but it is practically impossible to apply yourself to a job you cannot do. If the task had been within the child's ability and attached to his interests, the chances are he would have applied himself.

When we ask "Why this too early start in reading" the answer gives food for thought. First, it is possible that the parent of this child or all the parents of a community, insisted that the school begin teaching reading to all children in the first week or two of school, regardless of whether they were ready or not. Such parents had forgotten their past experiences in trying to force a child to do something before he had developed the ability to do it. Or the parents might have had the strange but too common idea that learning reading means memorizing the text in the reading book. Such memorizing was common in old-time schools but now we know that the purpose of the reading book is to teach a child to perceive the words so accurately that he will know those words when he meets them in new sentences. Memorizing the text deceives many parents, and even some teachers. But each year, the child gets new books which cannot be read unless the child has learned the words in the old books. An extreme case of this difficulty was a sixth grade boy who did not have even first grade reading ability; yet he "had been able to read in grades one and two." This obviously meant that he had memorized his books in grades one and two but had not learned one word from another.

Of course it may be that parents were not at all anxious to push the children into reading but that the school authorities had no other provision for them. Many first grades are lacking in activity materials and in the many kinds of learning that can go on without trying to recognize words. Likewise, the school may have planned for all children in grade one to do the same thing. Therefore, when the more mature children wanted to read, as they were quite prepared to do, the less mature children had to do the same thing. Or, the first grade may have had two groups, one for the fast and the other for the slow. Then if a few children were still not ready when the rest of the slow group were, they were then forced to start too soon. It is to meet this situation that so many schools have in grade one groups A, B, and C, the C group being kept busy and happy on things aside from reading until their second year in school. But whether due to misconceptions of parents, or lack of provision by the school, many, many children are discouraged from the start and set against reading to such an extent that their progress is permanently slowed down. Such children will tell you years later that they have never liked reading, and that they have never picked up a book unless they had to. So they became poor readers. What else would we expect?

2. Sickness and moving

Many of our poor readers will tell us that they liked reading when they started school and succeeded in it, but then some childhood sickness came along or some accident, which put them in bed for weeks and months. When they came back, things were different. The class had gone on and the child tried to join in with the others, but the page of the book contained many words he had not seen before, since they had been brought in while he was sick at home. And he had forgotten many other words which he had known before. Thus reading became hard and unpleasant. Perhaps the teacher did not realize his handicap and scolded him. He became discouraged and inattentive.

Still worse is the case of the child who was succeeding happily until his parents moved to some other school district or town where other books were being used. Such a child might be moved to a new school every year or perhaps through several schools in the same year. He may have mastered the first books he met, but the new books were quite different. The rest of the class had learned most of the words in the book but they were not the ones he had learned. To them, the book might have five new words on a page. To him, it might have twenty-five. In fact, some children whose parents move them around often get so confused with the constantly new vocabulary they meet in the new books they are not sure of any words at all and seem almost non-readers.

There is a method of dealing with loss from sickness, the provision in the school of a "special help" room where children who have been out are taken back to the work they have missed and brought up with the rest of the class, but few schools have such rooms. There is a partial solution to the difficulty of changing text books. It is an emphasis by all teachers on the very common words which appear in all school readers, rather than on the special words which change from one reader to another. But as yet teachers have not made this adjustment, and so children who are moved about get a feeling of failure and hopelessness. Thus many children who make a good start in reading find their progress blocked and get an emotional resentment through the difficulty caused by sickness or by the moving of their parents. Surely, we cannot hold them to blame for such circumstances.

3. Promotion into failure

Modern educators are completely convinced that the school must at all levels take the child where he is and help him to go from there. In fact, "take the child where he is," is almost a slogan of sound modern education. One fact behind it may be that modern schools have been giving tests and thus have discovered how far many children are from being where they are supposed to be. Another fact may be, the realization that you have to take the child where he is if you are to get him anywhere else.

Unfortunately, there are still many schools where the work of each grade is treated as though it stood alone and as though it did not rest upon and depend upon previous work. Thus, many fifth grade teachers start out in September teaching fifth grade work without any regard as to whether the children ever learned what they were supposed to in grade four. That is, they start, as it were, building the fourth floor of the house though there might not be any third floor beneath them. Naturally, as we have suggested, such work is only pretense. At least in the subject of reading, it is impossible to teach fourth grade work to children who have not learned first, second and third grade reading. One learns to read fourth grade books by reading third grade books, to read third grade books by reading second grade books, and so on.

Many primary teachers know they must take children where they are and therefore begin reading at the level at which the child can actually read. Thus second grade teachers may start some children in primers. Second and third grade teachers may have a group reading in first readers. If this plan were continued, each child would progress at his own best rate. But, sooner or later, the child is promoted into a room where he is given a book that all the others have and told to read it. If he had been a grade or two behind the previous year, he has now, frankly, been promoted into failure. He cannot do the work, he is scolded and marked down for not doing it, and his progress in reading usually stops right there.

If a poor reader is this kind of a case of arrested development due to promotion into failure, we certainly cannot blame him for it. Sometimes we may blame the parents because some parents insist on promotion when the result of promotion will be certain failure. Such parents may have the naive belief we have already referred to that if a child cannot read the fourth reader, for instance, he can in some mysterious way, be taught to read the fifth reader. Or we may at times have a case in which the parent does not care about the child but only about how she will explain non-promotion to the neighbors. Sometimes, of course, we can blame the school for making no provision for those children who cannot go as fast as the others. Some provision by subdividing classes is often made in the primary grades but the middle and upper grades often ignore the situation. Or the teachers may say that with so many subjects to teach, they must demand that every child do the same work. Such an attitude simply indicates ignorance of modern practices. In modern books on reading may be found the ways in which many schools now keep every child happily advancing at his own rate.[1]

An alternative to "promotion into failure" is non-promotion. Many schools have abandoned non-promotion, claiming that modern psychology teaches that every child must be promoted every year.

---

[1] See list of professional books on page 201.

Psychology does not teach any such thing. Psychology does teach that children develop at different rates, mentally, emotionally and socially. Wholesale promotion is certainly not adjusting to these different rates of development. Promotion into failure cannot be called adjustment. Non-promotion is definitely desirable when it would improve the child's whole pattern of development. It is certainly wrong if it is used only as an adjustment to failure or success in reading or arithmetic.

4. Too hard reading material

Many poor readers will tell you that all reading matter is hard. They have never seen any that was not. If you find for them a book suited to their interest and within their reading ability, they may discover to their delight that reading is fun. This is an idea that they have heard teachers talk about but they have never believed it. To them, for years and years, reading has been nothing but hard work, usually accompanied by a failure and a scolding.

It has until very recently been a fact that school reading materials were adapted chiefly to the more bookish members of the class. Teachers have in the past been sympathetic toward the good readers in their classes, and almost openly antagonistic to the poor readers who are found to be indifferent to books and to verbal learning. In addition, the writers and editors of text books have been quite unsympathetic to those whom they unconsciously regard as pre-destined failures. However, teachers who understand children have for many years been demanding easier text books, and students of reading have been demonstrating through scientific studies that many of the children were finding the standard text hopelessly over their heads.

The strange thing is that when a child is given reading books beyond his reading ability, he learns very little from them. For instance, a child with third grade reading ability may sit through the fourth grade, the fifth grade, and the sixth grade and still have only a third grade reading ability. The books that are too hard for him simply do not improve his reading. If instead he had been given third grade readers, he would have improved somewhat year after year. We might state the principle as "give a child a weight he can lift, and he will be able to lift more; give him a weight he cannot lift, and he gets no stronger."

Here again we can see that our poor reader has been strictly a victim of circumstance. He was given books and told to read them. He could do nothing about it. He could not go get himself other books. Surely, the blame, if any, is upon those who should have known better. The schools could have met the situation because for some years there have been available a quantity of books on many subjects at many reading levels. No matter what the child's interest, it is nearly always possible to find reading matter on that interest at or near his present level.

No matter what the school subject, there are books upon it at different reading levels. The trouble is that the schools have generally shut their eyes to the situation. They have also allowed themselves to be deceived. The children who could not read the books given them "covered up" by guessing and all sorts of other devices. Their teachers often do not realize that this is going on, but they should realize it. In any event, we have here a large explanation of why so many children are poor readers and remain poor readers.

5. Poor methods in teaching reading

Great strides have been made in recent years in study of the psychology and teaching of reading. We know which methods fit the learning process and which ones do not. We know the good ways of handling reading material and the poor ways. We understand the psychology of meaning and of motivation. In short, we know how reading may be successfully taught to nearly all children.

Yet many school systems and many teachers are very ignorant of this progress that has been made in methods of teaching. Principals and teachers who had their training thirty years ago have often failed to keep up with the times. They have not gone to professional meetings. They have not read the new books. They have slipped into the self-satisfying conviction that "what was good when I went to school, is still good today."

Of course, we cannot blame a poor reader if his early training was taken in such a school as we have described. Many of the poor readers began by memorizing their book, as we have mentioned above, and were highly praised for doing so. Many poor readers were taught to spell out every new word in the manner of a century ago. Many poor readers spent years in school where there were hardly any books to read or at least no interesting, easy books. The use of poor methods has continued to exist and will continue for a long time to come. As a result, some schools will continue to "turn out" poor readers just as a factory turns out trucks.

Poor readers are "made" (1) by a too early start, (2) by sickness and moving, (3) by promotion into failure, (4) by too hard reading material, (5) by poor methods of teaching reading. Can these causes be removed? We believe the picture is hopeful. Good schools everywhere are working on the five causes and getting results. Poor schools are unaware of the situation and are still blaming the individual child. Let us hope that enlightenment on this subject may be spread widely and soon. Let us not be guilty of "making" poor readers and thus contributing to the frustration and failure that poor reading almost inevitably produces.

CHAPTER XIV

THE FIRST STEP IN REMEDIAL READING

It is invariably found that a non-reader or a poor reader has an inadequate sight vocabulary. Yet the common words which constantly recur in reading should certainly be recognized immediately if the child is to devote his attention to the more difficult, less frequent words. The first step, therefore, in remedial reading is to teach the child to recognize instantly the basic sight vocabulary. Chapter IX lists the 220 words which make up 50 per cent or more of the reading matter used in school. This small number of words is of such wide usefulness largely because the list includes no nouns but is made up of the prepositions, conjunctions, adjectives, adverbs, and verbs which form the framework of expression and communication. Nouns cannot be of general use because the change from one school subject to another and from one topic in a subject to another topic necessarily means a change of nouns.

The first step in remedial reading, the teaching of the basic sight words, can be done with surprising ease if special cards prepared for the purpose are used.[1] An illustration is a recent remedial project

---

From the *Elementary School Journal,* Vol. 37, No. 4.

[1] Basic Sight Vocabulary Cards, Garrard Press, Champaign, Ill. 50 cents.

carried on with fourth-grade children. Of the 300 children in the grade, a fourth (about 75) knew no more than 194 of the list of 220 words. The number of words known by these 75 pupils ranged from 194 down to only 40. The children scoring below 195 were selected for remedial work. The number of words known as sight words by each child was tested with a pack of cards, each card bearing one of the words printed in primer type. The cards were placed directly before the child, and he was told that the game was to call the words, giving them only "one look." He was assured that he might know all the words if he took his time but that he was to help pick out the "one-look" words from the "two-look" words. The children liked the game. The tester sat at the child's right hand and took the cards from the top of the pack at a steady rate of from one to two cards per second. Those which the child called correctly were placed in one pile and those which he missed in another pile. Thus, the basic sight words that the child already knew by sight were separated from those that he was to learn.

From this start each child was to make progress toward instant recognition of the whole basic sight vocabulary. Each child had a manila envelope containing his individual pack of cards and bearing on the outside a series of numbers, one for each practice period. After the first was placed the number showing how many words the child had to learn and after the others the daily record of the number of words still unknown. Every day the cards were shuffled, and the child went over them with the aid of a "helper," a pupil who was a good reader chosen by the teacher to fit the particular case.

Sometimes this work was carried on in the classroom while the rest of the group worked at something else, and sometimes it was done in a separate room. The child who was the "player" read each card and handed it to the "helper." If the player was right, the helper put the card on the desk; if not, he kept the card in his hand. If the player did not know the word or if he miscalled it, the helper pronounced the right word, and the player repeated it after him. Both were eager to reduce the number of unknown words, or to "overcome the enemies," as some of them put it. When a child could call all the words correctly, he repeated the performance for the next two days to prove that he could remember them all. A final individual check was made by the tester.

The few children who, at the beginning, knew less than half the 220 words were not given all the cards, but only those that they knew and a few more that were especially taught. Their packs gradually grew as new words were steadily added. The "known" were emphasized rather than the "unknown." Directions that come with the word cards tell more of how to handle these very poor reading cases.

The record of what these children accomplished in from three to four weeks shows that children of fourth-grade maturity can, in a remarkably short time, correct the fundamental defect of lack of sight vocabulary. The figures in Table I (for sixty-five children instead of the original seventy-five, ten having been eliminated because of absence, removals, etc.) are those secured from individual testing by an experienced tester, not the results secured by the children themselves. They show that in all but a handful of cases this group of poor readers, after the special work, recognized instantly practically all the 220 basic sight words. A large factor in this success was the great interest of the children in reducing the number of unknown words to zero. They had a definite job that they were sure they could do, and they did it. In some schools a third of the room was working on this project, and the other pupils were as interested as were the "players" in winning out. A few extremely poor readers showed unwillingness to co-operate until given individual attention by the teacher or the tester. A few helpers had to be changed because of personal feeling.

A check on the results of this first step in remedial work was made by the use of a standard test. It is understood, of course, that no single reading test could directly measure the result of increasing the sight vocabulary, but it was felt that such a test should give some indication of easier reading or

TABLE I

Basic Sight Words Known by Sixty-five Pupils in Fourth-Grade Remedial-Reading Group Before and After Four Weeks of Special Work

Number of Known Words	Number of Children Knowing Words	
	Before Special Work	After Special Work
220	......	50
215-19	......	8
210-14	......	3
205-9	......	2
200-204	......	......
195-99	......	2
190-94	7	......
185-89	6	......
180-84	10	......
175-79	6	......
170-74	3	......
165-69	3	......
160-64	4	......
155-59	6	......
150-54	3	......
145-49	3	......
140-44	2	......
135-39	1	......
130-34	......	......
125-29	......	......
120-24	5	......
115-19	1	......
110-14	......	......
105-9	1	......
100-104	......	......
95-99	2	......
90-94	1	......
40	1	......
Total	65	65

greater reading ability. For this purpose the Gates Silent Reading Tests, Type B (Reading To Predict the Outcome of Given Events), was chosen because it comes closest to ordinary straightforward "reading for the story" such as average fourth-grade pupils are expected to be able to do. The results showed an average gain of two months in reading grade after the one month spent on the basic sight words, together with an increase in average correctness. These figures were encouraging, though they could not be taken as positive proof because of the large probable error.

The benefit to the poor readers and to the other pupils in the rooms was, however, decidedly more than can be shown by any standard test. The self-respect and the self-confidence of the poor readers increased remarkably. Their whole attitude toward school was improved. They actually tried to read their textbooks in geography and other subjects. It cannot be said that this improvement was due solely to the learning of the basic sight words, since at the same time the pupils had been given easy books to read in their room libraries. Knowing the basic sight words, however, undoubtedly enabled them to read those easy books more readily, for the 220 words made up 60 per cent or more of the running words of these books. The only cost was the cost of the cards bearing the sight words, and the only derangement of schedule was the setting-up of the practice period for players and helpers and a twenty-minute library period.

This project has shown two very important things: first, that sight-vocabulary deficiency can be corrected in a short space of time and, second, that the correction can be made with a large group of children under normal class conditions. Most work in remedial reading has been individual, and individual attention can never reach the great number of children who are in need. It can be given only to the genuine problem cases. Most poor readers, however, have simply failed to make the usual steps in reading progress when the rest of the class made them. Methods must be devised whereby they can make these steps later. The use of basic sight words on cards, as illustrated in this project, will permit a group of any size to make the first step in catching up with their fellows at any time that a school or a teacher may decide to bring poor readers up to grade.

The basic sight words are now presented in a bingo game that children can play without the need for teacher supervision. The Group Word Teaching Game, Garrard Press, Champaign, Ill.

CHAPTER XV

MASS REMEDIAL READING

Many superintendents who study the matter find that in their middle and upper grades a surprising proportion of the children are unable to read their textbooks. Teachers will report the same situation if they can do so without fear of criticism of their teaching ability. The giving of any standard test will reveal it, if the superintendent will disregard medians and study instead the scores of the tail-end of each class. Supervisors realize that there is a tremendous need for remedial work in reading, but do not know how to attack the problem.

Practically all the material on remedial reading in technical books and magazine articles describes individual remedial reading. Tests to discover individual deficiencies are described, as well as methods of individual tutoring to overcome them. But how can the already over-burdened teacher do much with individual methods in individual reading? One or two children may be helped in spare moments, but if there are a dozen children a grade behind and several children two or more grades behind, individual methods become impossible. To many, the situation appears hopeless.

From *Educational Administration and Supervision,* Vol. 23, No. 7, Baltimore, Md.

PREVENTION

If a superintendent finds this serious retardation in reading in the middle and upper grades, the first thing he should do is to change the conditions which brought this retardation about. First of all, he will undoubtedly find that his system is starting the beginners on a definite program which treats all of the children alike. The third or fourth of the class who are so immature that they cannot possibly learn to read by the usual classroom methods sit and do nothing and very soon the work has passed completely beyond them. By the middle of the year the class is beginning its second or third primer, while these immature children still hardly know a single word by sight. If the superintendent wishes to prevent the great retardation in his middle grades he must begin right in the first grades by starting his beginners when they are ready to learn. Then practically all of them *will* learn.

The superintendent will probably also find that the second-grade teacher assumes that the children she receives are much better readers than they really are. He should have her make no assumptions whatever. She should try them out and start the children with material that really suits their ability. The bright ones will read second readers, the average should probably begin with first readers, and the poorer ones will need to be given a primer or pre-primer. In this way, each child will go on from where he is, and will keep on going. A similar policy needs to be applied to third grade and later. If each child keeps progressing from his own proper level, there need not be the tremendous amount of retardation in reading. The basic cause for that sad condition is the consistent ignoring of children's actual ability and the continual giving to them of books they can not read. All children of a grade are given the books officially planned for that grade in utter disregard of the children's ability or inability to read them. The result is not only months and years of no progress whatever, but violent antagonism to reading, which makes learning almost impossible.

MASS REMEDIAL READING

While the superintendent is taking steps to prevent the continual production of poor reading by the system, he can take what may be called steps in mass remedial reading. They are called this because they can be carried out (1) with the entire room, (2) by the regular teacher, and (3) with equipment that can be secured by any school. These mass remedial measures are applications of principles that are used in individual teaching, but they make it possible for all systems to do *some* remedial work with all poor readers. As these measures are being put into effect, difficult reading cases may be discovered and studied and given individual diagnosis by clinics or otherwise. But no system need wait for special help. These mass remedial measures can be begun at once.

The first step in mass remedial reading is to secure *interested reading by every child at his present reading level.* The first purpose of this step is to change the children's attitude and to cause them to want to learn to read better. It is surprising how quickly this change can be made. Even those children who hate the sight of books will soon be asking for them. The method in this first step is to provide each room with a library which ranges from primers up to books of the room grade and higher. The grade levels of these books must be so concealed that they cannot be learned by the children. The best method to secure such a library is to buy one or two each of the various new series of readers which put no grade marking on a book or which have only a small mark which can be concealed by a sticker. The other way is to break up the sets of primary supplementary readers which are found in most systems, distribute them among the middle-grade rooms, and then put on manila covers so that the books look all alike. The title pages can be partly covered or removed, if necessary. When a room is supplied with this ungraded library, a daily free reading period is arranged during which every child must get a book from the library and read continuously in it. The time need not be more than twenty minutes; but twenty minutes continuous reading will let every one complete one or two stories. Even if a child reads as slowly as sixty words a minute, first-grade speed, in twenty minutes he can read one thousand words. If the child likes a book and wants to go on reading in it, he will put a card in his place with his name on it, the card being long enough to stand up above the book when it is on the shelf. The teacher, who knows both the children and the books, will try to see that each chooses something that he can read with pleasure. If a child shows too much tendency to change unnecessarily, she will encourage him to keep the same book during the whole period.

It will be seen that here are two ways in which this method tends to secure a favorable attitude toward reading. First, each child has a story book which he really can read and which he, therefore, immediately finds interesting. Second, there is the class situation; everybody is reading, most of them with obvious interest and pleasure. No one wants to be left out. Therefore, even the poorest readers make a desperate attempt to read also. And the results in a short time are truly remarkable. The good readers in the room can profit from the free reading period by reading books at their own level. The teacher will circulate about, helping and directing.

At times there is objection, spoken or unspoken, to the name, "free reading period," because to some traditionally-minded persons it sounds as if the children were not doing something worth while. In that case, the name "rapid reading period" can be used, using the reasoning that children learn to read rapidly only when they read a great deal, and that the only way for them to read a great deal is for each to read to himself. For those who fear the children are skipping and not getting much from the reading, it must be emphasized that the teacher is circulating about, sitting now with one child and now with another, asking them to read to her in an undertone, and even asking questions of the children about stories they have completed. The precautions must be taken because in some schools, any slightest variation from the traditional practice meets immediate criticism or condemnation. Of course, the real answer is the giving of tests before this practice is begun, and after it has gone on, to show definitely the progress made. This is one of the excellent services of standard tests.

The second step in mass remedial reading is *securing instant recognition of all of the "basic sight vocabulary."*[1] Poor readers have poor sight vocabulary, and the first step in remedying this difficulty is to make sure that they know instantly this group of words which make up more than half of all school reading matter. These two hundred twenty words are best taught by individual packs of word cards,[1] in a game which the children like to call the one-look game. The pupils are paired off into teams, one member of a team—the poor reader

---

[1] This step is described in detail in the preceding chapter as the "First Step in Remedial Reading" because it was assumed the teacher would have provided easy reading material. The cards used are the Basic Sight Vocabulary Cards, Garrard Press, Champaign, Ill. 50 cents. Less in quantity.

—being the player, and the other member—the good reader—being called the helper. The game is to see how quickly the player can call the whole pack correctly giving each word only "one look." The player has the pack in front of him and picks from the top one card at a time as rapidly as possible, calling the word and handing the card to the helper. If the word was called correctly the helper keeps the card; if not he put the card on the desk or table in another pile. If the player hesitates in calling a word it is counted as incorrect because he did not know it in one look. (This method of using the word cards is fully explained in the preceding chapter and in the directions that go with the cards.)

When the pack is finished the number of words missed is counted and entered on a chart. The helper then hands back to the player one by one the cards missed and as the player holds the card and looks at the word the helper tells the player what it says and he repeats the word so that he will know it next time. These cards are then shuffled back into the pack ready for the next practice period. This game can be repeated once or twice a day until the players call off all the words instantly after "one look" and can do so for a number of days in succession. They will then be able to recognize these same words instantly in reading. This ability will give them more confidence in reading because more than half of the words will be immediately known to them. These known words include prepositions and conjunctions and the more common verbs, and a recognition of these *will help a child greatly* in his attack on the other words in the sentence.

A third step which the superintendent who has a mass remedial problem in the middle grades should take is to secure for every child some kind of sounding *attack to help in identifying strange words.*[2] We may sketch here the essential steps in teaching sounding that concern mass remedial reading. Work on sounding can be done with the whole room, as most of the children will profit by it. (*a*) Certainly every pupil should be able to tell how a word begins, that is, know the sounds of beginning consonants. All the children know the names of the consonants, and they can be taught the sounds that the consonants indicate when they begin a word.

(*b*) Next in importance in sounding are the long and short sounds of vowels. Pupils know the long sounds because these are the names of the letters, but they have in many cases forgotten the short sounds which were taught back in the first grade. The best way to teach these is by giving key words, such as *bat, bet, bit, but, hot.* Then if a child wants to know the short sound of *e* he can think of the word *bet* and get it from that word. If the teacher will have the children of the entire room find in their reading books a large number of words which contain the same sounds as these key words,

---

[2] This step is described in more detail in Part II, Word Recognition and Phonics.

they will soon become conscious of the short vowel sounds, and be able to use them in word attack. If the children are sure of both the long and the short sounds of vowels, they may do a great deal of identifying of words by trial and error. The pupil is looking at a strange set of letters, but the word those letters indicate is probably quite familiar to him by sound. If he knows the consonants, he will try both the short and the long vowel sounds and in this way, with the help of context, will identify the word. The trial and error method, though crude, actually works most of the time.

(*c*) Vowel digraphs and diphthongs may be taught by key words, *meat, sheep, boat, rain, house,* or the like. Pupils can learn the sounds of these combinations of letters by finding in their reading other words containing those sounds. More phonic principles, such as the effect of final *e,* or of *r* or *l* after certain vowels, can be taught but they have nowhere near the value of the three items just given. Let the treatment of sounding be brief but thorough. Let the pupil become absolutely familiar with one point before another is taken up.

(*d*) Syllabication must be taught. The "beginnings" like *pre-* and *un-* and the "endings" like *-ing* and *-ed* will easily be noticed. Then children should at least be given the notion that there are as many "pieces" of the word, or syllables, as there are vowels, usually excepting when two vowels come together. Children readily recognize the "pieces" in words they know, and soon try to divide new words. They can be taught just how to make divisions, or the pupil can divide in any of a number of ways and still recognize the word. We are here dealing only with recognition, not with the sounding of words that are not familiar by ear. In short, calling children's attention to the presence of syllables will go far in causing them to use syllabication in reading.

Even as brief a treatment of sounding as just suggested will be of great assistance to middle-grade children in word attack, because those children have sufficient maturity actually to use these fundamental sounding facts. These children can use both context clues and sound clues together, which is the way an adult uses them. Some non-readers who have reached the middle grades will in a few months be able to use ordinary textbooks merely by intelligent use of sounding clues. In short, the superintendent will find a great deal of reading retardation may be due to the fact that his system tries to teach sounding too early and then consistently neglects it after the first or second grade.

The fourth step in mass remedial reading is *the developing of thought reactions.* This should be made a school wide campaign. Whether the reading matter is read orally or silently, the teacher will ask questions. These questions will sometimes call for repetition to emphasize *careful* reading. More often these questions will ask for comments to emphasize more *thoughtful* reading. Teachers have long used the device of giving the easy questions to the poor readers. Let them try to do this without embarrassing him. If the reading is silent and one child is very slow, he is given a question on the first part of the selection. Or if thought questions are being asked, the slow reader can be given one which fits his slower mental reactions. Thus the poorer readers can be helped to continue to try to develop habits of careful and thoughtful reading.

A superintendent who wishes to bring a whole system up to great efficiency should get the help of reading experts if possible, but without such help he can still do the work of prevention and remedy that we have outlined. The results will be surprising. Valuable as they are for reading itself, they are equally valuable for other school subjects. All subjects benefit tremendously from improved reading. The work with problems in arithmetic will become easier. The study and recitation in geography and history will become more intelligent. The resentment against lessons that cannot be read will diminish and disappear. The whole attitude of large numbers of pupils will change. Thus remedial reading furnishes at present the best opportunity for general improvement of work in our schools.

CHAPTER XVI

BAD HABITS LEARNED IN PRIMARY READING

It is a very common thing for us to speak of "failures in reading" in the first grade or in the other primary grades. Teachers are very likely to say that such and such a child "did not learn anything" during his first year or during several years under school instruction. The child may have been passed on to the next room just because the desk or table was needed for incoming children, or he may have been passed on in the hope that somehow he would "catch on" in the next year, or he may have been kept two years in the grade and then passed on because of the general custom of retaining no more than one year. At any rate, he passed on. In this same way many children are pushed through the primary grades. They learn a little, it is true; they somehow manage to guess or make a pretense of reading. They learn a few words. But they come to the fourth grade as "failures in reading." They "haven't learned anything," it is said, by teachers and parents.

When such children are brought to us for remedial work, we find, on the contrary, that they have learned a very great deal during their primary years. This is in accordance with the universal rule that each child learns something every day at school. If he does not learn what we want him to learn, he learns something we do not want him to learn. These "failures in reading" have not learned to read. But they have learned a good many very important and very powerful things. They are not just "failures in reading." They are far worse than failures. They have learned a great deal that they have to *unlearn* before they can ever become readers. If they had merely failed, then we could start "from scratch" as we say. But we are not able to start from scratch. We have to "unteach" various powerful attitudes and habits that they were taught during those years when the teachers and parents merely said that they were failing in reading.

First of all, these children have been taught *indifference to school books*. They don't care for such books. If you put before them anything that looks like a reader, they shy off from it as a horse will shy from something that scares him. The school reader means failure and often classroom humiliation. They want nothing of it. We have to "unteach" this very powerful attitude. We have to begin with books that don't looks at all like school books. We have to begin with charts, with advertisements, with anything except school readers. Of course, the more docile of the children will obediently look at a school book if you put it before them, but the aversion will still be there. So with such a case, we choose one of the new readers that is planned to look like a "regular book."

Second, these children have been taught that *reading is hard work* and a stupid bore. Reading is just the opposite of anything that they call fun. Why should anybody read if he can do anything else, they think. Reading is wandering amid a maze of unknown words, getting a glimmering of the sense, constantly worried because you know you are not succeeding, liable any instant to be scolded or told you are dumb, and so on and on. After children have been taught this for two or three years, the idea is very strongly set in their minds. You cannot just "talk them out of it." You have to "unteach" this conception of reading.

For these children who think reading is hard work, we have to use endless ingenuity to make reading fun. We have to find material that is strongly interesting to the individual child. Good readers will work on a very mild interest, but with these children a mild interest will not do. The material must be almost what we would call "fascinating." That is why each remedial case is such a special problem. That is why you have to get the child to talk freely about himself and his thoughts. That is why you need to know all about his home, his hobbies, his ambitions. Only in that way can you find the subjects that will really get his strong interest, and thus help unteach the idea that reading is stupid work. And this fascinating material must be found in a degree of difficulty far below his age. It must often be of ten-year-old interest and six-year-old difficulty. That is a large order. But in no other way can we unteach what the child has learned during his years as a "failure in reading."

Third, "guess-and-go-on" must be untaught, if these children are ever to learn to read. Perhaps, back in the very beginning, years ago, they may have looked hard at words but they have got over that. Now they give a look and guess and go on, saying something that makes sense or even that does not make sense. For years now, most of the words they have looked at in any book have been unknown to them. So they have quit worrying about them. They skip from one known word to another and fill in between. This method has been especially developed by the amount of "silent reading" that has been done. Other children went through the paragraph or story very fast, and to keep up, they had to go fast too. The main thing was to get some kind of answer to the questions asked. So you skipped along, reading a little, guessing most of it, and giving an answer that you hoped would fit. But this is not reading. So if we are to teach these children reading, we must unteach this habit of guess and go on. We have to slow them up. We have to have them point at each word if necessary until they learn that you have to read what is on the page and not what you make up in your mind.

This habit is a most stubborn one to unteach. It takes laborious days and weeks and months to teach these children that reading means first knowing what the words say, and that only by knowing what the words say can you tell what the sentences say and what the paragraphs say. The children resent this teaching very strongly because they have learned a very easy, "sloppy" method of reading that has served their purpose a good part of the time. If the child is quick mentally, he may have had considerable success with his guess-and-go-on method. Now we ask him to look at each word and know what each word says. Why go to all that trouble? So here is a real problem in unteaching what these children have learned very strongly all during the time when the teachers said "they were not learning anything."

Fourth, a little known result of this guess-and-go-on kind of reading is *the habit of "jumping eyes,"* as we might call it. An eye movement photograph of these children who were "not learning anything" reveals that they have learned a most disastrous habit of eye movement. We all know how a picture of good eye movements shows a pair of stair steps, as the eyes alternately shift to the right and then stand for a moment and then shift to the right again. We are often told that the poor reader makes a poor kind of stair steps, that is, he makes many little moves to the right instead of a few big ones, and he stands a long time at each point instead of standing only a short time. Now it is true that the poor reader does make such an eye movement record. But in comparison with it, some of these failures in reading make a most fantastic record. The film shows two lines, one for each eye, but those lines twist and loop and go in all directions. No trace can be found of any "following the line." The child's eyes just wandered over the page and back and forth and up and down.

The reason for this habit is most obvious. For years and years the child has got more from the pictures than from the text, so he has learned to look constantly up at the picture during the process of what he calls reading. Look at a few words and then up at the picture, back at the same words or different words and up at the picture. And so on. Then, if there is no picture, he looks along the lines from some words he knows to other words he knows and skips on to others and then back to the previous ones, trying to make sense out of it all. He has the eye movements of doing a jigsaw puzzle rather than of reading.

This habit of "jumping eyes" is a tremendous one to unteach. We cannot take pictures away for fear of killing all interest, but we have to keep the eyes on the reading. So part of the time we have to cover pictures or take material without pictures. We have to keep the eyes from wandering up a few lines and down a few lines, and so we often have to have reading through a window in a card. Sometimes we have to hold a card above the line so that the eyes cannot go back. Partly to control the jumping eyes, we have to have all reading aloud so that the child is compelled to read the words in the order they are in the line, and not in his own order, but even at that he will often read them out of their order. We have to watch carefully the oral reading to make sure there is no skipping of words. Sometimes when the child is tired or inclined to be inattentive, all other methods fail, and we have to point from word to word. It is surprising how this pointing will often speed up the reading. In fact, one of the tests of jumping eyes when a child is reading slowly, is to run a card under the line and see if the reading does not at once speed up when the jumping is partly controlled. Sometimes the reading will become much faster if you point from word to word, thus keeping the child looking at the right place. One of the tricks to overcome the habit of jumping eyes is to have the child count the words he has read, using his right hand and pointing from word to word as he counts. After a child has counted a page or two each day, his eyes have had very good training at following the line and not wandering around away from it.

These are some illustrations of the things that children have learned while everyone said they were learning nothing. These things the children have learned stand directly in the way of all good reading. These things have often been learned so solidly that it is a long and hard process to unteach them. The children who have learned these things are not just "failures in reading." They are worse than failures.

Obviously, an ounce of prevention is worth a pound of cure. If the children are not learning the right thing, we should not let them learn the wrong thing. How can we prevent the learning of these attitudes and habits that must later be unlearned. The methods can easily be deduced from the difficulties we have outlined. (1) The schoolbook should never be "too hard" for any child. School systems have worked in this direction by adopting easier texts, but this is not enough. When in any class, the textbook has become too hard for a number of the children the obvious thing to do is to separate this small group and give them an easier book, one that is not too hard for them. This can easily be done during the primary years. If the teacher cannot take care of so many small groups, the children can be trained to read in small groups to one another under a child leader. In this way, reading can always be easy enough, the child can like the book, and reading can be fun for all.

(2) If we want to keep children from acquiring the habit of "guess and go on" we must watch our use of silent reading. Make sure the children *can* read the material orally before you ask them to read it silently. If they can read every word, they will not skip because they will not need to skip. But just as surely as they read silently and meet words they do not know and cannot ask about, they will skip and thus begin the habit of guess-and-go-on. In later grades and high school, when we send children to reference books which are loaded with hard words, we must actually teach the habit of guess-and-go-on,

but during the primary years, it is safer to teach them to read every word.

(3) We can prevent "jumping eyes." If we keep the poor readers on oral reading, or have them read orally first and reread silently after, they will be kept moving their eyes along the line. If the children look too much at the picture we may even have to read the story first, referring to the picture, and then cover the picture and read the story without it. We can also check this habit of jumping eyes by often rereading easy stories rapidly. If we are sure the child knows the words, we can urge him to read them more rapidly, and thus keep him looking along the line. The child who is rereading a story as fast as he can, will be bound to keep his eyes on the line, and thus is being trained to this habit.

If children were merely "failures in reading" that would be bad enough. But the children who are called failures are in fact worse than failures because they have learned so many things that must be unlearned. If we will remember this fact at all times, we will so manage our materials and methods to prevent in large part the great handicaps which we are producing for these children.

CHAPTER XVII

WHAT TO DO WITH READING DEFICIENCIES IN SECONDARY SCHOOLS

Not very long ago the poor reader was practically unknown in high school. Such a pupil had practically no chance to get through the elementary grades. Nowadays he cannot quit school and he passes through the grades because we object to the maladjustment caused by continued retardation. Therefore the high school gets the poor reader.

One change gradually coming about is doing much to help children in high school who have reading deficiencies—the publishing of simpler books in all subjects. In most cases this means books that are easier to read, and naturally all poor readers benefit. This movement was started by the insistent demand of high school teachers for books with which the children would have less trouble and from which they could learn more. Poor readers benefit by getting more from their books, by finding their subjects more interesting, and by getting much greater benefit from the money spent on their education. This movement should continue. Most high school subjects are not *necessarily* hard. They are only presented in a hard way.

1. Whether school books be easy or difficult we must help children to deal with them. To this end

---

From the *Educational Outlook*, Vol. 15, No. 1, School of Education, University of Pennsylvania, Philadelphia.

the most effective step we can take is *to increase children's meaning vocabulary.* Meager meaning vocabulary is the greatest cause of poor reading in high school. Teachers report that many of their children find on every page so many unknown words that comprehension is impossible. With certain commonly used textbooks, this number has been found for poor readers to be as many as twenty per page. We need not necessarily blame the textbooks. They were written on the assumption that the students would have learned the words in their previous school texts and also that they would have read widely in popular classics and in current books and magazines. The poor reader now in high school has had no such experience. He has probably read nothing outside of school except the comic strips. In school he has moved along without much understanding of all the textbooks that have been put before him. He therefore does not have a meaning vocabulary essential to intelligent reading of high school texts. The teaching of the meaning of words therefore becomes our readiest method of helping the poor reader in high school and this applies to teachers of each and every subject. It does no harm to discuss a word that the children do know. It is a definite harm to fail to discuss a word that they do not know.

The best time to develop meaning vocabulary is in the assignment. Instead of merely telling children to read a certain chapter or certain pages, we should carefully examine those pages for words about which even some of the children may be in doubt. Many of these doubtful words will involve basic concepts that the teacher had assumed and that must be retaught before the class, or at least some members of the class, are ready to go on. For instance, a boy in a freshman history class did not seem able to understand his textbook. Investigation showed that many of the history words in the book, which everyone expected him to know, meant nothing to him. And he was a boy of at least average intelligence.

Some persons would say that new words in an assignment are easily taken care of by telling a child to go to the dictionary. This method may work with the good reader. The poor reader however would have to look up an impossible number of words, and, if he did, he would probably not understand what is given in the dictionary. Instead, "teach the words in the assigned lesson" must be the rule.

In the English class especially, meaning vocabulary can be emphasized. One good device is to discuss the word families which are suggested by new words which appear in the texts. The book may say: "The officer exceeded his authority." The class or teacher may point out that "exceed" means to go beyond. The teacher can ask for other words which have the sound "ceed," such words as "proceed," "precede," "secede" and the like. The children will be interested to see that all these in spite of differences in spelling mean some kind of "going."

Poor readers will get a new or a better meaning for some of these words, and a clearer notion of accuracy of word meaning. With this particular family they will also get some help in spelling. Unfortunately the study of word families has been thought of as something very complicated. Instead it is something that all children already know something about. They know *automatic, automobile, autobiography,* and so on.

2. As a second step to help poor readers in high schools, teachers of all subjects can aid all their students to be more skilful in *sounding out new words.* Children in high school may have an enormous hearing vocabulary; but when they meet many of these same words in print, they do not recognize them. A very little skill in sounding would, with the aid of context, enable them to get the words and read on. The words we refer to are practically all polysyllables. The first essential is therefore deciding how many syllables the word has and which letters belong in each syllable. Syllabication is often overlooked in the grades. Therefore every teacher in high school needs occasionally to give a class practice in syllabication because every textbook is full of long words that pupils do not at first recognize. The English teacher alone cannot possibly give enough time to this subject to develop the needed skill in the slow children. Any teacher uncertain of the rules of syllabication can find them in Chapter VI in Part II of this book.

3. We come now to the problem of *study habits.* Poor readers in high school do not know how to study. A natural suggestion has been that someone should undertake the special teaching of study habits. The person usually nominated is the English teacher. Many textbooks and workbooks have been published to be used in teaching high school children how to study. It is often assumed that if you have a good teacher and provide the class with these textbooks and workbooks the "poor study" problem will be solved.

Experience shows that improving general reading ability improves study more than teaching of study skills without the better general reading ability. Therefore many schools prefer to devote what limited time they have to improving general reading ability. We may teach a boy paragraph analysis to help him get his history lesson. But the trouble with this boy is that every page is full of words that he either cannot identify by sounding or does not know the meaning of. Paragraph analysis will still not enable him to get his lesson. It is only after general reading ability is satisfactory that special study skills can function. General reading ability is referred to in the first two sections of this chapter.

The second problem about teaching study is *what* study skills to teach. There is a tendency to attempt to teach too many skills with not enough practice given to any one. Every book designed to teach study skills should be examined from this point of view. A few skills well taught is what we want. Then there is a tendency on the part of most practice books, instead of giving much practice on a single skill, to go into great technical detail. For instance, every pupil needs some conception of outlining, at least to be always conscious that ideas are presented in sequence and in groups. But when one starts to teach outlining there is a temptation to go into fine points. It is easy to make an elaborate science out of study skills, but in high school we are just trying to help the children get their lessons better. They need to discover main divisions, and need much practice in doing so and little attention to fine subdivisions.

A third comment on study skills is that a strong case can be made for not teaching specific study skills at all, but instead, for the simple teaching of careful thoughtful reading. One widely used set of practice books, the *Standard Test Lessons in Reading,* is based upon this idea. Every page contains a paragraph followed by questions. The paragraphs represent all kinds of reading material. The purpose is to read the paragraph and answer as many questions as possible in three minutes. The goal is faster, more careful reading. This may be called either a skill or an attitude or both. It is a combination that is certainly needed in all textbook reading. All teachers can teach "more careful reading" without thinking of particular study skills.

What can English departments in particular do for poor readers? Poor readers in high school cause more concern to the English department than to any other. Many students can get along in other subjects, especially with study directions from the teacher, but seem hopeless when confronted with the usual work in English. Sometimes special classes are arranged for these pupils, but usually such an arrangement is impossible. For the poor readers in the regular classes, two types of provision are possible. The first has to do with outside reading. It recognizes the fundamental purpose of outside reading as not to cover certain books, but to develop *a lifetime reading habit.* This can result only from time devoted to books which the child finds both readable and interesting. "Readable" may mean books of fifth or sixth grade reading difficulty. If the English teacher uses a reading list, she must put such books on that list. The librarian must furnish such easy books to the poor readers. English teachers can easily find out about such books by consulting book lists for the grade schools. The American Library Association (Chicago, Ill.) has such lists and the Washington office of the Boy Scouts of America will provide an excellent list. Also get the lists of the Elementary Section of the National Council of Teachers of English (Chicago, Ill.)

The greater difficulty is to provide poor readers with outside reading books that they will find interesting. Their tastes are neither literary nor mature. Like the average adult they want stories of excitement, adventure and mystery. A story to suit their taste is the simplified version of *Treasure Island.* Modern stories of similar appeal are Western stories, detective stories and mystery stories. If these children ever acquire a life reading habit, it will be a habit of reading this type of fiction. We would like them to read novels of character, of social problems, and non-fiction of all types. But the chances of their ever doing so are slight. This difference between the children's interest and our plans calls for compromise. Experience shows that we must begin somewhere near the children's present interest if we are to get any outside reading done that will help increase their reading ability.

The other type of reading in the English course is that done for the intensive study in class, that is, the reading of the classics or the books of "standard selections." The vocabulary, style, and ideas of many English classics are a real problem for the average high school pupil, not to mention the poor reader. Teachers have been trying to solve this problem by assignments which include fuller explanation of content and of vocabulary. For poor readers these explanations have to be fuller still, or we must cease to expect the degree of understanding that has been our goal in the past. For instance, we have expected pupils to understand classical allusions. When we have so many poor readers, we may not stop for the explanations that were formerly made. We may frankly ignore classical mythology as unsuited to the needs of these children. In the case of poetry, many English teachers throw the emphasis upon the word music and emotional tone and read the poems to the children as impressively as they can. The children get enjoyment and a real message from the classic pieces even though some of the words and allusions are not fully understood. The poor reader can get something from great literature even if he cannot get all that we would wish.

In a large school it is sometimes possible to have a special freshman class for poor readers, usually a special English class, although there are sometimes special general science classes for poor readers. The best method of selecting the poor readers seems to be to give reading tests before the children leave the grades so that when they come to high school, provision is already made for them. If we must wait until they reach high school, registration must either be held up until the tests are given or changed for children who are selected. To change registration and move children into a special class, causes comment and embarrassment to all concerned. All children in the special English class must have all their other classes adjusted accordingly. There is the question of whether or not the special English class should receive credit for high school graduation or college entrance. What becomes of the children after they leave the special English class? Do they go back to the regular English of the first year? Do they go on to the regular English of the second year? Finally there is the problem of getting a teacher who will have genuine sympathy for these children and know how to make them better readers. The usual method is to ask the most sympathetic English teacher to study remedial reading. These problems are so many and so difficult that many large schools are slow to organize special English classes for slow readers.

The usual plan in a special English class is to try to cover most of the usual English work and at the same time include work to improve reading. The teacher finds this situation almost impossible. The usual freshman English program is already overcrowded. To drop a little of it and put in a little remedial work gets very little results in better reading. The one good point in this arrangement is that the teacher may give the pupils an outside reading list that is within the range of their reading ability. At the other extreme is the plan which drops practically all of the usual English curriculum and devotes itself entirely to the improvement of reading. This method assumes that intensive work on reading can make a great change in a short time and can bring many children up to normal reading ability. The fact is that good reading is a process of growth over many years. Poor readers in high school are three to five years behind. We can stimulate them to grow more rapidly and we can correct specific defects, but we cannot perform miracles in one year. These children should be growing in reading, but they should also be growing in the self-expression and the thinking which are an important part of the usual English work. The best part of freshman English should therefore be included.

Every teacher in every school can help poor readers by enlarging meaning vocabulary, helping in independent word attack, and teaching the study skills needed to get daily lessons. The English teachers especially can stimulate a life reading habit by giving children books that interest them and are within their reading ability. The English teacher can also emphasize the special message of the classics while minimizing their vocabulary and content difficulties. The special class can benefit extreme cases if administrative adjustments can be made and if a sympathetic, well-prepared teacher takes charge.

CHAPTER XVIII

A REMEDIAL-READING COUNSELLOR IN EVERY SCHOOL

When a school system cannot have a reading supervisor, an excellent plan is to have one teacher in each building make a special study of remedial reading and thus develop into somewhat of a specialist in the field. That teacher can then act as counsellor to anyone interested in remedial reading.

In every school there is, as a rule, at least one teacher who feels keenly the handicap suffered by the poor readers and who would find a distinct pleasure in learning more and more about the fascinating subject of remedial reading. By following this interest, that teacher could, year by year, accumulate a special knowledge about reading and a special skill in handling reading cases that would make her an invaluable consultant for other teachers in the school. She would be much pleased to have reading problems brought to her. If she did not know the answer immediately, she would know how to find it. Here is an opportunity for an aggressive and ambitious teacher to open up a field of absorbing interest and to be of outstanding service in the community.

The first step toward becoming a counsellor in reading is for the teacher to become familiar with

---

From the *Elementary School Journal,* Vol. 41, No. 3.

at least a few of the books in this field. The following would be a beginning.

Emmett Albert Betts, *Foundations of Reading Instruction.* New York: American Book Co., 1946.

G. M. Blair, *Diagnostic and Remedial Teaching in Secondary Schools,* Macmillan Co., New York, 1945.

G. L. Bond and Eva Bond, *Teaching the Child to Read,* Macmillan Co., New York, 1943.

Edward William Dolch, *A Manual for Remedial Reading* (revised edition). Champaign, Illinois: Garrard Press, 1945.

Donald D. Durrell, *Improvement of Basic Reading Abilities.* Yonkers-on-Hudson, New York: World Book Co., 1940.

A. I. Gates, *The Improvement of Reading.* New York: Macmillan Co. (Revised 1947).

Albert J. Harris, *How To Increase Reading Ability.* New York: Longmans, Green & Co., 1947.

Samuel A. Kirk, *Teaching Reading to Slow-learning Children.* Boston: Houghton Mifflin Co., 1940.

Paul Witty and David Kopel, *Reading and the Educative Process.* Boston: Ginn & Co., 1939.

Next, the teacher should have at hand many of the helpful magazine articles that are appearing constantly on the improvement of reading. She should, therefore, be a subscriber to the *Elementary School Journal* and to *Elementary English* (both Chicago). These magazine articles give the latest ideas and methods of the many teachers and experts.

Third, out of the vast number of reading tests, the teacher will want to begin with a few and later try more and more tests when she feels more sure of what she wants to learn from them. She will first want one or two tests which give a rough general estimate of a child's reading ability. For general grade placement of children who may be reading at the primary-grade levels, the Detroit Reading Test, Tests I and II for Grades II and III (World Book Company), serve very well. In the middle grades the poor readers may also need the Detroit Reading Test, Tests I and II, or they may be tried out with the Gates Reading Survey (Teachers College, Columbia University) or the Durrell-Sullivan Reading Capacity and Achievement Tests (World Book Company). With this experience as a basis the teacher will want to go on to still other tests, and she may well find some which please her more.

Fourth, the problem arises of analyzing the reading process and finding out in exactly what ways a child is handicapped. The silent-reading tests mentioned and perhaps others will not be found very helpful in making this diagnosis. The most dependable method is for the teacher to develop skill in listening to the child's oral reading and thereby telling what the pupil is doing when he reads. Only when the teacher discovers what methods the child is using, can she tell where the trouble is. For this purpose the teacher needs the first four or five books of a good series of reading textbooks in which there is no grade marking. "The Children's Bookshelf" (Ginn and Company) is one such series which is widely used. The teacher hands the child one of the books which the pupil is reasonably sure to find easy and asks him to read something, picking a selection which will interest him and which he will not think is intended for too young children. As the teacher listens, she will be estimating (1) sight vocabulary, (2) sounding ability, and (3) comprehension. Comprehension is shown somewhat by the method of oral reading but is best estimated by asking the child to tell what he has read.

During this period of oral reading the teacher will observe and make note of many bad habits into which the child may have drifted. The teacher who wishes to be especially prepared in remedial reading will get much practice in listening to children read and in diagnosing the difficulty as he listens. She will check the correctness of this diagnosis by further study and thus will rapidly learn what are the indications of the various troubles that children have. An additional method is for the teacher to use the Gray Oral Reading Paragraphs (Public School Publishing Company, Bloomington, Ill.). On the sheet containing this series of paragraphs, ranging from easy to difficult, the teacher will make a permanent record of what the child does as he reads. The sheet can be kept as a record for further study and for a comparison later on to determine what progress has been made.

Fifth, the teacher studying reading will become expert at finding the causes for a child's difficulties, since the causes must often be removed before much help can be given. Chief among these causes are home conditions, past school history, sensory defects, and low intelligence. The teacher who studies reading cases will learn how certain family situations may block a child's learning to read and how certain school experiences, especially the experiences of the first year of school, may do the same thing. She will learn how to test sight and hearing and to help correct any speech defects there may be. Finally, she will learn how to test intelligence by nonreading tests or how to estimate the child's intelligence from his actions. All this knowledge is part of the equipment of one who wishes to help poor readers.

Sixth, the teacher who is to be a counsellor in remedial reading will want to attend a reading clinic where she will see the methods used with actual cases. There she will see more and learn more about reading and about reading difficulties than she could learn by herself in a much greater length of time. Most large universities now have reading clinics or give courses which afford students practice in clinical methods.

Finally, the teacher reading counsellor will develop a battery of methods from many sources. The books and magazines on the subject give many methods. A teacher will find some of them useful and others not. She will develop methods of her own. She should have at hand the book *Reading Aids*

Through the Grades.[1] Any methods, to be useful, must be suited to the special case and be built upon some interest or purpose of the child. The reading teacher will become skilful in discovering a child's interests and in using them.

We have sketched a program which is within the reach of any teacher who loves children and who feels deeply their need for better reading. Every school has such teachers and would benefit greatly if they were encouraged to work in this field. All that is needed is a small expenditure for books and materials and some relief from the pressure of other special duties. The rest is a matter of time and experience, but the results are sure for the children and the school.

---

[1] David H. Russell, Etta E. Karp, and Edward I. Kelly, *Reading Aids through the Grades: Two Hundred and Twenty-five Remedial Reading Activities.* New York: *Teachers College, Columbia University, 1938.*

Part V

Testing Reading

CHAPTER XIX

TESTING READING

Many tests in school subjects are designed to suit the needs of the supervising officer. He wishes to know what results his organization is securing, and he therefore favors a test which describes achievement in terms of grades. Other tests are designed to suit the purposes of the psychologist. His desire is to dissect the skills and the kinds of knowledge taught in the schools, and he develops tests to serve his purpose. He does much of his work in the laboratory, and he then evolves from his laboratory work tests for use in the schoolroom. Many tests made from these two points of view are now available, but somehow these tests have not revolutionized school work as it was imagined they would. The general test devised for the supervisor tends to allow teachers of high-scoring classes to become complacent, while teachers of low-scoring classes are driven to do still more strenuously, yet blindly, exactly the kind of thing that they have been doing.

From the *Elementary School Journal*, Vol. 34, No. 1, University of Chicago, Chicago, Ill.

Many of the carefully devised tests of the psychologist seem to the teacher "impractical"; that is, they do not seem to fit into the possibilities of classroom work as it must be carried on in the average school.

If testing is to function in the schools as it should, tests constructed rather definitely from the teacher's point of view are needed. These tests will differ from many of the present tests in a number of respects. For one thing, they will differ in price. Present tests are put out in forms which are too expensive, and are distributed by methods which are too costly to make it possible for teachers to use tests freely. The teachers are forced to produce test material of their own by means of the mimeograph or the hectograph. The cost of tests made for teachers will have to be almost as low as the cost of these home-made tests. Tests will have to be produced in such quantity and distributed in such volume that they can be priced at not much more than the cost of the paper on which they are printed (and it can be cheap paper).

Other characteristics of tests made for teachers are more important than cost. The chief of these are indicated in the statement that a test must test (1) *some specific thing* (2) *which can be taught and* (3) *which should be taught* (4) *in a particular grade or range of grades.* That is, the test made for the teacher must show the child's standing in some particular knowledge or skill; the teacher must be able to teach that particular knowledge or skill; and the particular knowledge or skill must be a legitimate part of the educational program at a certain grade level. In contrast, (1) many present tests measure indefinite combinations of knowledges or skills. (2) Some test abilities that cannot be taught. These tests are nevertheless useful at times, as in the case of intelligence tests, when the abilities aid or hinder learning. (3) Many present tests measure skills which are not proper teaching objectives. (4) Finally, present tests usually cover a wide range of grades, and the result is that the individual teacher can secure little help from the small section of such a test really suited to her own group of children.

Let us now apply these principles to the teaching of reading. Is the teacher of reading actually aided in her work by the tests of reading now available? Are the present tests "teacher-tests" according to the requirements just laid down? To answer these questions, let us ascertain the specific things which the teacher of reading can and ought to teach in certain grades and then determine whether tests are available which measure exactly those things in a way that will help teaching. One by one, specific purposes of the teacher of reading will be discussed.

1. *The teacher can teach meanings of words.* From the start the child must know the meanings of the words before he can read them. In Grade I progress is so slow that the teacher can teach the meanings of any unfamiliar words encountered. Likewise, the primary reading books are so carefully

made that words of unfamiliar meanings do not often appear. As soon as independent reading is possible, the vocabulary broadens immensely. The child takes up books from the reading table. He attempts to read the newspaper. He tries to read magazines. At once the child with a small vocabulary is handicapped. He pronounces, but there is no meaning. He develops an antagonism toward the meaningless process.

Meanings of words can be taught and are taught constantly in school. Which words need teaching, and which children need to be taught these words? Here is the field of the *graded vocabulary test.* At present there is no adequate test in this field for the elementary school. Every test we have tries to cover a wide range of grades with a small number of items. Even in the case of a test giving a hundred items, the children of any particular grade will find the greater part of the test entirely too easy or entirely too difficult for them. Therefore, existing tests give only slight samplings of the vocabulary at any particular grade level, and there is entirely too much likelihood that the scores of individual children will be governed by chance. The need for vocabulary-testing is at present filled, if it is filled at all, by the speller when the teacher is careful to determine whether the meanings of the spelling words are familiar to the children. More direct help to the teaching of reading would result if tests were constructed which would test the children's knowledge of the difficult words contained in the reading books used by the children. Such tests could be based on textbooks in reading, arithmetic, geography, or any other subject. At any rate, it is clear that vocabulary is needed for reading, that vocabulary can be taught, and that the teacher needs a vocabulary test prepared with her special purposes in mind.

2. *The teacher can teach sight words.* Reading must begin with the learning of sight words. Do the children learn these words? The teacher should know whether they do or not because a child cannot go on successfully to a new set of words if the old words are still new to him when he meets them. In fact, progress into the first reader should never be permitted until the basic sight words of the primer are known. Otherwise, there will not be progress but only greater and greater confusion and discouragement. Many teachers assume that they can tell how thoroughly the children know the sight words, but they fail to realize how greatly children can deceive them by memorizing stories and by guessing from the context.

After Grade III the teaching of sight words is not emphasized but we should certainly know how children's sight vocabulary is developing. At present *tests of sight words* are used principally in the primary grades. Several such tests now exist, but they are not adapted to use with any particular group of children. Each group of children studies a particular book with its own vocabulary. The group should, then, be tested on the vocabulary studied, but any standard test fulfils this requirement only in part because only a small group of words given in the test occur in the books studied. Therefore, the local school must make its own test of sight words based on its own books unless the publishers will bring out such tests for individual books. The teacher must have a test that fits her work. No other kind will help her greatly.

3. *The teacher can teach the sounding-out of new words.* Before independent reading is possible, the children must have a means of sounding out words that cannot be recognized by sight. A teacher can teach children how to sound new words. She therefore needs a test to indicate how a child tries to sound new words and how well he succeeds in doing so. For this purpose the teacher now has word-pronunciation tests but none that entirely suits her needs. Most of the present tests are general word-pronunciation tests which include words of all kinds containing all combinations of letters. In using such a test, the teacher must note the methods of attack used on the different kinds of words, record the kinds of mistakes made, and then analyze the results. By such analysis she finds that the tests contain too many words of some kinds, too few of other kinds, and no words at all requiring certain methods of attack.

If a word-pronouncing test were made from the teacher's point of view, the test would try the child out systematically on the various methods of attack and the various combinations of letters contained in words, thereby giving definite diagnostic results. That is, the test would clearly indicate to the teacher whether the child knows that a final silent *e* makes the preceding vowel long, that an *a* followed by *r* has a particular sound, and so on. If the test told such definite facts, the teacher would know the exact kind of teaching which each child needed. Definite teaching brings results, and the test must help the teacher in such teaching. Word-pronouncing tests made distinctly from the teaching point of view are still lacking. Meantime, the teacher must do the best she can with the word-pronouncing tests now available.

4. *The teacher can teach fluent reading for story comprehension.* The teacher wishes to know whether the child is prepared to do recreational reading outside of school and for what kind of reading he is prepared. The reading matter used for this purpose will not be difficult, since the child will choose easy material, but such reading requires fluent recognition of words because fast reading is necessary to prevent the flagging of interest. Is the child able to read with fluent recognition? If not, the teacher can encourage the choice of easy, fascinating books for home reading. She can enlist the aid of parents. She will not have to stress understanding, since the story will do that, but she will endeavor to maintain

this essential out-of-school practice in rapid word recognition.

How much skill in this type of reading does the child have? It is most important that the teacher have a definite measure because she must recommend the books that are suitable to the child's ability. Therefore, the teacher needs a test of speed of easy reading. Scarcely any tests of this type are now published. Practically all reading tests now available give directions which slow the child up, make him try to remember, or use kinds of reading which are not typical of the kind used in the children's room of the library when the child is picking out or going through a book. As a result, most teachers test this kind of reading by timing the children as they read a selection from their reader if it is easy enough for them to read it freely. This method, though crude, is generally effective. It may be the only possible method, since any other kind of test is unlikely, unless very carefully managed, to cause the child to use the same methods used in fluent reading for story comprehension.

Any tests of speed of easy reading should be prepared for particular grade levels. The reading matter would have to be easy for the children but not too easy. That is, an average sixth-grade child could not be tested on a seventh-grade test because the test would be too hard for him. He could perhaps be tested on a fifth-grade test, but a fourth-grade test might be necessary to show the extent of his ability in this type of reading. It is this adjustment to grade levels which renders the test practical and sound for the reader, and it is lack of this grade adjustment which helps make most of the present published tests useless for the teacher's purpose in testing "fluent reading for story comprehension."

5. *A teacher can teach careful reading for meaning.* It is important for a teacher to know whether a child is a "careless reader." If he is, the teacher can require careful reading from the pupil. She can question him on his reading to make sure that he is getting the meaning. She can seek to establish the habit of understanding what is read instead of just running over the words. What the teacher needs, therefore, is a test of reading for thought. There are, however, many degrees of the ability of reading for thought, since the thought units vary greatly in complexity. The simplest degree is the reading of sentences, and this ability is the most important because all the others depend on it. Therefore a sentence-reading test is fundamental. Such tests are available, but not all indicate whether the child is a "careful reader." Some of these tests are chiefly vocabulary tests, since the problem is to understand the difficult words used in the sentences. Some do not require careful reading so much as fast reading, since they are made up of easy sentences to be dashed off under pressure. The most successful of the present sentence-reading tests, from the teacher's point of view, are tests giving directions,

each sentence telling the child something to do in such a way that he cannot do the right thing, except by chance, unless he understands all the word relationships in the sentence. The ordinary reading test merely tells us that the child got "part of the meaning of part of the sentences." Instead we want a test that tells us he got "all the meaning of all the sentences." This sort of test is what the teacher needs because it would indicate to her exactly the kind of instruction required for those making low scores.

6. *A teacher can teach how to study.* A further aspect of careful reading needing special attention from the teacher is learning to study. "To study" in school means to attack paragraphs or longer sections of reading matter and to get from them needed ideas. On this kind of study depends success in many school subjects. Therefore, the teacher needs a test which will tell how much of each particular study ability each child possesses. Then she will know which children need help in each special type of study.

It is true that study tests now exist. In fact, there are more study tests than reading tests of any other kind. Unfortunately, however, most of these study tests are based on the old idea of study. The child was assigned a section and "studied" it; that is, he memorized it. The teacher then tested the results of his memorizing by asking questions. A modern test which proposes detailed questions to be answered *after* the reading of a given paragraph is constructed on the assumption that "study" means remembering. Most of the tests of paragraph-reading are of this kind.

The modern teacher expects a pupil to study with a purpose, and modern textbooks are written with that end in view. The purpose may be to find out the important information in the section read or to find the main points made by the author. These purposes are assumed to be the objects of the reading unless other guiding questions are given before the reading is done. Sometimes, it is true, a modern textbook gives questions after the reading matter, but it is not supposed that the children will answer these questions from memory. Instead, the child is instructed first to read the material for a general impression, then to read the questions, and then to go back over the text to find the answers. "Remembering everything" is not the typical method of study expected from children today.

The existing study tests can be used in classes where "reading with a purpose" is done if we instruct the children to read the questions *first* and *then* to read the paragraphs. The test then measures what the teacher wants to teach in so far as the questions are the kind given children to direct their school study. The present study tests can be divided, roughly, into those that ask for the main point and those that ask for details. Each kind, if given as suggested, may suit some of the teacher's needs for measures of the children's ability in particular kinds of study. Some children will be deficient and need help in one kind, and some children in the other. Since teaching the children to find the main point of a selection is quite a different thing from teaching them to locate details, the teacher needs to know which kind of instruction is required.

New study tests, built from the teacher's point of view, will have the same purposes as the study reading now given the children and will use material such as the children are asked to study in school. The new tests will therefore use paragraphs very like those found in textbooks. Present study tests, unfortunately, give material that is appropriate chiefly for recreation reading, such as stories or artistic descriptions. The teacher wishes to test study ability in attacking typical study material, and such material should be used in the tests.

SUMMARY

The needs of the teacher of reading will guide the most advantageous use of present reading tests in the schools. These needs of the teacher may also guide other test-makers to prepare reading tests that (1) will test some specific thing (2) which can be taught and (3) which should be taught (4) in a particular grade. Because teachers can and should teach (1) meanings of words, (2) recognition of sight words, (3) the sounding of new words, (4) fluent reading for story comprehension, (5) careful reading for meaning, and (6) how to study, tests for these abilities at particular grade levels are needed. Given these tests, the teacher will gladly use them, and the children will greatly profit from their use.

CHAPTER XX

THE EFFICIENCY OF PRIMARY BOOKS IN TEACHING WORD RECOGNITION

One of the necessary functions of primary books is to teach word recognition. They must promote an interest in reading, a thought-getting attitude, correct eye-movement habits, and other desirable outcomes, but teaching word recognition is an indispensable function. How well does any particular primary book succeed in this work? Standard tests do not tell us very well because only a part of the vocabulary of any standard test will have been taught in any particular book. Standard tests are also seldom available because of cost. But it is highly desirable for supervisors to know what success is being secured with certain books as compared with other books. Very often new books are tried out, and there should be more than a mere impression as to how well they are succeeding in this fundamental phase of the teaching of reading. Teachers also benefit from having definite knowledge of the degree of success they are securing.

It must be recognized, of course, that the primary book is not alone in the teaching of word recognition. In addition there are experience charts, pre-primer charts, blackboard work, cards of all sorts, and seat work, including, perhaps, work books. There are

---

From the *Journal of Educational Research,* Vol. 28, No. 4.

further experiences with words in supplementary books, picture books, newspapers and magazines, and on signs and posters everywhere. Nevertheless the steady hammering of the teaching period is principally upon the book and most of these supplementary materials are, or should be, closely correlated with the book vocabulary. Their success is largely measured by the success achieved on the book.

The success of any primary book in teaching word recognition, due allowance being made for the factors just mentioned, can be discovered very easily by a technique that is quite in accord with that used by standard tests. Practically all primary reading books have a vocabulary list in the back. That is the material of the test. How this material can be used is shown in a recent experiment.

Two different series of readers were being used in two groups of schools. It was desired to know the relative success of the primers of these two series, that is, how well did each primer teach the vocabulary that it purported to teach? As noted above, this is not the only function of a primer, but it is a most necessary one.

The vocabulary of each primer was made into a test for that primer since each book was to be judged by the work that it set out to do. The word list in the back of the book was mimeographed in primer type, on thirty-one lines, on a single legal-size sheet. Each line was numbered at the left, and each line contained five words, separated by uniform spacing. The five words were not put in vertical columns because it was intended that they be easy to read from left to right. From this sheet were omitted, to conserve space, proper names, compound words, and words of less than four letters.

At the top of the sheet was placed a practice exercise of three lines, beginning with a, b, and c, and composed of easy three-letter words. This exercise was done first to make sure the children knew what was expected of them.

Each child was given a manila liner, since it was imperative that no one lose the place. An assistant went about the room during the testing to make sure that everyone understood directions and that no one lost the place. It was also necessary to watch some of the children to see that they did not copy from others. Those who insisted on looking on others' papers were removed from their seats to tables or to the teacher's desk.

The test was given near the end of the year, though the primer had been completed some time before. This introduced an element of uncertainty as to whether the words had been repeated in other books or otherwise reviewed. It would have been more desirable to give the test immediately after the primer was completed.

The tests were given in all the schools by an experienced tester, assisted by another person and by the teacher of the room. The tester first talked to the children about games they liked. The children all agreed that games were not fun unless everybody followed the rules. The tester then said they were to play a game, and they must be sure to follow the rules. The rules were to do just as she said and then to look right up at her so that she could tell when to go on.

The papers were distributed, face down, and all the children given pencils. Names were written on the back of the paper. Then all turned the paper over, and the practice exercise was begun. The children placed the marker under a line, and the tester told them to draw a circle around a certain word in that line. The tester and assistants made sure that all children did what was expected. By the time the three practice lines were completed, the children were moving their liners when told to do so and drawing the circles correctly.

The test consisted of one word chosen from each line. In this case, care was taken to choose words that had an initial letter different from the initials of all the other words on the same line. The test could have been made harder if the words chosen had had the same initial letters as others on the same line. Such is the plan followed in the *Basic Sight Vocabulary test,* after which this test is modeled.[1]

An important feature of this method of testing is that the same stencil can be used for at least two

[1] The Basic Sight Vocabulary Test lists all of the 220 Basic Sight Words in test form. Garrard Press, $1.20 for 100 tests.

years. New copies made from it can be used again and again by merely calling for the circling of different words. There is no unwelcome element of cramming for the test, because the words are all those of the primer and just the ones that should be stressed.

When two primers are being compared by the type of testing just described, it must be remembered that the tests do not necessarily contain the same words nor words of the same difficulty. Each primer is being judged by a sampling of its own vocabulary. If one primer has a harder vocabulary than another, it is the fault of the primer if the test results in low scores. A primer should ensure a large word recognition vocabulary. It may do this both by wise selection of vocabulary and by skilful presentation. To test the efficiency of the primer by a sampling of the words it purports to teach, is thus eminently fair.

In Table I are shown the averages secured from the use of the test as described in the two sets of schools using the two different primers. That is, each set was given the test of 31 lines of words, five words to a line, made from the vocabulary list in the back of the primer used by that particular set of schools. Since one word in each line was called for, each set of children were asked to circle 31 words. The table shows in the A schools a range of averages from 28 words right in the best school to 21 right in the poorest. In the B schools the range is almost the same, except for the lower score of the poorest school.

From consideration of the table, a number of questions at once appears. First, are these averages as high as they should be? In the case of the lower schools, perhaps not. But are the higher schools satisfactory? Only repeated testing, year after year, will answer this question, and establish some sort

TABLE 1

Scores on Word Recognition Test on Basic Primers Used in First Grade Rooms of Two Groups of Schools
(31 word sampling of vocabulary of each primer)

Test on Primer A		Test on Primer B	
Schools	Average No. of words known	Schools	Average No. of words known
A	28	1	28
B	27	2	27
C	26	3	25
D	23	4	24
E	22	5	21
F	21	6	18

of norm. We do not now know how efficient any primer should be, in the sense of teaching word recognition of the vocabulary it contains.

An important aspect of the testing does not appear in Table I which gives only averages. The complete figures from the tests showed that in most of the rooms of both sets of schools there were children who had practically no word recognition of the list of 31 words. These children had sat through a year of teaching and did not recognize even the word "mother." They had stumbled along, using memory of the selection as read by others or promptings from teacher or other pupils. This outcome could have been expected because these schools, like practically all others, admit to Grade I children who are simply too immature mentally to learn to read. This fact so clearly demonstrated by this test was brought more strongly than ever to the attention of all concerned. This result alone would justify the giving of the test.

It may be asked how well a sampling of 31 words represents a total list of 155 words as taught in these primers. To answer this question, one of the test sheets was given three times in one of the rooms, each time using fresh papers and a different sampling of 31 words. The results of all three tests were combined to give a score on 93 words. The results on the single tests of 31 words each were correlated with the scores on all 93 words. Coefficients of .96, .98, and .96 were obtained. Similar results appeared on repeated tests of other rooms. Therefore a single sampling of 31 words seems to give highly reliable results.

This simple but most effective kind of test can be prepared and given in any school system. It has the hearty approval of the teachers because they realize that the test is upon what they have actually taught, and they want to know what results they have secured. It forms a basis for planning the work of the grade, since those children who do not know the vocabulary of a book when they are through with it should not be pushed on to more difficult work. They should have further exercises on the material of the book or a second book using largely the same vocabulary. They should not go back over the same book because they will have memorized it page by page. Then at the end of the year, this same kind of test can be most valuable as one criteria for promotion. No children should be given advanced books who do not have a satisfactory recognition of the vocabulary they have been taught. If "social promotion" is practiced, the work in the next grade for such children should remain on the same grade level and should not be an advance into greater and greater depths of discouragement.

Part VI

Reading Difficulty

CHAPTER XXI

GRADED READING DIFFICULTY

Authors and editors prepare reading material for certain grades. Superintendents and teachers choose reading materials for definite grades. An important concern in both this preparation and selection of materials is graded reading difficulty. Is the material of third grade difficulty, for instance, or is it of second or fourth grade difficulty? Experienced persons have definite conceptions as to what is meant by reading difficulty of a certain grade. They glance through a book and will then tell you what its graded reading difficulty is. Where do they get their conception of what is the reading difficulty for a certain grade?

Grade reading difficulty may have two meanings. Some persons, when they say, "Fourth Grade reading difficulty," may mean the difficulty of the reading matter that fourth-grade children actually read with success. But what difficulty of reading matter can fourth-grade children actually deal with? We now know that every grade in school has in it children who read as well as those two grades ahead and others who read as poorly as those two grades behind. We know that any two consecutive grade rooms overlap 60 per cent or more in reading ability. Thus in any single school, the level at which third graders, for instance, read is very indefinite, unless we mean the average for the room, which would be the center of a wide distribution.

This level of reading ability is still more indefinite if we compare school with school, or city with city. In any good-sized city, there will be marked differences between "average reading ability" in a certain grade in the favored part of town and the corresponding grade in the less favored part of it. There will be an equally great difference in average reading level between what are supposed to be the same grades in two cities in widely differing parts of the country. Thus, from any angle, the notion that the grade difficulty of books corresponds to the actual reading ability of children does not stand examination.

Hence, if we cannot be sure just what children of any particular grade *can* read, we must conclude that the only conception of reading difficulty for any grade that is at present defensible is derived from *the reading difficulty of the reading books provided for that grade.* By this conception, third grade reading difficulty is the difficulty of the third grade reading books, fourth grade difficulty of the fourth grade reading books, and so on.

Again we must admit that here we also are dealing with an average. Third-grade books vary in difficulty and so do books for any grade. Consequently we do have to think of an "average difficulty" of books for any grade. But at least this difficulty will not vary from school to school or from city to city. It will be nation-wide in scope since the different popular reading books are sold and used widely throughout the country. In addition, the opinion that an experienced teacher has of graded reading difficulty is based upon this variety of graded books. The experienced teacher makes a subjective "average" from all the graded reading books she knows. She does not seem to have any difficulty in doing this.

It is true that "average reading difficulty" for any grade will change as the character of the supply of published reading books slowly changes. New readers are issued and old readers are abandoned, and standards gradually change as a result. At the present time, therefore, the current conceptions of graded reading difficulty are to be discovered from the reading books that are at present widely known and used.

This study on "Graded Reading Difficulty" deals therefore with the reading difficulty of present graded reading books. It makes the assumption that these books are graded for reading difficulty, that is, that these reading books become harder, grade by grade. The authors and editors of any series of readers plan to make each book harder than the book for the year previous. Superintendents and teachers think the books get harder grade by grade. The children seem to find a gradation of reading difficulty. We are therefore not demonstrating that graded reading difficulty exists; we are assuming that condition. We are not assuming that the differences from grade to grade are equal but only that there is some increase in difficulty at each grade.

If then, the reading books used in the schools become harder to read, grade by grade, it seems that in them we may find the clue as to what factor or factors make material either hard or easy to read. There must be differences between the books made for one grade and those made for the grades below and above. Somehow in those differences must lie the differences in reading difficulty.

Our attack, therefore, upon the problem of "graded reading difficulty" will be an attempt to discover and to describe the differences which actually do exist between the books for different grades provided by well-known series of readers issued by recognized publishers.

After differences between reading books for different grades have been identified, we may not immediately have the full answer as to just what causes graded reading difficulty. Some differences may be much more important than others or may be important under different circumstances. But we shall at least have definite knowledge as to what factors may possibly cause graded reading difficulty. Therefore definite ground will have been gained toward the solution of the whole problem.

PHYSICAL FACTORS

Attention is to be called to physical differences between books for different grades, although they are not part of the present study. These differences include (1) size and outward attractiveness of book, (2) amount and kind of illustrations within book, (3) type page, including size and style of type, space between lines, and length of line or width of margin, and (4) color and surface of paper. Variation in these factors causes two differences which have been studied by others and which need only to be referred to here.

Physical differences between books for different grades may make a difference in *ease of reading.* It has been almost universally assumed that as books are adapted to higher and higher grades the type can become smaller and the type page larger. It has been admitted that this change causes at least a potentially greater reading difficulty, though it has been assumed that the child's increased ability counterbalances this factor.

Physical differences between books also undoubtedly affect the child's attitude toward the reading of a book and thus indirectly affect the reading difficulty of a book. The *size* and *binding* of a book may make a child think it is easy or hard even before he opens it. It is well known that poor readers in general prefer thin, easy-looking books and those bound in bright colors. *Type page* certainly affects a child's mental set toward a book. A child will open a book and, without reading a word, say "that book looks hard." This is a real factor in getting a child to start a book, but its effect may wear off after a little reading.

Pictures also certainly affect a child's mental attitude toward a book. The primary child is repelled by continuous pages of type, whereas the child in the upper grades expects to meet such pages. There may here be a genuine effect on reading difficulty. Text without pictures must rely on imagination alone. The fewer pictures and the smaller pictures there are, the more sustained the imagination required. Children who lack the needed past experience cannot maintain imagination, or they do so with difficulty.

In the series of readers used in this study, the physical differences from grade to grade were those now conventional in text book publishing. There was (1) a gradual increase in thickness of the books, (2) a gradual decrease in size of type and of space between the lines, and (3) a gradual decrease in amount of illustration. In these respects the books differed grade by grade. The differences each year were somewhat the same in all series. We have no way of telling to what extent these physical differences actually do contribute to the differences in reading difficulty between the books of each grade and those of the next. We have made no tabulation of these differences. They are discussed here merely so that they will not be forgotten as we present other data.

CONTENT FACTORS

There is a second factor in grades reading difficulty that must be remembered but that is not part of this study. It is obvious that material for higher grades contains a different kind of ideas from that for lower grades. We say that we give the older children "harder material," meaning material which contains ideas which are harder to understand. Clearly here is a factor in graded reading difficulty. In analyzing this factor, we find three ways in which ideas can be "hard."

Ideas may be hard for children to read about, first, because of their *distance from children's immediate experience.* All series of readers begin in first grade with ideas which are close to the immediate home and school life of the child. From that immediate environment, a steady progression is made to things which are further away (a) geographically, even extending to distant countries, (b) in time, going back to previous historical periods, and (c) in maturity, going up to the adult occupations with which children can have little direct contact. All of this material may be very concrete but still distant from child experience. The assumption is that the greater the distance the greater the comprehension difficulty.

Second, ideas may be harder for children to understand because they are *abstractions.* The abstract is naturally foreign to the child's concrete way of thinking and therefore, insofar as reading matter contains abstractions, it becomes more difficult. However, if reading books expect to develop a deeper understanding of life, they must necessarily become harder to read on this account.

The third way in which content or ideas may become "harder" is that they may be presented in more difficult words, or more difficult sentences or in other more difficult "forms." It is obvious from our experiences that "form or manner of presentation" may vary enormously even though the content or ideas remain fundamentally the same. We know that a great wealth of ideas can be understood by children of any grade level if those ideas are presented in a suitable way. For instance, the stories which are read in the original by high school students or by adults can be told by a skilful narrator to first graders. In school readers by different publishers the same story may appear over a range of five grades but "adapted" in each case to the grade. In the field of science, teachers who try to answer children's questions find themselves telling to primary children things which are ordinarily supposed to be studied in high school or college. And in a series of health text books, the author finds himself compelled to explain some of the same facts about health and safety at almost all the grade levels.

A moment's analysis will cause us to realize, of course, that it is not exactly the same story or the same explanation that we give at all grade levels. As we address younger and younger children, we leave out some of the material described in the last section, that is, (1) things too far from the child's experiences, and (2) things which are too abstract. But the surprising thing is that so much material can be presented at all grade levels if the manner of presenting is truly adapted to the children of each grade.

MANNER OF PRESENTATION

Leaving aside, therefore, physical factors in reading difficulty and also intrinsic difficulty of ideas, this study is devoted to an analysis of the differences in manner of presentation of the material in school readers. Of course, intrinsic difficulty of ideas is included to some extent as it shows itself in difficult presentation. Truly difficult ideas tend to cause difficult words and difficult sentences. But we shall deal with difficulty of presentation regardless of whether the difficulty lies in intrinsic difficulty of ideas or in the presentation of ideas only.

Manner of presentation is the factor most readily controlled by the writers and editors of school reading material. The other two sets of factors just discussed are not so amenable to control. The first, physical characteristics, is determined by the demands of those who purchase books and by the question of costs. The second, ideas presented, is determined largely by curriculum considerations, since we must give grade by grade, the materials which are believed to contribute best to child development. But after physical limitations and curriculum material have been determined, the method of presentation lies largely in the hands of authors and editors.

READERS STUDIED

We have studied manner of presentation in Books I to VI inclusive of ten sets of school readers. These are all of recent publication, prepared by authors of unquestioned standing, and issued by companies that have skilled editorial staffs. They represent a range of types, from the literary emphasis on one hand to the social science emphasis on the other. Results from study of these sets are undoubtedly typical of good practice at present and for some time to come.

METHOD OF SAMPLING

There was neither time nor need for a study of all the text in these books. Instead, the sampling included somewhat more than ten per cent of the text, so distributed that all material was evenly represented. This result was secured by taking the first two sentences on each page in each one of the books. In the early books these sentences were short, but the pages were short also. In the later books the sentences became longer, but the pages became large in proportion. No attempt is made to state exactly what per cent of the total text the sampling was, but it was at all times more than ten per cent of the total.

Sentences were chosen rather than a certain number of lines since the sentence was one of the units to be studied.

Only material which was part of the regular text was included. No exercise material was taken. The attempt was made to study only the standard text material given in the one kind of type used generally throughout the book.

Previous investigations have studied differences in reading materials with a view to determining what makes some more difficult than others. One general comment may be made concerning all of these previous investigations. They did not use the graded reading materials of the schools as a basis, and therefore do not, in their conclusions, make a real comparison with those reading materials. This is unfortunate, because, as we have pointed out, the teacher, when considering the graded difficulty of any new materials, unavoidably compares them with the school reading materials she already knows.

ELEMENTS TENTATIVELY STUDIED

Tentative study was made of a number of possible differences between reading books of the different grades. Some of these were carried to a considerable length and then discarded. One of these was the *type of discourse,* especially as to whether the material was narrative or non-narrative.

The type of discourse to be used is the first consideration for an author or editor in the preparation of a book or selection to be read by children. Is the author to write a narrative or a non-narrative? Other things being equal, it is universally recognized that a story usually makes easier reading than explanation or than any other type of non-narrative material. The reasons are self-evident:

a. A story follows a simple sequence of time.
b. A story tends to be concrete.
c. A story tends to have less involved sentences.
d. A story may include much conversation.

A tabulation of the per cent of narrative or non-narrative material in the eight series of readers showed that grade by grade the percentage of non-narrative increased though not with any uniformity in all series of readers. Editors apparently had a definite feeling that the higher grades could use more non-narrative than the lower grades.

Because the series differed so much from one another, it was thought inadvisable to give grade averages for per cent of narrative or non-narrative. We can only say that most series began with no non-narrative in first grade (though one had 5 per cent) and ranged up to from 10 per cent to 22 per cent in Grade VI.

A second element that we studied was proportion of conversation. It is a universal experience to find the conversation in a story easier reading than the "solid parts." Children, especially, like to see pages broken up with conversation. Poor readers at all levels are repelled by "solid" sections of straight narrative or description in a story, and often read only the conversation.

The reasons for this situation are easily seen. In conversation we are likely to find:

1. Ideas closer to everyday experiences.
2. Concrete rather than abstract ideas.
3. Shorter and simpler sentences.
4. Simpler and better known words.

Analysis of the readers studied showed the general tendency for the primary books to have a high percentage of conversation and for this percentage to decrease in the books for higher grades. Some series showed considerable differences from others. Some series had some inconsistency within themselves. Yet, grade by grade, there was a definite progression, with less conversation found in the books for higher grades. We decided, however, not to use the per cent of conversation as an element for comparison of the readers. The per cent of conversation seemed an indirect rather than a direct way of measuring reading difficulty. If more conversation made for easier reading, what elements in conversation made it easier? Those same elements could appear in all reading matter whether conversation or non-conversation. It was felt we should study those elements directly wherever they happened to appear.

FACTORS FINALLY SELECTED

We finally decided to give intensive study to two elements of reading difficulty that appear in all forms of discourse, and in fact, in all reading matter whatsoever. These are sentence length and word difficulty. It is obvious that the reading process required recognition of words and knowledge of their meaning before the larger elements of thought can be understood. It is also obvious that words are used to make up sentences, and that the sentence is the real unit of thought and thus the essential unit of reading. Of course the sentences combine to make larger units of comprehension, but without comprehension of sentencs, the larger units would also not be comprehended. Thus at least two elements are clear, the word unit and the sentence unit.

GRADED SENTENCE DIFFICULTY

It is a common experience of all persons to find difficulty in the reading of long sentences. A long sentence may be hard to comprehend for either or both of two reasons. First, the mere *amount of material* between capital and period requires a duration of attention long enough to comprehend the sentence as a unit. This duration or span of attention is recognized as an element in maturity or mental age. The Binet-Simon test measures development in part by the ability to repeat sentences of greater and greater length, and obviously a large element in the ability to repeat is the ability to understand. Therefore we could expect that as reading matter became more and more difficult, grade by grade, the sentences would become longer and longer.

The second reason a longer sentence is more difficult is that length almost necessarily means greater complexity of thought. The simplest sentence includes a simple subject and a simple predicate. Then these may both be expanded or restricted by simple modifiers. Then there may be added prepositional and other phrases. Then there may be added clauses, either adjective, adverb, or noun. At the same time, any element may be compounded, as by having a compound subject or a compound verb, or the like. All these complexities of thought necessarily make the sentence longer. The sentence can hardly be made longer without having more complexity of thought. Therefore, as grade by grade, the authors of the readers wish to include more and more complex ideas, they naturally use longer and longer sentences.

Wishing to make the problem of measurement as simple as possible, we have adopted sentence length in words as a measure of the difficulty of comprehension of the sentence unit. We know this is a rough measure but it is the only practicable one if difficulty of reading matter is to be checked with any rapidity. Therefore, as explained above, we counted the number of words in the first two sentences on every page of the readers studied, and tabulated the result. Only regular text material was used, and not exercises and suggestions to the teacher and so on.

For each reading book the sentences counted made a wide distribution, ranging usually from one or two words to a very large number. How were we to express the situation so that the various reading books might be compared? First, we found the median or middle sentence for each book. This can be found just by counting up to the middle sentence, and without the amount of figuring that an average would require. Then at each grade level, we averaged these median sentence lengths for the various readers of that grade. This gave us for each grade an average sentence length. These averages came out with numbers of words and fractions of words. Of course a real sentence always has an even number of words. We therefore took the nearest even number for the sentence length for each grade. The results are as follows:

TABLE I

Typical Sentence Length in Words for Each Grade as Found in Ten Series of Readers

	Grade					
	I	II	III	IV	V	VI
No. of Words in Average of Median Sentences........	8	10	12	13	14	15

It may at first seem surprising that the increase grade to grade was so even, but it is not when you consider that this is a combination of the judgments of many authors and editors. They were all striving for a progression, and, all together, they secured one. Naturally, all series were not consistent. Of the ten series studied, seven had an unbroken progression of greater difficulty, grade by grade. Of the three which did not, two had only one book which was "out of line." One series of the ten seemed quite confused and varied irregularly grade to grade.

Were the series then consistent with one another? Of the first grade books, none was as hard as the second grade figure. Of the second grade books, two were as low as first and one was as high as third. Of the ten third grade books, three were as low as second grade and three were as hard as higher grade books. From the fourth grade on, about half were at the grade level given and half were lower or higher. Thus we see greatest consistency in the primary grades and less in the intermediate. This is just what experience with books would lead us to expect. We must remember that sentence difficulty is just one element. A book may be very well graded in all other elements but not quite consistent in this one. Therefore if a book seems to be too easy or too hard in this one element, we should also consider the other possible elements of difficulty.

The length of the middle or median sentences is not, however, a full enough description of the sentence difficulty in a book. We all know that most of the sentences in a book may be easy enough for a child but that there may be occasional long ones which are impossible for him to handle. Our distributions of sentence length in readers showed this fact very clearly. Some books with about the same median difficulty of sentences had a much larger proportion of unusually long sentences than others.

The problem then became, how to describe the unusually long sentences in any book. It would not do to take the very longest, for there might be just one of that length. It was finally concluded to consider the longest ten per cent of the sentences in any book. The method used was to find what was ten per cent of the number of sentences in the sampling, count down that number from the longest sentence, and thus find the sentence which had ten per cent of the total above it. This is technically known as finding the upper decile point. In practice it means that for each book we found the sentence that had ten per cent of the sentences as long or longer. This tabulation yielded the following figures for the six grades:

TABLE II

Typical "Long Sentence" Length in Words for Each Grade as Found in Ten Series of Readers

	Grade					
	I	II	III	IV	V	VI
No. of Words in Sentence With 10% as Long or Longer......	12	16	20	23	26	29

Of the ten series studied, eight show a continual progression grade by grade within themselves. But on this point of long sentences there was much disagreement between series. Every book has hard spots at one place or another. They may be certain hard selections or hard spots within various selections. The editors and writers are rather successful in keeping the general style and tone of the book at a certain level, but they did not think it desirable to keep all the sentences at that level. That is the conclusion we must come to when we compare the two sets of figures, as we do below.

TABLE III

Middle and "Long Sentence" Length in Words, Grade by Grade, as Found in Ten Series of Readers

	Grade					
	I	II	III	IV	V	VI
Middle Sentence..............................	8	10	12	13	14	15
Sentence With 10% as Long or Longer..............................	12	16	20	23	26	29

We should add that the "long sentence" as given in the table does not tell the whole story. Ten per cent of the sentences were "as long or longer," and some were much longer indeed. In practically every book there were a few sentences 50 per cent longer than the "long sentence."

GRADED WORD DIFFICULTY

Everyone recognizes that hard words are a major problem in reading difficulty. All studies of reading difficulty have dealt with hard words as a major factor. We therefore tried to determine how the actual reading books, prepared by experts for children's reading, grade by grade, differed in word difficulty.

The first study of word difficulty was based upon the very common idea that "long words are hard words." A study was therefore made of the polysyllables in the sampling of the readers. The material studied was the same as in the case of sentence difficulty, the first two sentences on each page of the books studied. The polysyllables in these two sentences were counted. Then the percentages of polysyllables in the books for each grade were averaged. The result for each grade was then expressed in rounded numbers.

It was soon seen that there were many two syllable words but not so many longer ones. It seemed that three and four syllable words would be a real element of difficulty with regard to word attack. Therefore two counts are presented, one for all words of more than one syllable, that is, all polysyllables, and then a count of words of three syllables or more. The results were as follows:

TABLE IV

"Word Length" Difficulty, Grade by Grade as Found in Ten Series of Readers

	Grade					
	I	II	III	IV	V	VI
No. of Polysyllables	14%	16%	19%	22%	23%	25%
No. of Words With 3 or More Syllables	½%	1½%	2½%	3½%	4½%	5½%

It must be especially emphasized that these percentages should not be applied to small samplings. The occurrence of very long words depends on many circumstances, especially upon the kind of material in the reading matter. Some kinds of material demand longer words than others. The element of chance in use of long words is very great. Therefore only in a large sampling of very diverse material can there be expected to appear any consistency of percentage of appearance. Our sampling was of two sentences on every page in an entire grade reader. Any smaller sampling could not be expected to conform to these results.

The type of "word difficulty" we usually think of is, however, not mere length but having meaning that is distant from the child's experience. This means, for practical purposes, the use of words that do not deal with the child's immediate environment or which he would not be so likely to hear and to use. The method of determining this kind of word difficulty is to secure a list of "common words" and then to find what percentage of the reading matter is not included on this "common" list. Words not so appearing are judged to be "hard words" to a greater or less degree.

For this part of the study, an unusually valuable list was available. In early studies, the first 1,000 of the famous Thorndike list had been used, but it was evident to anyone who studied that list that it contained many adult words in addition to those known by children. This was natural since much adult reading matter had gone into the making of the Thorndike list. Seeing this point, Edgar Dale had corrected this error of the Thorndike list by comparing it with the Kindergarten Union list which presented words found to be actually used by young children. He found 755 of the first 1,000 of Thorndike also on the Kindergarten Union list, and therefore proved to be familiar to children. This list of 755 words was at first used, but it was soon seen that it was too small. Because it contained a small number of words, it did not show enough difference between the school readers. Therefore the list was expanded to become "The First Thousand Words for Children's Reading" as shown and explained in Chapter X of this book. This list of 1,000 proved more satisfactory, and therefore "hard words" as used in this study means words not on the First Thousand Words for Children's Reading.

For this part of the study, all the words were used that were found in the sampling of the first two sentences on every page of the readers. Every word not on the list of 1,000 was underlined and counted every time it appeared. Therefore a percentage of hard words means a percentage of the running words, that is, the total words read. We are aware that if a word appears a second time it is not now a hard word if it were learned the first time, but there was no way of allowing for this factor. Since only two sentences were taken from every page, and the selection changed often, it did not seem that the same hard words would be likely to reoccur very frequently.

The percentages of hard words for the books of each grade were averaged, and then the figures were rounded to the nearest whole number. The result shows the following:

Table V

Word Difficulty, According to Appearance on First 1,000 Words for Children's Reading as Found in Ten Series of Readers

	Grade					
	I	II	III	IV	V	VI
Hard Words (Not on List)........	4%	6%	8%	12%	14%	16%

These figures show the well-known "fourth grade hump," a difference between the third grade books and fourth grade books that is twice the difference between the other grades. The steady progression shows a remarkable success on the part of authors and editors in securing gradation for word difficulty. Of the ten series studied, all but two show a continuous increase in percentage grade by grade.

Of the ten books for each of the first three grades, only two showed a word difficulty as great as the average for the grade above. Several of the intermediate grade books are as hard as the next grade above. However, the greatest differences from the group averages were found in a few of the newest readers. Three of the new series have first grade books that have only 2 per cent of hard words, or just half the standard given on the table. And two of these new series have second grade books as easy as the first grade standard. Here is a tendency that will change the figures in this table in time. As the harder books go out of use and new books come in, we can expect a considerable lessening of the per cent of hard words in primary grades.

SUMMARY OF STANDARDS OF GRADED READING DIFFICULTY

For convenience, we may now put together the various standards for graded reading difficulty that we have derived from a study of ten series of readers for Grades One to Six. They are as follows:

TABLE VI

Standards of Graded Reading Difficulty as Found in Ten Series of Readers

	Grade					
	I	II	III	IV	V	VI
Hard Words						
(Not on first 1,000 List)	4%	6%	8%	12%	14%	16%
Sentence Length in Words						
Middle Sentence	8	10	12	13	14	15
"Long Sentence" (10% as long or longer)	12	16	20	23	26	29

It must be remembered that these figures are only approximate, as each one represents a considerable variation between the ten series of readers studied. They are definite tendencies however. They show the trend, grade by grade. They tell us about the amount of increase in difficulty in the various factors that editors and authors have thought suitable for the children of the country at their different grade levels.

We must also emphasize that children of any certain grade vary within the particular room, grades vary between schools in the same city, and grades vary between cities in different parts of the country. If these figures represent the books published, it is then up to the principal and teacher to choose the books that suit the particular children. Certain fourth grade children may need a book that conforms to third grade standards, and other fourth grade children may need a book that conforms to fifth grade standards. This problem of adaptation of material is entirely apart from the tendencies in published readers.

Finally, we must call attention again to the factors mentioned earlier. Physical appearance may be very important and must be considered at all times. If the illustrations are clear enough and attractive enough, a book that seems fifth grade by text may be suitable to fourth graders, the pictures making up the difference. In addition, we must consider difficulty of ideas other than as represented in hard words. We have not as yet been able to measure this difficulty apart from the words used, but such difficulty exists. Hard words may make a simple idea difficult, but easy words do not necessarily make a foreign idea easy to understand. This is a problem for further research.

USE OF THE STANDARDS FOR GRADED READING DIFFICULTY

Anyone may use these standards to help find out the "grade" of a book by the use of the principles of sampling just described. It is advisable to take a sentence from each page to overcome the change in difficulty from section to section that is so common in all reading matter. Two sentences from a page make a larger and more reliable sampling. A sentence is taken to extend from capital to period, except when semicolons join independent statements without a conjunction; for instance, these two sentences have been printed together with a semicolon but they are still two independent sentences. A sentence of conversation includes the part beginning "said so-and-so." The different numbers of words in the sentences can be listed from one word on up to the longest. Then count the total number of sentences, divide by two, and thus find which one the middle sentence would be. Find that middle sentence and compare it with the table. Then divide the total number of sentences by ten to find where the upper ten per cent would be. Count down from the top to find the sentence that has ten per cent as long or longer. Compare that sentence with the table.

For the words, underline all which do not appear on the first 1,000 Words in Children's Reading found on page 123 of this book. Count the number underlined. Then from the sentence table already made, calculate the total number of words in all the sentences. What per cent are the hard words of that total? Compare the figure with the table. If you wish to consider length of words, count again for polysyllables and figure the needed percentages and compare with the table.

A little practice makes this process easy and rapid. The result will be a great help in estimating wisely for what grade of children any certain book is suited. That is, it will tell how that book compares with the standard readers. One must then consider which standard readers are suited to the particular children and be governed accordingly. Give children books suited to their abilities and most reading difficulties can be solved.

CHAPTER XXII

FACT BURDEN AND READING DIFFICULTY

We have all spoken of some school textbooks as being "heavy" and others as being "light." By this phrase we have generally meant that some textbooks are more loaded with facts than are others. Students at all grade levels have complained that their textbooks were too heavy with facts. They have complained that there was too much for them to remember. Teachers have complained that there was too much for them to teach. The situation has been most acute at the time of examinations. And many teachers have adopted new type tests in an attempt to cover facts by the hundred.

Trying to see just what the situation really is, we have been counting the facts in content textbooks. By this we do not mean the total number of ideas which any book contains. We are thinking only of the facts that belong to the content subjects and not of any others which may be used along with them. If it is a science textbook, we are asking what is the burden of science facts in that book. If it is a health textbook, we are asking how many health facts the book contains. The same approach is used with a geography text or a history text or with a textbook in any school subject.

From the *Elementary English Review*, Vol. 16, No. 4.

The question at once arises as to how one is to tell just how many facts there are on a page, in a chapter, or in a book. This is a much simpler process than one might imagine. The question is simply "what items are there which a teacher might ask pupils to reproduce when examining them on the special subjects." For instance, if the textbook says that "New York is on Manhattan Island," there are obviously two geography facts. The teacher might ask, "Where is New York?" If the pupil answered, "On an island," he would have only part of the answer. The other part is that the island is named Manhattan. If a science book says "Heavy rainstorms, snowstorms, and high winds may cause migrating birds to drop to the ground," there are at least three facts. If the teacher asks what may cause migrating birds to drop to the ground, she would expect three items and might give only one-third credit for each one. Thus it becomes remarkably easy to measure fact burden in textbooks if we apply the criterion, "What might the teacher ask in an examination?" and then note what facts would be needed for complete answers according to this particular text.

The importance of distinguishing between ideas in a text and fact burden of a text is clearly illustrated in a recent primary book on care of pets. The book is a series of stories about a family and a kitten. It has 114 pages of text. Every page presents many ideas but few of these are facts about pets and the care of pets. Actually from the point of view of the purpose of the series, which is to teach about pets and their care, there are only 41 content facts in this book of 114 pages. In one place there is a story of seven pages, presenting many ideas but only one fact about pets, that kittens do not like water. Thus the fact burden is determined by the purpose of the book. The content facts are those which the book plans to teach and which teachers may ask for on an examination on the particular subject matter.

Our first study of fact burden was made on five sixth-grade geography texts. We chose this subject because geographies are notoriously heavy in fact burden. Because geographies are illustrated so profusely, it was necessary to adopt some standard unit for sake of comparison. This unit was a full type page, which in four of the books happened to be about the same, that is, about 600 words. This unit was used in counting for all the books, even though two books actually have larger type pages. The equivalent of ten full pages of this size was taken from the beginning of each book, a similar unit also from the middle, and a similar unit also from the end of the book. It was found that averages range from 24.3 facts per page to 48.9 facts per page. Doubtless all will agree that 40 new facts on every page is a decidedly heavy fact burden. It is no wonder that so many children do not like geography if they are expected to learn it primarily from such reading matter.

These data on the fact load in geographies led us to wonder what the situation might be in other textbooks. A modern history series was counted for history facts. The series ran from grade five to grade eight, and we found the fact burden per page to range from 10 to 13. These were history books of the story type which tried to picture the past in terms which the children could understand. From these books, very many of the dates and names which have been common in history had been omitted. The size of page in these books is just about half that of the geographies. Thus the fact burden is 10 to 13 facts to about 300 running words. Therefore the fact burden is, for an equal amount of text, just about half the fact burden in the geography books.

Next we turned our attention to a science series and counted facts in the books intended for grades two to six. Here the science facts were found to range from 3.3 to 6.5 per page of from 125 to 250 running words. These books were therefore somewhat lighter in fact burden than histories, being about 8 facts per 300 words as against 10. Finally, we counted facts in health books for grades one and two and found them to average about 1.5 facts per page of 100 running words. These were still easier content books.

We have thus traced a progression from very heavy books to very light books, following through the subjects of geography, history, science, and health, and at the same time progressing from the sixth grade down to the first grade. This study has been only exploratory, however. We do not mean to say that most books in any one subject are heavier in fact burden than most books in any other subject. No one can state this conclusion without having rather thoroughly covered the books in each field. We cannot say just what fact burden is characteristic of any grade level because very extensive figures would be needed for such a conclusion. Neither can we say what should be the fact burden in any one grade. Wide experimental study with materials of different fact burden will be required to get at this situation. We do hope that the figures here presented will stimulate research in all these directions so that we may know more about how heavy, with regard to fact burden, school textbooks are or should be.

Leaving statistics, let us turn to some interesting suggestions which this tentative study has made. First, it was noted that as the books became lighter and lighter in fact burden, they came more and more to be story type material. The geographies were practically straight description and explanation. The histories contained much narrative or story type material. The science books were full of stories about children and their surroundings. The primary health books, finally, were almost entirely made up of stories about children, with health facts introduced quite incidentally. We therefore seem to have before us the hypothesis that one way to lighten fact burden is to use more and more of the story form. This seems logical, but also calls for verification. Perhaps there are also other ways of lightening fact burden. Explaining the new facts in terms of children's everyday already-known experiences may be just as effective in lightening fact burden as telling a story about it.

Second, it was very noticeable that the books with low average fact burden were uneven. Some parts were very light and some were very heavy. For instance, a fourth grade science book with an average of 4.3 facts per page has on one page 38 facts. An eighth grade history with 13.4 facts per page has on one page over 50 facts. A geography which averages 48.9 facts per page had 74 facts on one of these pages. Thus the average for a book, though useful in comparing it with other books, does not give a true picture of the book itself. There will naturally be some variation in any book, but how much variation should we expect? How far do the excessively heavy spots go in cancelling the favorable effect of the light portions? These are important questions.

Third, it might be said that heavy load of facts may not be as damaging in a book as failure to distinguish between important facts and unimportant facts. As texts are now presented, the child may find 40 facts on a page and try to memorize them all, or the teacher may try to teach them all. As every good teacher knows, one or two of these 40 may be of great importance and the others merely supplementary. The pupil cannot know which are the important facts because he is just a beginner in the field. The teacher, if she has not studied the matter, may not know either. And the book may make no distinction in the way the facts are presented.

Suppose, for instance, that a certain science book has 400 pages. It contains an average of 10 facts per page or a total of 4,000 facts. Now let us suppose that only 400 of these facts are so fundamental that we may ask the child to remember them. Who is to select which 400 out of the 4,000? Obviously the author is best prepared to do this. Therefore the way the book is written or printed should clearly point out these essential facts. Topical headings do not do this because they simply point out areas of knowledge and not definite facts. It takes a sentence to state a fact. This does not mean the teacher should not use her discretion to help fit the subject to the particular class, but surely the textbook should help much more than it does now.

Finally, we must recognize that there is an additional factor beyond quantity of facts. There is also the difficulty of the facts themselves. This means their relative strangeness, or remoteness from the child's experience. Some new facts in textbooks are only partly new. Others are so remote as almost to be meaningless. Textbook illustrations attack this problem. Authors attack it by detailed description or explanation. Our experience in this study seemed to show that an author's consistent attempt to overcome strangeness of fact usually resulted in greater lightness of reading matter. When he explained the strange by means of the familiar, the new facts were surrounded by ideas that were not new at all. Therefore the fact burden per page or per 1,000 words went down.

So far, most of the research on reading difficulty has dealt with method of expression, that is, with word difficulty, sentence difficulty, and the like. All the while we have known that the problem of comprehension includes more than the mere method of expression. It necessarily includes the content of the reading matter. We have here made a tentative approach to the problem of content by a tabulation of fact burden in grade school textbooks. The great load we have discovered, both in averages for entire books and on individual pages in otherwise light books, surely indicates an important aspect of reading difficulty that needs attention. We trust that these figures will be supplemented by those of other students in this field. We suggest therefore for further study: (1) Is there an essential difference in fact burden between books in different fields? (2) Is there a suitable fact burden for books for different grades? (3) Can textbooks be made more even throughout with regard to fact burden per page? (4) Cannot textbooks clearly distinguish important facts from unimportant ones? And finally (5) what methods are best for the lightening of fact burden?

Part VII

Literature

CHAPTER XXIII

LITERATURE IN THE GRADES

LITERATURE AS TRADITION

For several generations, literature has had an established place in grade school readers and in grade supplementary reading. Not so long ago it was thought of as the whole of material for reading instruction. Such is no longer the case, but we still have special literature readers, literature sections in most sets of readers, and the use of the library for literature study.[1] Apparently literature has a solid and permanent place in the elementary school. If we asked why it is there, most persons would undoubtedly answer that it is an essential part of a liberal education. They would make this claim with great confidence, but would usually be quite unable to explain further. If pressed, they would probably assert that everyone knows that literature is an essential part of an education. They would even claim that it had always been so considered. They would in fact be taking refuge in a tradition.

---

[1] An excellent account of how the literature emphasis in reading arose will be found in "American Reading Instruction" by Nila B. Smith, Silver Burdett and Co., New York, 1935.

The traditional place of literature in the school is due to its traditional place in society. An "educated" American is supposed to know certain things. In conversation he must not display ignorance. If he did not know who wrote "The Raggedy Man" he would be considered ignorant. He must also know about "The Land of the Counterpane" and "The Cheshire Cat." These are matters of "common knowledge." Literature contains thousands of such items, and if the graduate of our schools is to be "educated" he must have a fair knowledge of them. We are faced here with a rather unworthy trait in human nature but a very strong one. Those who possess certain items of socially approved knowledge have always looked down upon those who did not possess them. We do not want our children to be looked down upon. Therefore we insist that the school teach "literature" in this sense of a body of facts that "all should know."

There is one real difficulty with this notion of literature. Opinion as to what one should know in order to have social approval is steadily changing. The educated person nowadays is expected to know more and more about science, economics, sports, and such subjects and less and less about classic literature. In fact he is even expected to know something about living authors and current books. School text books and readers have not kept pace with this tendency. They contain selections which the teachers themselves realize are no longer well known. They discuss authors which a modern man or woman can completely neglect without being considered ignorant. In short, times are changing and the traditional conception of literature must change with them. It is still true that there are certain facts about books and writers which educated persons should know, but each generation of teachers needs to revise the list. The teacher using an old reader must therefore make a selection from the literature and literature study which it presents, emphasizing only those items which are held to be important by the present generation. The teacher can base her judgments chiefly upon the references to literature which she finds in the conversation of educated persons and in the text of good current magazines which she reads. For instance, it seems evident that nowadays less and less emphasis is being placed upon classical mythology. The people are not now expected to know the names of all the Greek gods. Similarly the number of Longfellow's poems with which a person is expected to be familiar is decreasing.

A teacher may feel that some of the knowledge about literature that used to be common ought still to be taught, and she must use her best judgment on this point. We are only emphasizing that as each new generation produces new works of art and at the same time gets further and further away both in time and in spirit from the older works, our emphasis in teaching *facts about* literature must change. This problem is a continual difficulty for the makers of text books and courses of study. They must decide somehow whether selections which were formerly considered "standard" for school text books are still supposed to be familiar to educated persons. They realize that many teachers would like to keep all of the old selections and that many other teachers would like to introduce new ones. The books which result are therefore compromises. The teacher who uses the books may accept the judgment of the publishers, or she may work out a compromise of her own between emphasizing the same things that used to be emphasized or making an adjustment in the light of ever changing opinion. No final answer to this difficulty will ever be made, but we cannot meet the problem intelligently unless we frankly recognize it.

LITERATURE AS ART

Having granted a place for the ordinary meaning of literature, let us turn to the true meaning of that word, the meaning it had to the men who wrote the works and the meaning it has to those who understand the true purpose of the writers. Literature does not really mean books. It means re-living the author's experience. If it be travel, we travel just as the author did. If it be history or geography, we see the people and places just as the author saw them. If it be a story, we live through the thoughts and feelings of the characters just as the author lived through them. Thus literature is not something to know or know about. It is something to experience. It is something intensely individual. What is literature for one person may not be for another. It must be to us something alive, vital, meaningful. This is the artists' conception of literature. It is what it means to the men who create it and what it means to the real appreciators. The question is, to what extent can it mean this to children in the grades?

It is important to note that we *do* use the true meaning of literature in our work with small children. To them the fairy stories, the animal stories, and the stories of other children are really alive. The little children show this plainly by their weeping at the sad parts and their delight at the happy endings. Primary teachers, as well as writers for small children, are so close to those children that they instantly sense when a story has not made contact with its audience. Literature in the beginning grades is therefore a delight to teachers and to pupils. It is an indication of what literature should be at all school levels.

Unfortunately, somewhere around the fourth or fifth grade the close contact between literature and the children begins to be lost, and we begin to give the children stories or books that they "ought to read." By the phrase "ought to read" we usually mean stories we think they ought *to know about*, because traditionally those stories have been included in literature courses. In other words, the conception of literature as art, or a reliving of the author's experience, is often supplanted by the conception of literature as tradition, or "knowing about" famous books. In these grades the "standard juveniles" begin to appear in reading books and on reading lists and on the room library shelves. The few very good readers attack them as good readers have done in the past and find them a thrilling experience. The average and poor readers are left "cold."

This sad loss of contact between school literature and the child need not take place. The standard tales such as Robinson Crusoe and the Arabian Nights could fire the imagination of all the children *if these tales were skilfully presented in children's language.* Instead, children's libraries, gift books, and all the editions with which publishers seek to attract the teachers and parents who buy books, persistently use the original text which was written for adults of the last century, or some slight variation of that text. Almost equally futile are "retellings" of those tales by writers who lack the gift for making literature. As a result much of what we fondly call children's literature fails to touch at all the imagination and the life of most of the children in school. *It is, in fact, not literature for them.* What we are urging is simply that the vital contact between the child and the story, which is the essence of the concept of literature as art, and which is so characteristic of our literature for young children, be maintained through all of the grades and in fact through all of school life.

If, in our text book, we do find stories or selections which have been written or adapted by true literary artists, and if both ideas and language are suited to the experience of the children, we can truly teach literature as art. We can have the stories read rapidly and easily just for the imagined experience that they give. Then we can talk of how "true" they are, how real the people are, whether they did the things they would be most likely to do in real life. We can ask what idea the author had in mind in writing the story, what he was trying to say. We can even ask if we think he said it as clearly and as strongly as possible. We can pick out the more successful parts from the others. We can appreciate the writer's imagination, his skill, in description, in planning and so on. If the interest is strong enough and the children will not feel that we are going too far, we can even notice especially happy phrases or skilful choice of words. Such a real artistic appreciation of a truly artistic piece of writing is a delight to all concerned. But the writing must be suited to the audience; and the children must be getting real enjoyment from it.

"GOOD" LITERATURE

The definition of real literature which we have given will be seen to fit a good many kinds of reading matter of which parents do not approve. The cowboy stories, gangster stories, girls' boarding school tales and the like may be re-lived by the children just as vitally as the classics have been by their most ardent admirers. These "cheap" books, we must conclude, are in a very real sense literature to the children who read them but we do not call them "good" literature. It is not sufficient merely to tell the children they are not good and to forbid the reading of them. Our literature teaching should show the children why they are not good. Literature is life experienced in the imagination, but it is not "good" literature unless it is *true to real life* as it goes on about us. The "cheap" story may seem like life to a child because he does not know what life really is. It becomes our task then to give him the true picture so that he can detect the false. We may do this by telling of our own experiences, but the best way is to give him stories which will be *real to him* and which are at the same time "true to life."

Here is a dilemma in which teachers have found themselves. The good literature which has been put in their hands has been either so foreign to children's lives or to children's language that the pupils have been unable to get any vital experience from reading it. At the same time the children have been getting vital but false imaginary experiences through funny papers, picture shows, and sensational books. Teachers have felt the impossibility of forbidding the false experiencing and have had to resort to what may be called counter education.

That is, they have encouraged the children to talk about picture shows and books just so that at some point they could ask, "Do you think things really happen that way?" These teachers have seen that if they could implant the principle, "Is it true to life?," the children might go on getting recreation from poor reading matter just as adults do but would not be misled by it. On the other side of the dilemma, the teachers have struggled to make the prescribed literature become more vital to the pupils. When the language was a barrier, they often read the selection to the class so that the children might use their imagination more freely. If the setting or background was too strange, the teacher might begin with an explanation or the showing of pictures, in this way making it more possible for the children to experience what they were reading about. Both of these attempts to meet the situation are good and must be continued until more real literature for children of these ages is provided.

"SUITABLE" LITERATURE

Literature presented to children may be real literature to them, it may be true to life, and yet it may not be suitable to children. There are kinds of imaginary living that we do not think will do children any good. For this reason, there has always been a very strong attempt to limit the range of things children read about. Here we have the old principle of "sheltering" about which parents disagree so violently. One group says children should have no knowledge of evil. The other says that the children are going to get that knowledge outside of school and that therefore the school should prepare them for it by letting them know the place which evil does have in real life and how it may be controlled. These two groups disagree violently as to whether certain literature is suitable for grade children.

Without trying to settle the dispute, we may point out one important fact. Parents let their children see many picture shows. Those shows are planned for adults and not for children, and from them the children certainly get ideas about all aspects of adult life. In this situation, it would seem that the only sensible thing is to help children see things in their right proportion. We would not then ask whether a book to be read by children is suitable in the sense of adapted to a state of ignorance. We would ask only, first, whether it was true to life and whether the teacher or some other capable adult were going to make sure that the piece of life was properly understood. This does not mean we should purposely introduce stories of passion and evil, but that we should not keep on trying to present an entirely idealistic picture. Grade school literature should keep pace with the development of the children's out-of-school life and help children to see that life in proper perspective.

BOOK LISTS

Many persons long for a book list which will tell us just which books to give to children of certain grades or ages. There are now in print many lists as a result of this demand and more are constantly appearing.[2] All of these lists tend to have two faults. First they are much affected by the tradition that certain books are children's books whereas in the past many of those books have been more or less forced upon children's attention by bookish parents. Second, the lists are always optimistic. For example, they suggest for ten-year-olds books which only the really good readers of that age can handle. That is, book lists are not willing to admit what poor readers a vast number of children are and how narrow are the interests of the average school child. For these reasons, teachers have not found book lists as useful as the makers of the lists had hoped. It is a good thing for a teacher to have the best and latest lists, but she will find them simply sources of information to use in her stimulation of her children's reading of literature.

GUIDING READING

Guiding children's reading is a difficult matter, first of all because reading is pretty hard work for most children. It is not so much that they do not

---

[2] One of the most useful lists is "The Right Book for the Right Child," John Day Co., New York. The American Library Association (Chicago) makes a practice of getting out lists of various kinds.

know the words as that it is hard for them to sit still and give the continued attention which reading demands. We as adults must remember that reading puts a greater strain on children's attention than on ours because their eye span is less and their eye movements are slower. In the case of a poor reader, any reading at all may be quite a chore. In the second place, the life of an active child does not leave much room for reading. After school he should be outside playing with his fellows, and not long after supper he should be in bed. If outside of school a child averages half an hour a day with a book, and in that time reads fifteen to thirty pages it would take him several weeks to finish a book. Reading a book is therefore no light undertaking.

Because of these obstacles in the way of reading, it has begun to be recognized that children will simply not read outside of school except with strong motivation. In the past, this motivation has often been the presence of striking pictures or the enthusiastic recommendation of a chum. Teachers' recommendations have been much discounted. To meet the situation there has been a systematic endeavor to discover children's interests and to find books which meet them. Children have been asked which books they liked best and why they like them. Children's choice of books in libraries has been studied. As a result we are told that children like stories of animals and stories of adventure, and so on. But if the teacher expects to arouse in a child enough interest to get him to read a book she cannot rely upon such general conclusions as these. She must find the subject which the particular child is eager to read about at the particular moment. For this purpose it has been suggested that we use an interest inventory which asks the child what he likes to do, what he wants to be, and so on. In any case, the class room teacher will naturally be conducting a continuous interest-inventory with each of her children. She will be making mental notes of his reactions to selections in the reader, of what he says in class discussion, of what he does in activities or outside of class. If in doubt, she will make it a point to converse with him. In this way she will hunt for some strong urge of interest which will get him to take up a book and to carry through the difficult job of finishing it. In short, therefore, the rule for guiding reading is *for the teacher to know the books and know the children and to bring the right ones together at the right time.*

POETRY

In our discussion so far of literature in the grades, we have purposely omitted mention of poetry. If a poem tells a story, the principles which apply to other stories apply to it, but the grade school is more concerned with poems which are not narratives. Such poems present a special problem which has not been successfully handled if we are to judge from the fact that so few older children will say that they like poetry.

The school's chief difficulty has been that it has paid too much attention to certain aspects of poetry and not enough to others. Perhaps the greatest mistake has been the emphasis on figurative or poetic language. The beauty of such language is not greatly appreciated except by people who have become self-conscious of the way in which they say things, and who get delight from the beautiful appropriateness of well-chosen figures of speech. Some children are thus conscious of the qualities of language but most of them are not. Most college students are not either. Yet the teachers who themselves enjoy the language of the poet have been trying to get the children to enjoy it. This misdirected effort has tended to conceal the other qualities which children can and do find pleasure in.

Word Music. The thing above all else that children should enjoy in poetry is its music. That is what makes it poetry and that is why poetry must be read aloud by a good reader. To assign a strange poem and have the children stumble through it is therefore the very last thing to do. Every poem deserves a skilful reading by the teacher or by some child who has practiced reading it and has been coached in its presentation. No pupil receiving such a first impression of a poem can fail to respond somewhat to its effect. He will enjoy it as word music even if he does not completely understand what it says. The poet strove to produce word music, and children, being human, will respond. We do not even have to mention rhyme or rhythm. We should address the ear, and the ear will get the effect.

Thought. Every poem necessarily contains some central thought, and this thought will be appreciated by the children if it is within the range of their experience. Now the thoughts expressed by poets may be thoughts about anything in the world and may range from a mere clever fancy all the way to the most profound observation about human existence. With the young children we naturally start with the clever fancies. Sometimes these are cute or funny, and sometimes they are serious, but the children catch the idea and have a glow of pleasure from doing so. From such a beginning we should lead by gradual steps through eight or ten years of school life to the deep reflections of the great minds of all times. In doing so, two problems are always with us.

First, poetry must always mean enjoyment of word music. The music may become more complex but must never cease to bring the reader a reaction of pleasure. Some children's appreciation will not develop, and they must therefore be given simple word music all their lives. Hence the popular newspaper poets. The other problem is to make by gradual degrees the transition from the clever fancies of the children's poets to the more serious poetry. The truth is, we are far too anxious to bring to the children the great thoughts of literature and especially of poetry. We give children adult thoughts while they are still playing with dolls and marbles. Instead, the poetry for children at any point in the grades needs to be close to their view of the world. The change to adult thinking and adult philosophizing needs to be kept gradual.

Imagination. Poetry, more than any other kind of literature, gives rein to the writer's fancy and imagination. The whole conception may be a stroke of originality. The title in itself may be. Every word, every phrase may be sparkling with it. The figures of speech have received most attention, but the writer's imagination goes much further than that. It includes every part or aspect of the poetry, even at times the way it is printed. This enjoyment of the writer's imagination is very evident in the case of the poems for small children. It is a strong factor in the enjoyment of any poem. Figurative language is only a part of the whole. We can call figures to children's attention when they are fresh and vivid, but we need also to look for all the evidences of imagination, one of the striking qualities of the poet's mind.

Feeling. Because poets are more emotional than many persons and feel deeply about their experiences, every poem was conceived in some state of feeling and is intended to arouse that feeling in the reader. This is a fact imperfectly understood. First of all, feeling does not necessarily mean intense emotion. It may mean mere delight in the beauty of some object or landscape. It may mean mere wonder at some thing or idea. It may mean simply pleasure in fun. From such relatively simple feelings, it may range to the strongest and noblest emotions of which mankind is capable. Second, the feeling or mood of the writer is all of a piece with his thought, his fancy, and his word music. All four are, in the best poems, combined in a perfect whole. In poems not so successful, one can see an imperfect combining of the four. Here is one of the criteria for judging poetry, and one that even children can gradually begin to use if we call their attention to it as favorable occasion offers.

Since true appreciation of poetry is impossible unless the audience responds to the writer's feeling, we need so to present poetry that children will get the feeling experience. One way of doing this is sympathetic reading by the teacher, who, for the moment, is putting herself into the proper mood or frame of mind, much as an actor would. We have all heard readers of poetry who could somehow make us respond to the poet's mood. We can all do this for children to some extent at least. Another way of producing in the children the right feeling experience is to prepare them for the poem by telling the right things about the author and showing what the experience was to him. This really means reinforcing the poem by a story, but the method is entirely justifiable and is very effective. If a writer is a real person to us, and we can imagine how he felt about the thing or idea the poem deals with, then we can respond more fully to his words.

Through methods such as we have outlined, the elementary school should be able to make a much greater success of literature teaching than it has in the past. Our anxiety to "push" knowledge of literature has defeated its own end. Children have refused to read the "heavy," "older" books that they have been assigned. If, instead, the true conception of literature as reliving the author's experience were followed, much reading would also follow. Quantity of reading leads to better and better reading if there is even a little friendly guidance. As the children mature and become more adult in their thinking, and in their tastes, they would find themselves reading with pleasure the best books and poetry that they are capable of enjoying. But unless they follow this natural road, no such happy result is likely to be attained.

CHAPTER XXIV

TEACHING LITERATURE IN HIGH SCHOOL

When we say we appreciate a work of art, we mean that we find something in it to enjoy. When we wish to learn to appreciate a form of art that is strange to us, we have to learn just what there is to enjoy about it. That is the task before the high-school pupil, to find what there is about the classics that he should find enjoyable. Strangely enough, the almost universal practice is to make him read the classics and assume that he will, in the nature of things, find what he is to appreciate. Quite in the nature of things, he does nothing of the kind. When he reads a story ordinarily he looks for excitement, for swift action, and for adventure. In practically none of the standard works studied does he find any of these things in the degree necessary to attract him. Nor does he find in a "good" story the kind of characters or setting he looks for. He wants men and women of today, millionaires preferably, who do the things he would like to do when he has won success. From such a point of view, of course, standard literature is a flat failure. And to our high-school boys and girls it will remain a flat failure unless an entirely different point of view is given them, unless they learn to regard the classics with the attitude one must have toward a work of art.

From the *English Journal*, Vol. 9, No. 4.

There are two separate conceptions of art, the artist's and the artisan's. The dictionary puts the artisan's first, defining art as "skill in performance." It is this conception that is almost universally presented to the students. That is, they are led to think, or allowed to think—whichever it is—that the value of a piece of literature consists in the skill in technique shown by the writer. When they study poetry, they have the technique of poetry impressed upon them. When they study a novel, they have the technique of the novel or technical qualities of narration and description presented to them. When they study a short story, they must perforce take up "ascending and descending action, complication, climax, dénouement," and similar machinery of short-story construction.

Now all such work is good enough in its way, but the question is, Will it give the boys and girls a desire to read, and will it enable them in their reading to distinguish "good" from "bad"? Observation says that it does not. And a moment's thought will show that it inevitably cannot. How many persons out of every thousand will, when reading a story, think of the technique which the writer is exhibiting? Does the teacher who has all the details at his fingers' ends ever think of them while he is actually reading? He may think of them afterward, and perhaps does, but is the average young person, without academic interest and in search of amusement only, to be expected to do so? Surely he is not. For to detect excellence or deficiency in technique takes an amount of serious thought and consideration that no one outside of the story-writing and the teaching professions will give to his reading. For this reason, teaching of literary technique in any class but the one in advanced college composition is practically certain to leave the students' reading just where it would be if no such teaching had been done. Study of literary art from the artisan's point of view has failed and is bound to fail.

Instead, literature should be considered as what it is, creative art. Classics should be judged and appreciated as are the masterpieces of any class of artists. The great writers were not interested merely in showing their skill; that was a minor matter to them, and it should be a minor matter to any student of their works. The great question they asked themselves constantly was, "Am I representing life truly? Am I faithful to human nature and to the world in which men and women find themselves?" Generations of readers have found this truth in their work. Therefore generations have acclaimed their writings as masterpieces and have called them classics. Accepting this verdict, we place these works in the course of study that we require of all pupils in secondary and higher schools. Is it not strange that we should fail to present them as works of art at all but only as skilfully done pieces of writing?

Presenting our literary selections as works of art would have various far-reaching results. In the first place, it would give a wonderful unity to what is at present a long, dreary train of isolated and unrelated pieces of reading. At present we take up a tragedy of Shakespeare, a short story of Dickens, a poem of Scott, a comedy of Goldsmith, and other material of still greater outward diversity, the pupil wandering, as it were, from one to another with no notion that these authors were all trying to do the same thing—present men and women and the world in which they live. The first thing requisite for passing judgment on works of creative art is some standard of comparison. And the standard of comparison is not plot structure, methods of characterization, and the like. It is faithfulness to the thoughts and actions of men and women and the probabilities and inevitabilities of life. With such a conception, the student can carry what he learns in one selection to the study of the next. As he will have to be constantly comparing each author's observations of people and events with his own, he will naturally enough be called upon to compare one author's view of life with another's. Are George Eliot's women truer than Shakespeare's? Do Scott's men possess the reality that those of Dickens seem to have? The fact that some works are in verse and some in prose will become inconsequential. Other external differences will likewise become insignificant.

Studying literature as art will have a still more far-reaching effect. It will bring to the same bar of judgment the classics in the school library and the magazines in the rack at the drug store. It will put the question, If Shakespeare can create real people, can the man who wrote the latest best-seller? Or, if the events in *Silas Marner* would be likely to happen, would also the events in the *Scarlet Scorpion,* or similar stories? It would show that where evil or ignorance would by all the laws of the universe lead to tragedy, the honest writer scorns the "happy ending."

If literature is to be studied as art, we need not then necessarily exclude contemporary writing. For the meaning of art is emphasized by imperfect examples as well as by perfect ones. As much profit may at times be gained from the contemplation of a failure as from the study of a masterwork. Indeed it is by comparison with those attempts that fall short that the masterwork is singled out. Nothing quite brings out the worth of a good story as well as the comparison of it with a really bad one. For this purpose, the current cheap magazines are a mine of material ready at hand. A class can buy copies of a ten or twenty-five-cent magazine and learn a great deal about literature in consequence. A contemplation of the impossible actions of some "successful" story writer's paper-pattern creations will bring about an entire new enjoyment of the assigned work of the school.

Will not such a study of literature be certain to bear fruit in the voluntary reading of our pupils? Not that it will perform the impossible. The boys and girls will read for excitement and for glamor the same as ever, but they will not be so ready to accept these in the trash they would otherwise pick up. If they found that their favorite magazine presented only impossible people in improbable actions, they would lose something of their enjoyment in reading it and try to find another that would better convince them of the reality of its mimic life. For entertainment and truth are both to be found if one but care to look. And the surest way to cause one to search for the true is to convince him of the falsity of the counterfeit.

Though the classics represent perhaps the most successful attempts in our language to record artists' observation of the life of man, they present great difficulties to the understanding of our pupils. Perhaps the greatest are caused by the fact that each artist necessarily expressed himself in the vocabulary of his own class and time, and pictured the men and women of his own age in the activities—physical and mental—that belonged to it. Of the two difficulties—difference in language, and difference in customs—it is hard to say which is the greater obstacle to present-day American girls and boys.

Perhaps the harder to overcome is the second—that the people of the artist's creation act in circumstances that are so very different from those that surround us now. Teachers are slow to realize the enormity of this difficulty, because they are themselves great readers and are well versed in the historical settings of the classics. But the settings and action of the works of Shakespeare, Milton, Scott, Eliot, Dickens, Tennyson, and the rest are almost hopelessly foreign to the average pupil whose whole reading has consisted of the newspaper and a few magazines. We laboriously explain this custom and that, this allusion and the other, but our words carry little information. What it has taken volumes to teach us it will also take volumes to teach others. In consequence, the class flounders on, getting but grotesque caricatures of what are to us living, breathing persons and of events truer in our eyes than those actually recorded in the histories.

Surely, if we are to cause our boys and girls to recognize truth in imaginative art, we must present to them something that is within their grasp. On this score, a lesser classic well understood is of much greater value than a great classic not understood at all. For it is not the intrinsic worth of the course of study that counts at all; it is the results actually gained in the minds and characters of the class. It might be possible, for instance, that a class might get infinitely more comprehension of what good literary art should be from study of a novel of Edna Ferber than from study of any of the classic novels that portray Englishmen and English life of a century or more ago. The real greatness of the model is beside the question; the comprehension of the student is the thing.

The other difficulty, the difference in language, is also little appreciated by most teachers. Every teacher should at some time make the following test with any classic which he is about to take up. Without previous warning, and before any of the piece has been studied, he should have the class read over several pages of the text for the first time. Each member should make out on paper two lists, one of the words of whose meaning he is entirely ignorant, the other of the words about whose meaning he is not certain.

A study of such a set of lists will be very interesting and enlightening. It will reveal the fact that very many words that one would think were familiar to everyone are entirely unknown to many. It will also show an astonishing percentage of words of uncertain meaning. The worst of the thing is, it will be found in every case that such lists of uncertain and unknown words include nearly all of those upon which the real meaning of the passage depends. If one finds such a state of affairs with a few pages, what is the situation with a whole selection of several hundred pages? A study of the dictionary will help the situation, but not a very great deal. The real value of words that are somewhat archaic or unusual is in their connotation, the atmosphere they suggest. No dictionary definition will give such atmosphere. We ourselves secured such a sense of their meaning from finding them frequently in our wide reading. Without this reading the boys and girls cannot possibly get anything like their force or value.

With these difficulties to overcome, we are of course forced to a compromise. The question for us is, Which works of those available combine real merit as interpretations of life with comprehensibility to most of our students? Good art with comprehensibility to present-day adolescent Americans —a difficult combination, surely. But a combination that is absolutely essential, none the less, for either quality without the other is useless.

If works which meet these two demands can be found — and I believe they can be — we must so present them as to make their study operative in our students' choice of reading matter when they are choosing for themselves and primarily for the entertainment which they hope to find. We can do this only by causing our study in school to furnish a standard of judgment that will be readily and even unconsciously applied to all of what is called "fiction." Such a standard is furnished by the test which distinguishes all good art from bad—the test of faithfulness to life.

Part VIII

General Educational Problems

CHAPTER XXV

EVERY SCHOOL AN ACTIVITY SCHOOL

We have all heard a great deal about activity schools, and the activity program. We have read the attractive books telling of the things that the children in activity schools do. In nearly every number of the educational magazines, we find illustrated articles showing interesting projects carried out by children in activity schools. Many universities have schools where they study the way that children can learn through activities. New courses of study for cities, counties, states, are constantly coming out, giving long lists of activities for children. All this is telling us of a wonderful development in American education, and a new school life for our children.

Then, after thinking of all these splendid things, we think of our own school situation. We think of the room in which we ourselves work. We think of our lack of equipment and materials. We think of the way we are expected to teach textbooks. We think of the attitude of parents toward all new things in the school room. And we are likely to become quite despondent and discouraged about keeping up with the pace set by those fine, fortunate schools where they work with activities and projects all day long.

This contrast has concerned me most deeply during all these years that the discussion of activities has been increasing. I think something should be done about it. And I think something can be done about it. That is why I wish to discuss the problem of making every school an activity school. I mean securing more active learning in every school, the poor school as well as the prosperous school, the school in any and in every community. And I mean more active learning without any revolutionary methods, in fact, with much the same methods we are now using. Let me point out how this may be done.

First of all, let us never forget that children must be active if they are to learn. Learning is an active process. A child who is passive cannot be learning. He is merely doing nothing. One way for a child to spend the time at school is by doing nothing. But that will not get him very far along the road to an education. We want him to learn. That is the same thing as saying we want him to be active during all the five hours or more he is in school. The active child is the learning child. Our problem is to direct that activity. In that way, we will be directing the learning. Here we are accepting altogether the fundamental philosophy of the activity school. But how can we apply it in the "regular" school? That is the question before us.

To find an answer, let us ask ourselves in what ways children *can* be active? What kind of things *can* children do? If we can make a list of these things, we can then see how many of them we can find a place for in the school that we actually have charge of. Now you will find that this list is not very long. In fact, there are just five things that anyone can do. Each of these five is a kind of activity. And I think you will find that all five of these kinds of activity you can have in your school next week and every week thereafter. Let us consider them one at a time.

The *first* kind of activity that children need to carry on is *perceiving*. That means using eyes, ears, sense of touch, and all the other senses to learn about the world they live in. It means stocking their heads with mental pictures. It means getting the raw material for all other kinds of activity. Perceiving is the fundamental, first kind of learning. It is active. This is not fully realized. A child who is looking, or listening may not be moving a muscle, but if he is really getting anything from his looking and listening, he is actively responding. If he is not reacting, the chances are he is not getting anything. We perceive not with the eyes merely, but with the mind, and with all our past experience. If we do not react with our minds, what we see or hear will mean nothing to us. So *the fundamental activity of any human being is perceiving.*

Here is an activity that belongs in every school room of the land. It is one that every teacher can emphasize just as far as she wishes. Do you say to yourself in the evening, "Well, whatever my children have done, they have seen something, heard something, felt something that they never saw, heard, or felt before. They have stored away some new mental images. They are to that extent wiser, richer persons than when I saw them first this morning." This goal is so easy to attain. Do you take a Sunday paper with a rotogravure section? Do you take two or three of them? Then every Monday morning you will have a stock of pictures of the whole universe to bring to your children.

Do you take picture magazines? Much in these magazines is not suited to children, but you can cut out pictures and bring them to school. From these pictures, the children will have active perceiving of bits of life and of the world that will forever after be part of them. So much for pictures. Then, have you ever tried to collect from the community as loans to the school the many articles of geographic and historic interest there? You will find objects from all parts of the world that will fill the children with wonder and give much active learning. Have you developed year after year a little museum of your own, of articles from other countries, or of things which come with a message from the past. Such a thing as a collection of books in other languages, books in French, books in Greek, books in Chinese, will bring to the child who looks through them a new experience, an active experience, that will strike home. Newspapers in other languages are marvels to them.

In the same way, do you bring to the child objects from nature? Has he perceived collections of leaves, birds nests, minerals, and the like? Has he gone out and perceived all the world of nature within the few miles about your school? Isn't there much there that he has never looked at? Then, has he seen the human activities in his own town? Has he stood, for instance, beside a linotype in a printing office and watched that almost human machine operate? Has he been amid the whirr and seeming confusion of a factory? I have said that perceiving is active learning. It is doing something. Have we gone as far as we could in having our children indulge in this kind of activity? I fear we have not. To emphasize this activity we need make no revolutionary changes in our school. We need only emphasize this aspect of learning to the full. So, let me repeat, we should be able to say at each day's end, "Well, at least the boys and girls have seen, heard, felt something today that they never saw, heard, or felt, before." Then we will be sure that there has been some active learning that day.

What is another of the five kinds of active learning? The *second* that we shall list is *imagining.*

Imagining is being active. As a child sits absorbed in a thrilling story, he is not inactive. His body may be at rest, but his mind is far afield. He is having great and novel experiences. He is doing things. We see the same situation as the teacher is reading to her class. The children slump back in their seats or sit forward on the edge. They make no motion. But the teacher's voice brings to their ears and paints in their minds wonderful things. They may be traveling through an equatorial jungle. They may be rushing a sick friend to a hospital. They may be princes and princesses meeting their subjects. They are actively doing something. They are living in imagination more actively perhaps than they will ever live in reality. And after the imagining is over, those children are not the same children they were before. They have learned; they have changed.

Here is again a kind of activity that we can have in any school. Geography, vividly taught, is an active adventure in foreign lands amid strange things and people. History, vividly taught, is a thrilling adventure amid the powerful and violent personages of history. The teacher who sees these things and persons vividly in her mind's eye and who can as vividly tell about them, is getting great activity behind the rapt eyes of her class. If she has not the words herself, she will find the stories and descriptions that will do the work for her. This does not mean the dry language of the usual textbook. It means the supplementary book or the novel. Do you have a stock of these that like magic carpets take the children on far journeys? You can gather such a stock from year to year,—books or stories that catch the children's imagination. They stir up the activity of imagination. They get real active learning. And let me remind you that most of the world we live in and most of the world of the past will always be a world of imagination. We have pictures to perceive, but not nearly enough pictures. The rest is imagination. Imagining is active learning. Let us develop it. Then we can say when the day is over, "Well, at least my children today have been on a journey and have seen something in the mind's eye that they will never forget."

What is the *third* of our different kinds of activity? Let us take *feeling,* because it grows so well out of *perceiving* and *imagining.* Feeling is a kind of activity. To feel love, hate, respect, curiosity, reverence, is actively to do something inside ourselves, whether we do anything outwardly or not. Feeling is a very personal activity. We do not often speak of it. It therefore goes often unnoticed. But we can most positively say that feeling is the most important of all the activities, for it forms the most important part of our personality. We are what we feel, much more than we are what we know or what we think. And what we do is controlled far more by what we feel than by anything else. The educated person is the person who feels certain ways about things. The good citizen is the person who feels certain ways. The school is finally an instrument to cause children to feel rightly about things. So we must realize the fundamental importance of feeling as well as its active nature.

To the teacher, the question of what her children have *felt* at school is very fundamental. If they did not feel anything at all, they were indifferent. That is obviously opposed to any learning. If they felt irritated or antagonistic, that also produced no learning. We want them to feel attracted, pleased, and enriched. Here we see the connection with perceiving. It is a pleasurable and exciting feeling to perceive the new and strange. It gives also a feeling of growth, of becoming larger and more important in the world. It is a pleasurable and exciting feeling to take the trips in imagination to other times and places. At the same time, there are all the thrills of all kinds of experience. To live in imagination with the poor and down-trodden of other lands gives us a feeling of pity and sympathy. To suffer in imagination the hardships of pioneers and explorers gives us a feeling of courage and resolution.

All the stories of literature develop a wide range of human feelings, for stories make us live in imagination many lives of many kinds. In short, we may say that feeling is a part of every kind of activity. It is an important part that we must not overlook. And we must try to see that all the other activities give the *right* kind of feeling. Feeling is an active kind of learning. It is a kind we can develop in any school. Every school develops feeling whether of the right kind or the wrong kind. Because feelings are not always outwardly shown, we overlook them. But the teacher who wants active learning in her school will want to say when the day is over, "Well, my children had some splendid, worthwhile feeling experiences today. They are finer boys and girls and will be finer men and women."

The *fourth* kind of activity which we shall consider is *thinking*. Thinking is doing something, and doing something with a most important part of us, the mind. We are constantly told that American citizens do not have enough practice at this most important activity. Business men say we should train the children to "use their heads." We can only learn to do something by doing it, and children will not learn to think unless they do think. Here is surely a place where any school can have active learning. Any school can cultivate thinking, if it goes about the thing in the right way. Our failure in the past has been that we have *demanded* thinking. We have *insisted* that the children think. We have *pleaded* with them to think. We have done everything but go about it in the way in which thinking is actually secured.

For to get thinking, we must realize how we ourselves think and when. What is it that teachers think about? What is it that anybody thinks about?

There is only one answer. We think about the things we are interested in and about nothing else. This interest may be pleasant or unpleasant. That is, we may think hard how to get out of trouble. In school, we have found in the past that children did do a lot of thinking of this kind. They have thought hard how to avoid their tasks, how to circumvent the teacher. They have thought about the wrong thing. But still they were thinking about the thing they were interested in. They were *not* interested in learning and they *were* interested in avoiding work.

Let us apply this principle to the job of getting real thinking activity in school. Children will think about the things they are interested in. Let us interest them in geography, and there will be no trouble in getting thinking about the why and how of geography. Let us interest them in history and they will think about history. Let us interest them in health, in science, in improving their handwriting, in what is in the newspaper, and unavoidably, they will think about these things. You cannot stop them from thinking about them. Here then is one of the most important activities we can have in school, and also the way of getting that activity. The path to interest has already been pointed out. It is chiefly through perceiving, imagining, and feeling. If any situation is real to children and if they feel its importance, whether it is in Africa or in the field of arithmetic, they will think about it.

Children think about their own lives, in school and out. They will think about the lives of others if those lives have the same reality that their own life has. Children do a lot of thinking as to who is to be on the basketball team. They can also do a lot of thinking about why the Revolution lasted so long if they can see that war as vividly as they see basketball. The challenge is to make those distant situations real and close. It has been done by many teachers. It can be done by each of us. But we have to see those situations vividly first. Children will think about what interests them. Let us get that interest. Then we can say, when we leave the school house, "Well, at least those youngsters have used their heads today. They can use them better tomorrow."

The *last* of the five kinds of activity, what is it? It is *doing* with the muscles. It is getting up and walking about. It is hammering and painting. It is making things. It is construction. It is the thing that you think distinguishes an activity school. In support of the activity schools, let me say that they are not primarily concerned with doing with the muscles. They want doing with the mind. They want the other four kinds of activity I have just discussed. But they think that the best approach to those kinds of activity is often the making of things, or they think that doing with the muscles is necessary if perceiving, imagining, feeling, and thinking are to result. We need not argue that point. We are not here confronted with the question of what is the best approach, since the school we work in determines our approach for us. We cannot start with *doing* with the muscles and we cannot have a continual *doing* of that kind. We have to start with where we are, with seats screwed to the floor, with textbooks and examinations.

What, then is the place of doing with the muscles in the ordinary school, the kind you and I have to deal with? There is some place surely. First, there is a certain amount of hand work that can be done without disturbing too much the general set up. There is the making of scrap books or note books of all kinds with the art work that goes with them. This can be done at the regular desks. There is the making of models, which can be kept upon a table and which will not disturb the traditional school room appearance too much. There is the decorative art work that can have its place on the walls. Frankly, the doing must not look like disturbance. It must not violate the set ideas of "neatness" that principals and patrons are so accustomed to. It must not be noisy.

Then there is the second kind of doing, the social doing. Clubs of all kinds provide for social doing. A club does not have to look like a traditional schoolroom. The children manage it themselves. They talk out of turn and otherwise mix naturally as equals. Then there are all sorts of social doing in presenting programs and performances. These are accepted as part of school work. They furnish opportunity for self expression, for use of the whole body, for the clash of personality that is so important in learning. Every school can have some kinds of extra curricular work, or special work that results in programs and exhibitions. These bring in doing with the muscles. Of course this is not their chief purpose. It is the mental doing that is important. But the bodily activity must be cultivated as far as it is possible. We may as well admit that the child outside of school will have much more bodily activity than the schoolroom can ever give him. Let us have every sort of bodily activity in play before and after school and at recess. Let us see that the play is social doing also. The bodily activity in the schoolroom we must develop as a means to an end. It is used in order that the pupil may *perceive, imagine, feel,* and *think* to better advantage.

Our subject has been, "Every School an Activity School." We have pointed out how children in any school can actively learn through perceiving, imagining, feeling, and thinking. This is the active learning we want. Let us not worry too much about the great projects that we read about and that make such splendid pictures in the magazines. Such activities do give one thing that our classrooms are not quite so well equipped to give. The activities of the activity school are intended to give the children practice in self-direction, in finding and in solving of their own problems. Let us recognize that fine purpose. Then let us try to give this same practice, as we have said, through playground activities, through extra curricular activities, through encouraging clubs of all kinds and even by stimulating individual hobbies. But at the same time, we can have constant active learning in our school rooms with largely the usual set up if we will emphasize that the child must perceive the world about him, he must imagine the world he cannot see, he must feel in response to all these experiences, and he must use his head to solve problems. Let us have more of this active learning.

CHAPTER XXVI

DEFINING EDUCATION FOR THE LAYMAN

Writers on education seem to have largely neglected the world of parents and of those students who are not intending to be teachers. They seem to have assumed either that these individuals know what education means or that it does not matter whether they do or not. Of course neither of these views can be correct; for the general public has no definite notion whatever of what it means to be educated and it makes all the difference in the world whether it has or has not. The kinds of schools children attend, the time they spend in them, the courses they take, and, more than all of these, what they do outside of school and after they have left school behind, are determined much more largely by public sentiment than by all the learned opinion of the few who conduct the school machinery.

In order to make ourselves understood by these "outsiders" and to secure their much needed coöperation in our work, we must frame a definition that to them will really define. A word or phrase will not do, for no word or small group of words can carry the amount of meaning we need to convey. Essays, chapters, books, will not do, for the public will neither read nor understand lengthy discussions. What we must do is to work out some state-

---

From the *Educational Review*, Vol. 66, No. 1.

ment that is simple but complete, couched in ordinary words but covering the breadth and depth of meaning the word *education* should cover.

Below appears an attempt at such a statement. To avoid verbal difficulties, it is expressed in the vocabulary of the average man. To convey the most concrete meaning, it is made a definition of the "educated man" rather than of the term *education*. To be more easily understood and remembered, it is put in diagram form.

The educated man is one who

knows of,		of things,
understands,	the world	of people,
participates in,		of thought,
and enjoys		and of feeling.

This is a description, of course, of a man who might be considered completely educated. Perhaps no man living can measure up to it; and that is the first thing the parent or student needs to realize—that to be educated is an ideal forever to be striven for but never fully to be attained. It is not that some are educated and some uneducated; *all are educated, but in various ways and in varying degrees.*

In addition to emphasizing the breadth of the idea of education, the statement brings out at once its tremendous complexity. One might say that instead of there being an education there are educations; one in each of the four worlds indicated. Though the four overlap, the character of each is distinct. There is the *world of things,* comprising all that is known about matter, from its analysis in chemistry to its final use in some form by men and women in their daily lives. There is the *world of people,* comprising all that is known about men and women in their social, economic, and political relationships. There is the *world of thought,* the reflections of men and women, past and present, upon all that life has offered or has to offer to mankind. And, last, there is the *world of feeling or emotion,* of sorrow and of enjoyment. Education in any one of these worlds does not merely mean knowledge, but implies that the individual becomes through sympathy and reflection a part of it. There must be in him a reaction by which what he learns becomes, as it were, an active part of himself. Such is the ideal, the impossible ideal perhaps, of true education.

With such a definition before him, the average man can begin to exercise some real judgment on educational questions. The first query that will occur to him, no doubt, is: "Can a man who left school when he could just read and write ever become educated?" A moment's consideration will give him the answer. There is nothing in the definition that says a man cannot, if he has sufficient initiative and capacity for work, become educated without the help of schooling. But the definition also clearly indicated that for all but the one in a thousand, lack of schooling means lack of any great degree of education.

Without study in school, a man is almost certain to remain largely ignorant of nature and natural laws. His ordinary experience will never bring before him the world of natural science which the school presents as astronomy, physics, chemistry, geology, biology, commercial geography, etc. If a man has had no schooling, his knowledge of people also is certain to be limited to those of his own time and almost certainly to those of his own locality and class. Without the help of the school, a man's world of thought is not likely to extend beyond the ideas presented to him by his circle of acquaintances and by the newspapers. Magazines may give him a wider world of modern thought, but the school alone will introduce him to the thoughts of former generations. In the world of feeling, the lack of schooling will do a man perhaps the least harm, for here the schools sadly neglect their opportunity. Yet here also the school can give some experiences that will come to few men otherwise. In short, lack of schooling—and a great deal of schooling, too—forever limits all but the most exceptional in the breadth and depth to which they can become educated.

The definition also answers the question: "Does the school necessarily educate?" It shows at once, for one thing, that the school does not introduce the pupil to all of the world that an educated man must come into contact with. The school does not pretend to furnish more than an introduction to the natural sciences. It can never bring the student thoroughly into touch with the business, social, and political world. Though it devotes a great deal of its time to impressing upon the student the importance of the world of thought, it rarely succeeds in giving him any idea of the riches a library can contain and still more rarely lets him know that men of his own day are having thoughts that are worth reading about. And, as we have said, the school almost ignores the world of the feelings. Of course art and music are being added as concessions to the insistence of a few, but the school assumes no responsibility for directing its pupils' emotional reactions to their experience. Though one would think the literature courses would perform such service, they quite universally do not. It is plain, therefore, that the school even at its best cannot more than partially educate.

The school's efforts, even when exerted with the utmost earnestness and wisdom, may still be thwarted by the pupil's attitude or his lack of capability. Suppose, as is often the case, that a boy is attending school on compulsion, feeling all the while an antagonism to anything the school presents to him. The school can force such a boy to come into contact with the various fields of endeavor that it presents, but it cannot force upon him any educative relationship to them. It can compel him to "know of" various facts about nature, mankind, or man's activities; it cannot force him to make the effort that alone brings understanding, reaction, and pleasure. Thus a pupil may quite thwart the school's endeavor to lend a hand in his education; as a matter of fact, a large percentage of pupils do so thwart it to a greater or less degree.

The pupil's lack of innate capacity may also prevent the school from doing its educative work for him. For many pupils indeed are unable to perform their part in the process. The school presents the experience to them, but they are not able to make it their own. They may memorize statements but be unable to see the meaning behind them. They may commit to memory facts innumerable, but not be able to relate them to their own sphere of action. That is, they are able to "know of," but not to "understand," as our definition has it.

Though there are many who are thus handicapped, there are very many more who, though acquiring some understanding, are unable to go further. The definition uses the word *participate,* meaning to digest, to reflect upon, to recreate in imagination. The school finds few indeed that are thus able to handle even the little given them. Of course, it is not to be expected that it should find many, for it is at this point that the few gifted individuals outstrip the rest of us.

The definition given should also make clear two facts concerning education that are little understood by most parents and those outside the educational machine. The two are closely connected and have practically the same implication, the *first* being that school-boys and -girls are much too young to understand many things that one must understand to be educated, and the *second* that for anyone to become truly educated in the few years of school life would be completely impossible. The process of education is continuous and never ending. However valuable and necessary the best schooling may be, it is but a beginning.

The definition we have given also points out to the men and women over school age how they should continue their search for education. Continuous observation and reading will be necessary for them to extend their knowledge and understanding of the world of things. There are many magazines devoted entirely to this field, and still others constantly present material belonging to it. They will find travel very valuable in extending their appreciation of the physical world; it will at the same time enlarge their contact with people. Their knowledge of people will grow in two directions; they will learn to know more people and more kinds of people, and they will also learn to know certain individuals much more intimately and profoundly. They will find it necessary to resist the natural tendency to remain within their own "set"; their pursuit of complete education will demand that they know people in all stations and conditions of life. They will have to overcome the likes and dislikes that so readily form and must strive to reach the position of the poet who said, in translation: "I am a man, and nothing that concerns mankind is foreign to me."

Then there is the world of thought forever lying open to the adults who have left school behind. If the school has done its duty for them, it has aroused an interest in books that it could not by any possibility satisfy. To the one who desires to be well educated in the world of thought, the library presents attractions that even a lifetime of reading cannot more than touch upon. Lastly, there is the world of sensory, intellectual, and emotional enjoyments. Our definition implies that here too a lifelong effort and search would be needed. Extension and refinement of physical enjoyments are forever possible; intellectual activity constantly has new pleasures; and the world of art calls for ever wider exploration. Surely education as the worthy object of a lifetime's effort should become the goal of all those who come rightly to understand its meaning.

It is this right understanding of education that the world in general lacks. The few specialists who are concerned with the subject have strangely failed to enlighten those outside their own narrow circle. They have discovered for themselves the ideal of the educated man, but they have not succeeded in making their discovery known to the world. Perhaps they would secure a better hearing if they presented the matter as the definition we have given strives to present it, simply and most explicitly.

Part IX

Spelling Problems

CHAPTER XXVII

DO SPELLING-BOOKS TEACH SPELLING?

PURPOSE AND PROCEDURE OF THE INVESTIGATION

Children do learn to spell. Can teachers claim, however, that this learning is a result of their teaching? The schools have in the past generally made that claim. Is it well founded? As a means of investigating this situation, a simple but thorough experiment was tried out in the schools. The results were rather surprising and should cause educators to re-valuate all the work in spelling, especially that which follows day by day the present standard textbooks in spelling.

The pupils of the schools in question for three and a half years used a standard series of workbook spellers which were made by specialists in the field and which are widely known and used throughout the country. The day-by-day directions of these spellers were carefully followed. From all appearances, the teachers were doing the correct thing in the correct way and were securing typically good

---

From *Elementary School Journal,* Vol. 39, No. 8. H. A. Curtis, Joint Author.

results. Certain indications, however, caused the superintendent to wonder exactly what function the textbook was serving in the children's learning of spelling. He therefore devised a testing program to secure evidence on this point.

For testing purposes a spelling list was made up of seventy words from each book from Grade II to Grade VII and eighty words from Book VIII, a total of five hundred words. These were chosen at random and represented one word out of each 7.63 words in the entire spelling program. From these five hundred words, ten tests of fifty words were made, each test consisting of seven words from each of Grades II-VII, inclusive, and eight words from Grade VIII. The tests provided for pronunciation of each word, use in a sentence, and a final pronunciation. The tests were mimeographed. All tests, with directions for administering and scoring, were assembled in booklet form, and a copy of the booklet was placed in the hands of every teacher. Each Friday the same list was given in the same manner by all teachers in all grades. This testing was done for ten consecutive Fridays, starting five weeks before February 1, and ending five weeks after that date.

Each teacher understood that the purpose of the tests was to evaluate the whole spelling program, not to ascertain the effectiveness of the individual teacher's work. There were no intimations at the time, and there have been no indications since, that any teacher did not do his best to secure an impartial score for his room.

The results for each class were recorded on a report form. For each test the forms provided fifty consecutively numbered spaces after each child's name. The teacher indicated in the proper space whether the child spelled correctly the word corresponding to each number. Thus, if a particular child misspelled words numbered 20, 35, and 45, marks were placed in the spaces which were so numbered. The records, therefore, showed how each child from Grade II to Grade VIII spelled each of the five hundred words selected from the spelling books for Grade II to Grade VIII. They also showed whether the child had already encountered that word in his spelling lesson. From these data the conclusions of this study were made.

GRADE RESULTS

Grade results were first computed. Computations were made of (1) the average percentage of correct spellings by each grade of the words that they had studied in their books during the twelve calendar months prior to the date of the test. This gave for each grade its score on the words taught that year, meaning the preceding 12 months. (2) The average percentage of correct spellings of the words studied previous to the past twelve months. This gave for each grade its score on the words taught them in previous grades or years. (3) The average percentage of correct spellings of the words not yet studied. This gave for each grade its score on words that they would study in later grades or years. These grade results are shown in Table 1. The last column headed "total" gives the grade score on the 500 words, or the words of all grades combined.

TABLE 1

Average Scores of Each Grade on Words Taught to Each of Grades II-VIII

Grade Tested	Percentage of Correct Spelling of Words Taught in Grade								
	II	III	IV	V	VI	VII	VIII	Not Taught	Total
II........	58.6	22.9	11.8	9.5	7.0	4.8	3.5	2.6	13.5
III......	79.7	71.8	41.4	36.9	24.0	18.4	14.4	10.5	36.6
IV.......	86.1	79.6	77.4	56.8	43.8	32.3	28.3	23.1	53.6
V.........	86.8	83.7	75.5	75.8	58.4	47.9	37.8	39.9	63.2
VI.......	96.5	95.1	90.5	89.1	90.0	71.2	63.1	65.5	82.9
VII......	94.6	93.6	85.6	84.5	83.9	80.2	64.2	67.1	81.8
VIII....	98.1	97.4	93.2	91.9	90.6	87.1	85.2	82.3	90.8

By reading the table horizontally, one may secure information concerning the ability of each grade to spell the words in each of the groups designated at the top of the columns. For instance, children in Grade II made 58.6 per cent on the Grade II words, 22.9 per cent on the Grade III words, and so on. No grade group made a perfect score on words studied in previous years. All grades made scores on words not yet studied. If one reads across, it is clear that every grade group knew how to spell some words assigned to every grade.

To examine the scores made throughout the grades on any specified word group, the table should be read vertically. For instance, the percentages of correct spellings of words in the second-grade list were 58.6 per cent for the second-grade pupils, 79.7 per cent for the third-grade pupils, and so on. To look at the other end of the table, we find that on the eighth-grade list of words, the second grade children scored 3.5 per cent, the third-grade children scored 14.4 per cent and so on. If this is true, in what sense did the list for any grade "belong" in that grade?

The scores underlined diagonally across the table are those earned on the word group which each grade had studied during the twelve months just before the dates of testing. These scores range from about 60 per cent to 90 per cent, most of them being near 80 per cent. These percentages seem to indicate satisfactory learning, as a grade average, resulting from routine teaching. It must be remembered that these words were not merely those taught during the current week. They were taken from all the words taught in the twelve calendar months prior to testing. For this reason the average seems high for a year's work in spelling.

When one looks at the scores *above* those which are underlined, a different conclusion is suggested. These scores show the percentages of correct spellings of words *before the children had studied the words.* Sometimes these scores are very close to the scores made after study; for instance, the sixth-grade children, without study, made a score of 71.2 per cent on the seventh-grade words, while the seventh-grade pupils, after study, made a score of 80.2 per cent on these same words. The scores above the lines indicate that in some cases, two years before they had studied the words, children did more than half as well as the children who had just studied the words. In short, these figures indicate that an astonishing amount of learning of spelling takes place without any formal study and takes place years before the words are supposed, by the authors of this typical spelling textbook, to become appropriate for learning.

It is also interesting to look at the figures *below* the lines. These show that in most cases the children kept on learning how to spell these words year after year, after the teaching of the words had ceased. For instance, the second-grade pupils made a score of only 58.6 per cent on the second-grade words, but learning of these same words had kept on year after year without teaching until the eighth-grade pupils made a score of 98.1 per cent. Here again there was learning of spelling without teaching.

Finally, there was a group of words which in Table 1 is designated "Not Taught." These were words which are assigned to the latter half of Grade VIII and which had not been taught at all up to the time of testing, because the testing came in the middle of the year. Each grade spelled some of these words correctly, and the eighth-grade pupils made a score of 82.3 per cent.

This table conclusively shows that most of the learning of spelling in the schools studied was done either before the year in which the words were taught or after the year in which they were taught. It has been pointed out that grade scores on words taught ranged from 60 per cent to 90 per cent and that these percentages would ordinarily be considered satisfactory results of teaching. If, however, the score *before* teaching is subtracted from the score *after* teaching, Table 1 shows a very small gain from the daily grind of spelling lessons.

RESULTS SHOWN BY ANALYSIS OF INDIVIDUAL SCORES

The figures in Table 1 are misleading because they are averages. For instance, the table shows that in Grade II the average percentage of correct spellings on the second-grade list was 58.6. The individual results show, however, that the lower end of the grade spelled hardly any of these words correctly, whereas the upper end of the class spelled nearly all of them correctly. Every figure in Table 1 must be interpreted in a similar way. Table 1 gives the grade averages, but the scores of individual children range all the way from almost zero to almost 100 per cent. In every grade there was a wide range.

The range within each grade is of special importance with respect to the learning of spelling before teaching. Characteristically, the upper end of the class spelled words far beyond their grade, and the lower end did not learn words until the words were taught. Table 2 shows the spelling achievement of the second-grade pupils divided into ten groups according to their total scores.

TABLE 2

Spelling Achievement of Second-Grade Pupils Divided Into Ten Groups According to Score on Total Test *

Score on Total Test	Percentage of Correct Spellings of Words Taught in Grade							
	II	III	IV	V	VI	VII	VIII	Not Taught
91-100	92	66	58	47	28	26	16	13
81- 90	85	50	26	21	13	9	8	5
71- 80	75	35	18	14	10	6	5	3
61- 70	70	26	12	10	7	5	2	2
51- 60	65	20	8	4	5	3	1	1
41- 50	57	15	6	2	5	2	0	0
31- 40	46	11	4	2	3	1	0	0
21- 30	36	8	2	1	2	0	0	0
11- 20	28	3	0	0	1	0	0	0
0- 10	11	1	0	0	0	0	0	0

* The figures across the table show that, for pupils in the highest tenth of Grade II, the average percentage of correct spellings of second-grade words was 92; of third-grade words, 66; of fourth-grade words, 58; and so on.

For the uppermost tenth of Grade II, the average percentage of correct spellings of second-grade words was 92; of third-grade words, 66; and so on, to 16 for eighth-grade words. For the next lower group the average percentage of correct spellings of second-grade words was 85; of third-grade words, 50; and so on, to 8 for eighth-grade words. Each lower group did less well until for the lowest group the average percentage of correct spellings of second-grade words was only 11; of third-grade words, 1; and of words above the third-grade level, 0. The average figures for Grade II given in Table 1 are correct only for the spelling of the center groups of the grade. They are not correct for the greatest number of children, who are shown by Table 2 to have done either distinctly better or distinctly worse than the center groups. This important fact holds for all grades, though space permits a detailed analysis of Grade II only.

The statement, suggested in the last section, that spelling is learned without being taught is now seen to be incorrect. It is more correct to say that spelling is learned by some children without teaching but by others only after teaching, even if then. It seems suggested, therefore, that classes should be divided and that certain children should be excused from spelling. Obviously many children are suffering a tremendous loss of time in sitting through spelling lessons that they do not need.

RESULTS ON DIFFERENT WORDS

It has been pointed out that children differ in spelling ability, and it must now be emphasized that words also differ in spelling difficulty. It has been suggested that some children learn spelling without being taught but that other children need much teaching. The results of this experiment also suggest that certain words do not need to be taught whereas others do need real teaching.

As explained above, this study yielded the record of each child on every word of the five hundred included in the experiment. From these records it was possible to tell what happened to each word in each grade. Table 3 gives the results on ten typical

TABLE 3

*Spelling Achievement on Ten Fifth-Grade Words by Fourth-Grade Pupils Before Studying the Words and by Highest and Lowest Quarters of Pupils Divided According to Score on Total Test **

Word	Percentage of pupils in Grade IV knowing word in year prior to teaching	Grade at Which Ability to Spell Word Was Attained by 90 per cent of—	
		Highest Quarter of the Grade	Lowest Quarter of the Grade
address	83	IV	......
aim	37	V	VI
appeared	25	V	......
bones	71	III	VI
boots	77	III	VI
breath	67	IV	VI
certain	2	V	......
chief	41	V	VIII
cities	27	V	VI
contest	70	IV	......

* "Address," a word taught in Grade V, was spelled correctly by 83 per cent of the children in Grade IV. The word was spelled correctly by 90 per cent of the highest quarter of Grade IV, but it was not spelled correctly by 90 per cent of the lowest quarter of the pupils in any grade.

words for Grade V. The second column shows the percentage of fourth-grade children who spelled these words correctly before they were taught. It will be noticed that the word "address" was spelled correctly by 83 per cent of these children who had not yet studied it, whereas "certain" was spelled correctly by only 2 per cent before studying. The other words range between these extremes. On the basis of learning without study, these ten words vary greatly, and the same is true for all the five hundred words tested.

The last two columns show what happened to the words after they were taught. Here the results are shown in terms of learning by the highest quarter of the grade and the lowest quarter of the grade. Satisfactory learning was assumed to be 90 per cent, since this score happened to be the passing mark in spelling in the local system. The two last columns, therefore, show at what grade level these words were actually spelled correctly by 90 per cent of the highest and the lowest quarters of the grade. Here the results also show great difference in difficulty between words. Two words ("bones" and "boots") were known by the good spellers as early as Grade III but were not known to the poor spellers until Grade VI. Five of the words were not known even by the good spellers until the words were taught in Grade V, and two of these ("appeared" and "certain") never became known to the poor spellers, even in Grade VIII. Half of the words had to be taught to the good spellers, or were learned by them in Grade V, where the words were taught; and half of the words did not need to be taught to these good spellers because they knew the words before reaching Grade V. The last column shows that all ten of these words needed to be taught to the poor spellers and that, even then, the teaching did not cause them to reach 90 per cent in Grade V.

CONCLUSIONS

The figures from this testing program seem to say three things: (1) Most of the learning of spelling seems to have been done before the year of teaching or after that year. (2) The good spellers do most of the learning without teaching, while the poor spellers apparently need the teaching and even more teaching than is given them. (3) Certain easy words, rather than all words, are learned without teaching by the good spellers. Hard words are not even learned through teaching by poor spellers, many of these words never being learned at all by this group.

The question, "Do spelling-books teach spelling?" does not seem to have a simple answer. At least this investigation points out that it is not entirely satisfactory merely to buy a good spelling-book and carefully to follow its directions. Much still needs to be determined before a particular faculty knows just what the school should do about spelling. One solution is the adoption of a thorough language-arts program. Such a program gives attention to words primarily as tools of thought and expression, but it brings in, at appropriate points, attention to word forms and to ways of learning word forms and thus encourages the continual, natural learning of spelling.

CHAPTER XXVIII

THE MODERN TEACHING OF SPELLING

Teaching spelling is an unpleasant necessity. We would rather not have to teach it, but we must. Our students are not actually better men and women when they can spell. Their character is not more developed. Their knowledge of the world of men and of things is not increased. But they must know how to spell simply because failure to spell correctly is a definite handicap. Poor spelling hinders communication and brings on ridicule. Everyone looks down upon those who cannot spell. So we must help our students to learn to spell correctly.

There are two approaches to spelling. One approach seeks to teach certain lists of words, and it may therefore be called the "list-approach." Its logic is very simple: Children need to write words in any writing they do. They must spell the words they write. Therefore, let us list the words which will be needed and teach those words. Then the children's spelling needs will be taken care of. Accordingly, many word lists have been prepared for use in the teaching of spelling. These lists[1] are of four kinds: *First,* there are the lists of common words which make up such a large part of all writing that every person, child or adult, should know their spelling

[1] See the end of this chapter for descriptions of typical lists of each of the kinds discussed. The material of this chapter is expanded in Better Spelling, Garrard Press, Champaign, Ill.

automatically. A list of only 1,000 words makes up 90 per cent of all writing. A list of 2,000 makes up 95 per cent of all writing. It would therefore seem a simple and worthwhile precaution to see that these fundamental words are taught so well, and reviewed so often, that no one could ever make a mistake on them. *Second,* there are lists of words commonly misspelled. To know these words would seem a safeguard against the common spelling errors. Teachers very often make up their own error lists, and find that these lists help the children under their charge. *Third,* each school subject may have its own spelling list. Children who have to write examinations or papers in any subject should know the words that they will be likely to write. Teachers often make up their own "subject lists," based directly upon the books they use and the material covered in those books. *Fourth,* there are combination lists, made up of words which are in common usage, which are important for certain subjects, and which are often misspelled. Makers of such lists consciously or unconsciously use all three of these criteria in securing a list of "important words" which should be taught in spelling. All four types of lists have their value, and some or all of them will continue to be used. The "list-approach" is not however the only one, and it is not sufficient if our students are actually to qualify as good spellers in all their writing activities. An additional type of attack on the problem is necessary.

There is a second approach to spelling which we may call the "learner's approach." That is, this approach tries not merely to teach certain words, but to make the student an efficient learner of spelling, so that no matter what may be the situation in which he finds himself, in school or out, he may spell efficiently. This approach to spelling begins with the premise that no list or combination of lists can entirely take care of anyone's life spelling needs. Lists can take care of the more common words, but it is not those words that really cause the trouble for most people. We do write the common words every day, but we also write an ever-increasing and an ever-changing list of words that no one can foresee.

Every student writes English compositions about the things in his own past experience, and he needs therefore to spell many words that others may not need to spell. Every student writes examinations in his own set of high school subjects, which is likely to be different from the set of subjects taken by many other students. A student in any subject writes papers which are different from the papers others write, and which therefore require the spelling of different words. Every student writes personal letters which use words different from those of the personal letters of other people. And every student at some time gets a job which requires the writing of words that belong to that job rather than to any other job. So the life spelling needs of an individual are his own life spelling needs, and the life spelling needs of each individual are different from those of any other. These life needs are tremendous. What will be the number of different words that any individual may have to write at some time or other? Ten thousand words is a very conservative estimate. The true number may be three or four times that. And how is one going to be able to do this enormous job of spelling? Obviously, not through the study of limited lists. In fact, the only way is through the learner's approach, through becoming an efficient learner of spelling.

Using the learner's approach means that the schools must teach the "habits of the good speller." The good speller somehow succeeds in spelling at any and at all times. He writes about anything or everything and still he spells correctly any words he may need to use. How is he able to do this? The fact is he has certain habits which make this universal and continued spelling possible. These habits include at least the following:

(1) *The habit of checking guesses.* Whenever we come to a word that we do not know how to spell, or that we are not sure of, we naturally "think" it is spelled with certain letters. Do we take a chance and put those letters down? Perhaps most of us do, and that is why we do not continually become better and better spellers. The good speller "thinks" or guesses just as we do, but he also checks his guess. He asks someone, or he looks the word up. Every day or two he is checking some guess as to spelling,

and so every day or two he learns the spelling of some new word. He keeps this up, day after day, and year after year, and nothing can stop his steady increase in spelling ability. Thus "checking your guess" is the first habit of the good speller.

Now it is evident that very many pupils do not check their guesses. There are two reasons for this. *One* is that we frown upon pupils who are constantly asking how to spell something. We make them feel inferior. So to avoid our condemnation, the children take a chance, and as often as not, they "get away with it." The difficulty here is that no one learns a habit until he *wants* to learn it. We cannot force anyone to get a habit. We must attract him to do so. Suppose we praised the children who asked us how to spell a word? The effect would be quite the opposite. When uncertain, they would ask, and so they would learn. Of course there are children who would lean too much on others, and with such children we would first ask, "How do you think it is spelled?" If they were right we would tell them so, and praise their success. A *second* reason is that we want the children to learn to use the dictionary. But it is a lot of trouble to use the dictionary if there is just one in the room, and if a student has to make himself conspicuous by walking over to it. In such a situation, any student is likely to guess and go on. This is why there is the movement for dictionaries in every desk, or at least on every desk during any writing. If the dictionary is there, and if we have taught children how to locate rapidly any word they are doubtful of as to spelling, there will be more checking and thus more learning of spelling. The way to get children to do the right thing instead of the wrong thing is to make the right thing easier to do. Finally, it is the enthusiasm of the teacher that will do the most to develop this desire to check all guesses. If she feels that it is very important to make sure what the right letters are, and if she is well liked by all the children, they will naturally feel that checking is important too. Attitudes are caught rather than taught.

(2) *The habit of proofreading* also is characteristic of the good speller. Every English teacher knows how she may point to a misspelled word and the pupil will say, "Oh, I know how to spell that. That's just a slip." Now children may talk of "slips" but in the adult world there are no slips. Every misspelling is a misspelling, and is just as much ridiculed if it is a "slip" as if it were an "error." In fact, a slip is more reprehensible. We can excuse one who does not know better, but we do not excuse one who knows better but does not use his knowledge. This is the attitude that the teacher should take. If a child makes a mistake, but thinks his spelling is right, we will not blame him. He just does not know the correct form. But if he lets slips get by him, that we cannot excuse, for he is showing laziness or carelessness. So the rule must be, "Proofread for Spelling," no matter what the paper is,—

letter, examination, term paper, or what not. We may even go so far as to require that every paper handed in have the notation, "I have proofread for spelling." Then if a misspelled word appears, we can ask the pupil how to spell the word, and if he spells it correctly, we can justly consider the pupil has been guilty of inexcusable carelessness.

Contrary to common belief, proofreading must be taught. The average person thinks he can read for thought and at the same time catch slips in spelling. It really takes a good deal of skill for one to do this. The average person must first read for thought, and then must proofread as a separate process. Proofreading for spelling means looking at each word individually, disregarding for the moment what the sentences say. And the way to look at each word is to read the word syllable by syllable, looking at each syllable as it is read. Only in this way will the untrained student catch errors in spelling.

(3) *The habit of spelling analysis,* or a study of the spelling of new words, is also characteristic of the good speller, and this habit can be taught in the school if we will devote ourselves to it. The motivation, or the desire to learn this habit, results from an interest in new words. Every new word should be treated as something very interesting. Though at times we may wish to hurry on, usually there is an opportunity to consider the new word and something of its interesting characteristics. This is especially true with the words which appear in the various

high-school subjects. They are likely, whether they are literary or technical, to have an interesting origin, either in our own language or in Latin, Greek, French, Spanish, or other foreign source. Time devoted to the meaning of the word can also be made to serve for a study of the spelling. Teachers of all subjects can help in teaching this "habit of spelling analysis" of new words by following the steps we shall now describe:

The *first question* to be asked about any new word is, "Exactly what is the correct pronunciation?" This fact is important because the student wants to read the word correctly; he wants to say it correctly, and, incidentally, he will often use the correct sounding to tell him how to spell the word. The longer, more learned words are very likely to be spelled phonetically. If no student in the class can give the exact pronunciation, the teacher will give it to the class. Then the teacher should have the students say the word, not in concert, but one after the other until a number have said it. The reason is that if children are to be called on, they will be much more likely to listen closely to the sound. If the teacher alone pronounces the word, the same effect is not secured.

The *second question* about the new word is, "Does the sound tell the spelling?" The purpose of this question is to locate the hard part if there is a part which will cause trouble. The way to check sound and spelling is to say the word slowly, by syllables, and to look at each syllable carefully as it is being said. This is the way to do it, because it is the way we spell a long word with which we are not familiar. We say it syllable by syllable and try to spell the syllables, one at a time. In doing so, we are actually trying to spell the sound of each syllable. So the question is, "Does the sound tell the spelling?" Here we cannot be absolutely exact since very often the sound and the spelling do not agree absolutely. Yet the real question is whether they agree closely enough for the sound to tell us which letters to use. What we really do is to take the rules we learned in reading, that certain letters indicate certain sounds, and try to make for ourselves rules that certain sounds indicate certain letters. There are, however, differences between these rules which often cause trouble. For instance, in reading, we know that *-er, -ir,* and *-ur* have all a certain sound, but when we start to spell that sound, which of these three sets of letters should we use? Yet with all this difficulty, we find that all of us confidently use some method of spelling the sound, when we do not actually know the spelling by some other method.

Answering our second question, "Does the sound tell us the spelling?" will locate those parts which cause the real difficulty in spelling. For instance, *sympathy* is spelled *sym-* and not *sim-*. *Lettuce* is not spelled with *-us*. *Steady* is not spelled *stedy*. Such discoveries are absolutely necessary if we are to head off the errors which this disagreement between sound and spelling is likely to cause for a great many students. So we come to our third question.

Having found the hard spot, we ask, "How can we remember the right letters at this point?" Here a number of methods are possible. The best method is to use some kind of thought device. Thought devices make a great impression and are long remembered. For instance, we can point out that *lettuce* is not spelled like *let us*. Neither part is spelled that way. There are two *t's* and the ending is *uce*. We can also explain why *uce* is pronounced as *uce;* there is the rule that "*c* before *e* or *i* is pronounced like *s*." Or in the case of *sympathy* we can explain that the word is from the Greek, meaning to "feel with," and the first syllable *sym* means *with.* We have many words from the Greeks having this same syllable which uses *y* for *i* as *symphony, symbol,* etc. We have here illustrated thought processes both from logic and from mere chance association, but any thought process is a good memory process. Thought processes take time, but they add interest. And, as said above, they give us more permanent remembering.

If no thought process seems possible or advisable, then the students should visualize this spot in the word. There is no need to visualize the rest of the word; the sound takes care of that. But there is need to visualize the "hard part." The student may do this merely by looking long and hard at the particular letters. He should say the syllable as he does so, in order that the sound, when he thinks of it, may bring back the letters. Or the student may write the word, thinking of the hard part. Or he may underline that part, or write it more heavily, or use any method that will make a strong impression. For if he can remember how to spell this part which does not agree with the sound, he can spell the rest just by accurate sounding.

So the "good speller" (1) checks his guesses, (2) proofreads for spelling, and (3) studies the spelling of new words, which means, (a) he gets the exact pronunciation of each new word, (b) he asks if this sounding tells the letters, and (c) where it does not, he finds a means of remembering the exact letters at the difficult spot. He makes this rapid check in all subjects, in English, in History, in Science, or what not. He habitually makes this check, and does it in a few seconds only. As a result, he is at all times prepared to spell any of the words he knows and might use. Only by being so prepared can he be in fact a good speller.

HELPING THE POOR SPELLER

We have suggested that if the "learner-approach" were more widely used in the schools, there would be a higher level of spelling efficiency for all. This is because the "list-approach" takes care only of certain words, whereas the learner's approach prepares the student to attack any word in any field of knowledge. However, because spelling instruction in the school is still somehow ineffective, some students still come to us very much handicapped in spelling. Somehow they are poor spellers without knowing why, and they tell us they have always been poor spellers. In addition, most of them expect to be poor spellers for the rest of their lives. They have given up. All their efforts have proved vain, and they think they just cannot learn to spell. These are the students who need our special attention. They do not need more censure or ridicule; they have usually had nothing else from their teachers for years. First of all, they need sympathetic understanding. They are not wilfully misspelling. They are not just lazy. They are handicapped. That is the position any teacher must take if she is to help the student to improve. He has some difficulty that has to be located and corrected, and then he will become as good a speller as others.

First of all, the teacher needs to find out how the student does his spelling. There are in fact five different ways people spell. Which of these is being used by this individual? To discover this, the teacher will ask the student to spell some words orally. First, the teacher will give easy, everyday words. The chances are the student will rattle off the letters just as all the rest of us do. That is lip-spelling, or a mere habit of the speaking apparatus. Then let the teacher give harder and harder words, always watching closely what the student does. He may continue to rattle off the letters by lip-spelling until the words become too unfamiliar, and he may then refuse to try, saying that he just doesn't know how. This will indicate that saying the letters is his only method of spelling. It is one that serves in the early grades and with the common words, but it is an impossible method for the spelling of the harder words, either in school or in later life.

In the second type of case, the student, when given harder words, may look out of the window, or his eyes may go blank, indicating he is trying to "see" the word in his "mind's eye." This is eye-spelling or visualizing. The student can use this method up to a certain point, and then, as the words become harder and more unfamiliar, he will begin to make mistakes. He will mix up the letters, or leave some out. He cannot see the word clearly in his mind's eye, and he either fails to see some letters or sees them in a random order. He will often give the first letters, then the last letters, and then some of the middle ones. This kind of spelling, eye-spelling, is the one usually taught in schools. It does pretty well for the easy words of the language, that is, for the words which appear on the usual lists. But it does not do for the unusual words, the ones that are not on the lists that are studied. Try the student, for instance, on historical or geographical words and see what happens. Those words were not spelled day by day through the eye-spelling method. The results will probably be very peculiar.

A third possibility is that the poor speller may try to spell everything by sound. He may try to spell even the easy, everyday words by sound, thus making many mistakes, since the common words are the most unphonetic of the language. But this student unlike the others, will continue to try the harder and harder words. Even with the longest and strangest words, he will say the sound and then try to translate the sound into letters. He will have pretty good success, too, since so many of the long words are entirely or almost entirely phonetic. But obviously, sounding is not the one and only perfect method of spelling. It might be in Italian or German, those languages being spelled very systematically. But English has had such a strange history of mixture from different sources, and of shifts in pronunciation, and of development of traditions in spelling, that the result is far from simple. They say that, going by syllables, English is 85 per cent phonetic, but the other 15 per cent of syllables which are not phonetic are very important.

The lesson from this testing of how the student spells is clear. Uusually the poor speller tends to use only one method of spelling, either lip-spelling, eye-spelling, or sound-spelling. Any one of these serves some purposes, but no one serves all purposes. Therefore he continues to make mistakes and he will go on making mistakes all his life until he learns how to use the right method at the right time. The only way we can help him to do this is to show him the various methods and how to use them all for their various purposes. Explain how the common words need to be spelled by "seeing" because they are so unphonetic, and how the long ones need to be spelled by sound because there are so many long words and they are used so seldom that most of us cannot keep clear pictures of them in mind.

The situation is complicated by the fact that these poor spellers are often lacking in one or the other of the two essential natural abilities needed for spelling. One is the ability to visualize. Those of us who can easily "see" any word we desire do not realize the situation of the persons who just cannot "see" words and their spelling. They try to visualize the word they want to spell, but all they get is a vague picture which does not show the individual letters. Or they may see the beginning and end, but not the middle. This is why practically all spelling errors are in the middle of words, and not at the ends. This does not mean that these individuals have no visualizing power. They all have some, and this ability can be increased by practice. But if the handicap is great, we cannot hope to change it very greatly. The second needed ability is the power to "hear" accurately the sound of a word and to change that sound into letters. Many of the poor spellers just do not hear words accurately. Ask them to say some words, syllable by syllable, each syllable clear and strong. You will find that most of their syllables are blurred, if not incorrect. It is true that our ordinary pronunciation in English is blurred. We all know that nearly every unaccented vowel in a long word becomes *uh,* such as *puh-ta-tuh,* instead of *po-ta-to,* or *au-tuh-muh-bile* instead of *au-to-mo-bile.* Most of us use this blurred pronunciation, but when we want to we can use the "formal" pronunciation which gives every syllable a clear and distinctive sound. Formal pronunciation is used by orators; we do not expect it to be used in colloquial talk. But these poor spellers know only the colloquial sound of words, and they do not even know that sound very well. And when they try to spell that sound, only a vague resemblance to the word results. Here also we can say that everyone can improve to some extent his ear for words and his sounding of them. We can train a student to say words distinctly and thus increase his ability to hear the exact sounding. But if this handicap is a very bad one, we will have difficulty making much progress.

It is by now obvious that perhaps the best cure for all these spelling handicaps is the development of the habits of the good speller. If the student "checks his guesses" he will get to hear words more clearly and to see them more clearly. If the student proofreads for spelling, he will develop his visual images of words, and may have to check the sounding of many words, thus developing his auditory images. Then the process of "analysis for spelling" gives the poor speller just what he needs. The question,

"What is the exact sound of the word?" catches the one who has a vague sound image. The question, "Does the sound tell the spelling?" catches the one with sound difficulty, and also the one with poor visual imagery. He must look at the word hard, syllable by syllable, as he says the syllables. So, whichever the handicap, it is to some extent corrected. Finally, "How remember the hard part?" brings in a process that the poor speller has obviously neglected, "using his head."

In fact, the use of "thought spelling" or figuring out why the word is spelled that way, and how to remember it by some association, is the best solution of poor spelling, no matter what the cause. If a student knows that *finite, infinite,* and *definite* are all of the same family, it does not matter if he hears the word wrong or if he cannot see the word in his mind's eye; his reason will tell him that there cannot be an *a* in *definite.* If he knows that *procedure* is the exception to the *precede-proceed* group, which have two *e's* after the *c* or one on each side of the *c*, he will get the word right whether he has poor auditory or poor visual imagery or both. All students can well use more thought spelling, but the poor speller especially needs to depend on it more than he does. "Thought spelling" is the fourth method of spelling, lip-, eye-, and sound-spelling being the three already mentioned. The fifth method is hand-spelling, a muscle habit that results from the other four methods after long practice.

SPELLING, A CHALLENGE

Finally, the problem of the poor speller is in the last analysis one of attitude. Suppose we show the poor speller why he makes his mistakes and why he does not improve. Suppose we show him the method to overcome his difficulties. Nothing will happen unless we have developed in him a determination to overcome the difficulty. This does not mean a determination to please his teacher. That determination will last only so long as the student is with us. But the poor speller's problem is a lifelong problem. He will find out his errors, day after day, year after year. Someone will call his attention to a word that he thought he could spell but really could not. Then he must attack that word and overcome it. There will be more and more words, year after year, long after school is past. It is like the case of the farmer who finds with his plow the stones in his field. The stones will never get out of that field unless the farmer stops whenever he finds a stone and carefully takes that stone to the pile in the fence-corner. So, word by word, the poor speller must progress. He will not do this merely to please us. He will not do it merely to get a grade. He will not do it unless he has developed a feeling of pride that spelling "cannot get him down," that he can learn to spell as well as anybody. So there must be no censure. We are sorry when he shows such poor spelling. We are sorry for the unpleasant consequences that are ahead of him. We are glad to show him the various ways of overcoming these words. Sometimes it will be one way, sometimes another, for as experienced teachers, we have already discovered ways of remembering the difficult spots. And we encourage the student to feel that his case is not impossible. We show him his improvement. No matter if the new theme shows a half dozen new words misspelled. He did not misspell the one we called attention to last week. And so on and on, we must build up pride and self-confidence. Only in that way can lifelong results be attained. And no other results will mean much to the person who is handicapped in spelling.

LISTS OF WORDS FOR SPELLING

The 2,000 Commonest Words for Spelling. This is an Appendix in *Better Spelling by E. W. Dolch,* Garrard Press, Champaign, Ill. (1942). "These words are so selected as to include those words which make up 95% or more of all the words written by the average person." This list may be purchased in lots of 25 at 10c per copy.

Words Misspelled Most Frequently by Children of the Fourth, Fifth, and Sixth Grade Levels in Life Outside of the School. James A. Fitzgerald, pp. 216-217 of *Journal of Educational Research,* November, (Univ. of Wisconsin, Madison, Wis.) 1932.

The Teachers' Handbook of Technical Vocabulary, Public School Publishing Co., Bloomington, Ill. 1940 (50c). Has separate lists for thirteen school subjects.

Spelling Difficulties of 3876 Words, A. I. Gates, Bureau of Publications, Teachers College, Columbia University, New York (1937). "Compiled from twenty-five different widely used spelling textbooks and state and large city spelling lists.'' This list shows for each word the ''hard spot'' or the part most commonly misspelled.

BOOKS ON SPELLING

DOLCH, E. W., *Better Spelling*, Champaign, Ill., Garrard Press, (1943) 270 pp. A discussion of all the problems in teaching spelling from the ''learner's-approach.'' Emphasizes the psychology of learning spelling and the psychology and methods of remedial spelling.

FORAN, THOS. GEORGE, *The Psychology and Teaching of Spelling*, Washington, D. C., Catholic Education Press, (1934) 234 pp. A very complete summary of research on spelling up to the date of publication.

GATES, A. I., *Generalization and Transfer in Spelling*, New York, Bureau of Publications, Teachers College, Columbia University, (1935) 80 pp. Report on researches on spelling rules.

Review of Educational Research, Language Arts, Amer. Educ. Research Assn., 1201 Sixteenth St., N.W., Washington, D. C. A summary published every three years of research in the language arts, including Spelling.

Part X

Miscellaneous Reading Problems

CHAPTER XXIX

POOR READING AS SHOWN BY ARMY TESTS

To the question, "What should the schools do about the poor reading on the part of our young men, as shown by the tests given draftees?," the answer is very simple. The schools should keep on doing just what they are doing and do it more widely and energetically.

THE OLD WAY

The point which this seemingly embarrassing question fails to note is that the present twenty-one year old draftees were in the first grade fifteen years ago. They got their start fifteen years ago. But we are not teaching beginners as they were taught fifteen years ago. Then nearly every beginner was at once handed a book and was supposedly taught to read immediately. He may never before have sat still in a seat for more than a minute at a time. He may never before have had to do any assigned

From the *Elementary English Review*, Vol. 19, No. 7.

task. He may never have tried to look at things so small and so similar as words on a page. No matter. He was supposed to learn to read at once. But he failed and spent an unhappy year or two. Many were thus permanently set against reading and have hated reading and books the rest of their lives, at least until they have become twenty-one and been drafted for the army. Many others acquired bad habits of many kinds that have retarded their reading ever since.

THE MODERN APPROACH

Nowadays we do not handle beginners in that way. We think of *reading readiness.* In the past few years every series of reading books has been provided with a prereading book or prereading program. The endeavor is made to have every child like school, to have him become a part of the child community, and to have him take part freely in the discussion of his group. The endeavor is made to enrich his experiences so that everything in his book, when he gets his book, is meaningful and interesting. If the present group of beginners are examined fifteen years from now, their success in reading will be far more than that of the present draftees.

Easier beginning books is a second factor. When the present draftees were in first grade, they were usually given a primer which contained perhaps 250 new words, sometimes eight new words to the page. Failure or discouragement very often resulted. Many children discovered that memorizing the page was easier than telling one word from another, and the teacher often accepted glib memorizing as "knowing how to read." We do not do that now. Present series of readers have two or even three preprimers before the primer. These preprimers have never more than two new words per page, and sometimes as little as 20 new words to the book. After the preprimers, the children come to a primer that is easier than the old primer, and, in addition, a third to a half of the words in the primer are not new because they have been taught in the preprimer. The preprimer words are repeated in the primer, and the primer words in the first reader, and the first reader words in the second reader, and so on. Thus the child always meets more "old friends" than "strangers," and reading is possible and easy for the great majority of the children. This was not the case fifteen years ago.

We do not mean to say that the books published fifteen years ago were all so much harder than the books published now. Most of them were, but another fact caused the chief difficulty. In those days, it was much more the fashion to use the same old readers that the same school had used for years and years. There was still a feeling that any good textbook was good for all time and should be used by children and their children's children. So the books actually in the schools fifteen years ago were very difficult indeed. Now we find only occasionally an "antique" reading series being used in school.

Now it is much more the custom to get the new reading books and to keep all texts "up to date."

Reading readiness is coming to be recognized as a factor in success in reading in every grade, from the first through the twelfth. Our rule is "Challenge, but don't discourage." Ten or fifteen years ago, when these young men were boys in school, the rule for a great group of the children seemed to be "discourage and discourage some more." Grade after grade, the job was too difficult. Some boys learned how to evade the job by getting someone else to do their school work for them or by guessing when they could not read, or by reading pictures or depending on prompting from friends, or by the use of other "dodges." Some boys practically quit trying, and became "sitters." Nowadays, we know that the children entering any grade vary three to five grades in reading ability and we try to do something about it. For one thing, we are lowering the difficulty level of the prescribed textbook, thus bringing it into the reach of a larger number. Then we are finding means of helping the few who still are out of their depth. We realize that reading readiness is always with us. Are the children ready to do successfully the work of the grade? If not, we must get them ready or adapt the work.

Quantity reading has come into the picture since the draftees "went to school." Little reading was available in any grade in many schools fifteen years ago. There were not the easy science readers and health readers and art readers, and the like. There were not the many supplementary books of all kinds. There were not the school magazines that give easy interesting reading. Remember, we are speaking of the ordinary schools and not of the favored school. There are many schools now that do not have much reading matter. But the ordinary schools fifteen years ago were so lacking in reading matter that a visit to them would be a great shock to the average teacher today. Nowadays, average schools may have a dozen supplementary books per child, or several dozen. And most of these books are suited to the children in both interest and reading difficulty. The few schools fifteen years ago which had a supply of reading material had little that the average child could actually read. Such reading matter as there was in the schools was often of distinctly adult type, and usable only by the better readers.

Quantity reading in all subjects, such as exists today, did not exist even ten years ago, when present draftees were in the fifth grade. Then each subject had its one book, and the child learned the subject from that book, as that book gave it, and often in the very words of that book. Now we are more and more getting the idea that there is much to read on any topic that the children may be studying. If it is Africa there are stories about Africa and travels in Africa, and even a number of texts on Africa. There is much to read, and we get all the children to read from a number of sources. In the same way if the topic is health, or transportation, or government or what not, there is much reading matter, and much of it is written especially for children of low reading ability. Quantity reading on all subjects will give children a chance to get reading practice at their own level. And this quantity reading will raise all to their best possible reading level.

THE NEW WAY MUST BE EXTENDED

Yes, in answer to the question, what about the poor reading of young adults?, the answer is, "We are doing things better now." The only sad aspect of the situation is that we are not doing them better in enough places. We have mentioned reading readiness, better books for beginners, and each child reading at his own level in books in which he has a vital interest. The reasons for these changes in materials and methods are very simple and admitted by all. If we could all carry them into effect, what a great change there would be in the reading levels throughout the schools all over our country! And with this change in reading levels, there would come more reading and also a higher quality of reading. And with this better reading would come more adequate citizenship, a better understanding of world problems, and therefore a better outlook for a just and enduring peace in which the next generation of young men and women might live.

CHAPTER XXX

MEMORIZING IS NOT READING

Seeing a primer on the library table, I said to the proud father, "Why, is Jimmie reading now?"

"Sure," was the answer. "He knows that book by heart."

At school the next day, Jimmy's teacher showed me proudly a long row of experience charts and said, "The children can read all of these." When the children came in they did "read" them, actually reciting what the chart said at about a fourth grade reading rate, and half the time not looking at the charts at all.

Any child is likely to memorize a simple story word for word after he has heard it a number of times. If he is a bright child, he is almost certain to. If, as he heard the story, his eyes were on a page distinguished by any attractive picture or on a chart distinguished by a particular pattern of lines, he will associate the story with the page or the chart. All of this is natural. It is a helpful first step. It can be used to good advantage. But it is memorizing and not reading.

The child who merely knows "what the second line says" is not reading. He simply repeats from memory a line that he associates with a certain place on the chart or on the page. Many, many children

---

From the *Elementary English Review*, Vol. 11, No. 8.

do their "reading" lesson this way and continue to do so long after they should be doing something else. Test it out some day by taking a chart that the children can "read" and without their knowledge changing the lines around. Then have them read it line by line. If the title of the chart is "The Park," the children will insist that the first line says "We went to the park" even though you have changed the line to read "We saw fish in the lake." Test the same thing in the reader by making a cover for the page with a slit or window through which only one line can be seen. Then put this cover over the page so that the child can see one line but cannot tell what part of the page it is on. Mary, a child who read the page glibly before you used the cover, will now be quite at a loss. This will be sure proof that she had been only repeating from memory.

The child who merely knows "what comes next" is not reading. Watch the children who "read" looking at you instead of the book. Watch the ones who rattle off a line as fast as an adult when their actual *reading* speed is one word a second or less. One word a second is very slow but it is approximately the true reading speed of most children in the first grade. Any "reading" that goes faster than that, except in the case of the brilliant child, is showing "guessing speed" or "memory speed." It cannot be reading but instead must be just "remembering what comes next." Test this by having children read "mixed pages." Didn't you ever do it as a child just for fun? You take a page and fold it back so that it is just half as wide. Then you lay this half page against the next page and you will usually find that the half lines on the one page will almost fit against the half lines showing on the next. Then you read the mixture to see how funny it sounds. But the child will have to *read* this. Because two stories are mixed, he can not remember what comes next. Try this to see which ones are reading and which are memorizing.

Every teacher of long experience will know of cases like the following: A bright boy, son of intelligent parents who gave him an excellent home environment, apparently went along very well through grades one and two. Then in grade three he began to have trouble at once with reading. His mother wished to help and got a simple book different from the ones used at school. She tried the boy out on this and found he could hardly read a word in it. She was amazed and at once consulted the third grade teacher. This teacher explained the difficulty. For two years that bright boy had been memorizing his reading books so perfectly and easily that two teachers had never found him out. Memorizing is not reading, but for many children it is far easier than reading, and they will do the easier thing if you will let them.

Parents also need to be taught that memorizing is not reading. An indignant mother brought her child to the superintendent's office. The little girl had been retained in grade one. But the mother brought the book, and thrust it before the superintendent with the order, "Now, Milly, show that you *can* read your book." Of course the superintendent reached into his bookcase, brought out another book, and showed at once that the child could hardly read a word. Parents as well as teachers are deceived.

Make sure that your children are really reading. That means getting meaning *from the printed words,* not from the place on the chart or page or from the memory of what comes next. Use simple tests to demonstrate the situation to those who are being deceived or even to the children who are getting a false idea of what reading means. Memorizing is natural at the start. It is even a good thing in giving confidence. But it must be discarded as soon as possible for reading, or the getting of meaning from the printed words, in any place or position, and without pre-knowledge of what they are going to "say."

CHAPTER XXXI

HOW TO CHOOSE A DICTIONARY

The recent appearance of new school dictionaries naturally causes us again to give serious thought to how we should select such a book for use in school. Considerable stir was caused a few years ago by the appearance of the first book in a new series. That dictionary was said to be the first to be based upon a scientific word count, the first in which the definitions and explanations were specifically written for children and not reduced or condensed from definitions originally intended for adults, and the first which followed the principle that definitions for children must be longer than those for adults instead of shorter, both because simpler words must be used and because more explanation is necesary if one is to make contact with the child's more limited experience. New books in other series have been prepared with the same point of view. We need to ask how they compare with one another.

First of all, we want the children to use a dictionary with ease and pleasure. Unless they do, there is little hope they will turn to this type of book unless required to do so. The dictionary, like any other book, therefore, should be as attractive as possible both on first appearance and through all its use. Suppose we open on a table a number of school

---

From the *Elementary English Review*, Vol. 18, No. 5.

dictionaries. We will find that most of the junior dictionaries have open, readable type of good size, with leading or space between the lines to make for readability. If then we turn to the senior or advanced school dictionaries, we immediately see a much closer page with small type and little space between lines. Even an expert reader must look very closely to read the solid paragraphs. The reasoning is that older children are better readers, that they use the dictionary only occasionally, and that when they do so it does not hurt them to look closely. Some new dictionaries do not seem to adhere to that reasoning because the page looks more like the junior dictionaries in openness and attractiveness.

After appearance, one naturally considers the number of entries. One new dictionary has 63,000 entries. Other dictionaries of about the same level say they have 83,000 entries, 100,000 entries, or 110,000 entries. Here one is in doubt what to think because practically all the dictionaries fail to tell us certain facts. First, how many of the entries are on the margin in the main alphabetical series? Many persons believe that in a dictionary to be used by a child every entry that we expect him to find should be on the margin along with all the other words. Others believe that the child can readily be taught to look for some forms of words under others. Someone should do some research on this point, but in the meantime we will all follow our own ideas as to what is practical. Second, the dictionary should tell us how many in their total of items are "customary variations." A striking case is words which indicate the doer of an action, such as "runner," "baker," and the like. Should a dictionary add *-er* to practically every verb in its list and count these nouns as new entries? Some dictionaries do not do this. Competing books which claim many more entries often do this, as in the case of "bailer," "baiter," "balancer," to mention a few found right together. Then, should a dictionary for children take every adjective and add *-ly* and *-ness,* and count these as two new entries? On points such as these, all dictionaries should give the teacher specific information, but one suspects that sometimes the adding of customary variations is not a help to the child, but rather a method of padding the word list.

Before one can decide whether to adopt one new dictionary or some other volume, it is necessary to come to some opinions as to whether meanings should be arranged under parts of speech. This is the custom of all adult dictionaries, and has been the custom of most school dictionaries up to now. It is hard for a teacher to form an opinion on this point because her training has been on the traditional type of dictionary and because publishers which follow the tradition will play up this time-honored custom to the full. One new dictionary gives meanings after each word in one numbered series from the most common to the least common, without regard to part of speech. It claims that this method works more efficiently because the child is not looking for an adjective or a noun but is looking for a meaning. Other persons have said that they doubt whether anyone not a school teacher knows what part of speech he is looking for. The ultimate answer, of course, is the child's success in using the book to locate the right meaning, and we need to wait for research to tell which method works best.

A special feature of new dictionaries is the use of sentences to clarify meaning and to make usage clear. One volume has over 15,000 such sentences. Here it is hard to make comparisons because other dictionaries also use sentences or illustrative phrases. They do not, however, tell us how many they use. Here as in the case of kinds of entries, we should be given more facts.

To answer many of the questions suggested, what we really should do is to equip a room with a number of different dictionaries and find out from actual use which ones the children preferred, which they used more efficiently, and which seemed most suitable for building the dictionary habit. Lacking such an experiment, we should make a systematic comparison on points such as we have discussed. The best way to do this if one does not have time for a large statistical study, is to open one dictionary at random and then to turn to the same part of the word list in another. Compare, let us say, 50 consecutive words. See exactly which entries each book includes that the other does not. Then compare the meanings shown under corresponding entries. Then compare explanation of identical meanings in each book to see which will be of most help to the children who are going to use that book. Then, turn at random to another place and make a similar comparison of entries, meanings, and explanations. If one sampling seems to favor one book and the second the other book, make more samplings until you have satisfied yourself that you have fairly compared the books and have a real reason for saying that your children will profit more from one than from the other.

CHAPTER XXXII

READING PICTURES*

Very few people realize that we have to teach children to read pictures. The average person assumes that he has just to look at a picture to see what is in it. He knows what he himself sees in a picture. He does not realize that others may see something quite different or may see vastly more than he does. Of course, if he had ever discussed a picture at any length with a group of other people, he would have discovered what the psychologists have long since demonstrated: one sees in a picture only that which arouses his own past experience. He sees what he knows.

Someone has asked, "If we see only the familiar, how do we ever see anything new?" There are at least five answers to this. (1) We often see new things which are just variations of the old. A child may see an animal of a different color and size. (2) We may see combinations of the old. A child who knows an elephant and also a box may see a box on an elephant's back, which is called a howdah. (3) We may see "new things in a picture," meaning more and more of the familiar. If you have a picture hanging on your wall, you keep seeing things in it that you had not noticed before. (4) We may acci-

* From the Eleventh Yearbook of the Claremont College Reading Conference.

dentally see things which are largely, though not entirely, new by having our eyes accidentally fix upon an object or a relationship that they have always passed over before. We may, for instance, be familiar with a horse in a picture and a figure on that horse, but some day our eyes may shift from one to the other and we may notice the relative size of the two figures that we have never been aware of.

(5) Finally, we may see something new by having someone else call our attention to it. That is a job constantly being done by the parent at home and the teacher at school. In any picture more is generally seen by the adult than by the child. The teacher especially will have the wider experience which causes her to see more. She wishes the children to see all that she sees. That is why she teaches the reading of pictures.

When young children receive picture books, they have their first experiences in the reading of pictures. Adults or older children point out things in the pictures and give them names. The name is useful in talking about the picture, but the child is learning to see more in the picture than he did before. The same process is very important in grade one. The children in the class discuss the picture on a page. Different ones see different things in it. The teacher points out still other things. Thus the picture comes to have a common meaning for the group, a common meaning that is needed for understanding the story. One of the striking differences between teachers in the primary grades is in the way they teach the reading of pictures. Poor teachers have the naive view of the average person, that the children need merely to look at the picture to see what is in it. Skilled teachers spend considerable time with the class in picture reading. They will even read pictures over and over again because they know that the children will see more each time.

Primary teachers are, however, more skilled than later teachers in teaching reading of pictures probably because they understand children better. It is in the middle grades and later that the reading of pictures is most neglected. Consider, for instance, the subject of geography which, strange to say, so many children dislike. Modern geographies have most beautiful pictures. They are large enough to give a sense of space. They are clear enough to show much detail. Every picture shows dozens of interesting facts. Yet, too many teachers just assume the children will look at the pictures and see what is in them.

For instance, one geography picture shows a busy street in the chief port of the island of Trinidad. The children would look at it and see just an ordinary street of small stores with a lot of people going up and down. A teacher might ask which way the automobiles are going, and the children would discover that the traffic moves on the left, as it does in England. The teacher would call attention to the kind of cars, as an indication of how long ago the picture was taken. She might ask the children to count the bicycles, and they would find out there are many more than you would see in any American city. The children should then notice the balconies that give shade to the second story and to part of the sidewalk. They should read the signs as far as they can. They should notice the telephone wires and street lighting. How the people are dressed is an interesting point. And probably few children would notice, unless their attention was called to it, the fact that about two blocks away the street runs right into the mountains.

Many more things can be seen in the picture, but we have indicated enough to show how much children would not see unless they were taught to read the picture. If all the pictures in any geography were adequately taught, the subject would have an interest and vitality that is now practically unknown in the grade schools. The important facts of the text would come as a natural supplement to the pictures. And most of all, there would be a vast deal of thinking about the problems of other peoples and our own related problems that would make geography a real preparation for vital citizenship.

Failure to teach pictures has been one of the large reasons why the great movement toward visual education has failed to give the results that we all at first expected. Pictures are only one method of visual education, but a most important one. Still-pictures have not been adequately taught and even less attention has been given to the teaching of moving pictures. Adults go to the movies every week and naively assume that they see the movies they look at. They never realize that a really worthwhile moving picture needs to be seen a number of times. Only a few have discovered this fact by having accidentally or purposely seen some film over and over again.

This is not to recommend that everyone stay and "see two shows." It is much better to see the film a second time some time later. But here is the suggestion you can make to any of your friends. The first time you see a film, you focus your attention all the time on the main characters. The next time, you should purposely not look at those characters, but watch the other people in the picture. You will find their work very interesting and worthwhile. Then, the third time, you should not look at characters at all, but see the infinite pains given to settings, to decorations, to clothing, and other details. The next time you can find immense interest in watching the work of the cameraman, the way the sets are lighted, the direction of the shots, and so on. If anyone takes the trouble to apply this method to a good film, he will discover that there is a great deal to learning how to see a motion picture. Our suggestions have been only a beginning. This experience will lead one to see that we can do a great deal in teaching children to see moving pictures.

So far, we have urged that children get more from the pictures that we put before them. We must now ask whether we can so teach the reading of pictures that they will get more from all pictures they see the rest of their lives. That is, are there any general results from teaching children to read pictures in school? Obviously, the first and most important result is the idea that pictures need to be read, that the full meaning does not, as it were, leap into one's mind on first sight. Continued experience in careful reading of pictures will surely give this idea.

Second, there may be the habit of giving more time to a picture. We might call this the "slow reading habit for pictures" or the "study habit for pictures." Surely, if each one of us dwelt longer on any picture we were interested in, we would get vastly more from it.

The third habit may be called the "habit of exploration." That is, one may explore a picture part by part. In this way, one is giving the parts of a picture more of a chance to arouse associations. It also encourages the accidental seeing of relationships that we have mentioned earlier.

Finally, real discussion of pictures, like real discussion of any paragraph in a book, develops the habit of thinking about what we perceive. This is one of the most needed habits in American civilization today. People travel but do not think about what they see. People go to the movies several times a week, but do not discuss what they sat and looked at. People see picture pages in the daily paper, picture sections in the Sunday paper, whole picture magazines, and fine illustrations in all magazines, but they do not ponder over this constant mass of perceived material. In one sense they are having experience, and in another they are not. So much comes before their eyes, but their brains do so little about it.

These considerations will emphasize that a major neglect in our educational system is neglecting to teach the reading of pictures. We are, in fact, providing pictures more and more. But children do not see in the pictures that which they should. And they do not get from seeing the pictures the general conceptions and the general habits which will make them good readers of pictures outside of school and in later life.

INDEX